To Bear Witness

Holocaust Remembrance at Yad Vashem

On the cover: Concentration of the Jews of Lubny and the surrounding area,
16 October 1941

The texts in this book were based on "The History of the Holocaust"
by Israel Gutman, and materials from the Yad Vashem Historical Museum

Translation: **IBRT**

Language Editor: **Leah Aharonof**

Copy Editor: **Leah Goldstein**

Proof-reading: **Pearl Weiss, Richelle Budd Caplan**

Graphic Design: **Stephanie and Ruti Design**

Collection of material: Shira Porat, Niv Goldberg

ISBN-978-965-308-584-8

POB 3477, Jerusalem, 91034, Israel

E-mail: publications.marketing@yadvashem.org.il

Additional printings:

2006, 2007, 2008, 2009, 2010, 2011, 2014, 2016, 2018, 2020, 2023

Printed in Israel

Contents

To the Reader

Half a century has passed since the establishment of Yad Vashem, the Holocaust Martyrs' and Heroes' Remembrance Authority. We mark the jubilee by dedicating the new museum complex, which tells the tragedy of the planned extermination of the Jewish people—an act nearly carried out to completion. The "surviving remnant" who lived to experience the moment of liberation began their return to the land of the living in a process of personal and national rehabilitation, overshadowed by interminable memories and nightmares.

Founded under a law enacted by the Knesset (Israel's parliament) in Jerusalem—the city from where the prophet Isaiah delivered a vision of eternal peace—Yad Vashem has become the center of remembrance of the Jewish people. Seared into this memorial site is the commandment to preserve a memory of universal significance for posterity—as a warning and, concurrently, a hope. In its activities, Yad Vashem maintains the unbreakable bond between memorialization at the Hall of Remembrance and other sites, documentation in the archives and repositories that contain inexhaustible sources for generations of research, study at the International Institute for Holocaust Research, and education at the International School for Holocaust Studies, which spearheads a discourse that spans generations and nationalities alike.

The new museum complex is one of the tools in this discourse, designed to meet the changing needs of each generation, and serve as a bridge between the world that was destroyed and the life that resumed. The complex contains the vast knowledge amassed in Holocaust research over the past 60 years. At the forefront of the permanent exhibit, however, is the individual—the human being and, particularly, the Jew—and the tapestry of Jewish life that predated World War II. Jewish homes, families, and population centers had to confront a fate unprecedented in world history—an evil scheme driven by inexplicable hate that aimed to systematically carry out the murder of eleven million Jews as well as millions of other "undesirables" who fell into its clutches.

This book will lead the reader through the events, as they are displayed at Yad Vashem. The reader will share the bewilderment of Holocaust scholars in attempting to explain the almost total willingness of human beings to accept the dictates of a ghastly ideology and to commit mass murder without a second thought. The Jews' struggle to find a safe haven anywhere on earth was met with the obtuseness and indifference of an estranged world—except for several thousand Righteous Among the Nations who empathized with the suffering of the downtrodden and rescued Jews and, at mortal risk, offered them life.

Amidst the hunger, disease, and death that beset the Jews in the ghettos, camps, and hideouts, the best of human qualities were also revealed: mental fortitude and values of mutual assistance, concern for others, support of the weak, and the tenacious struggle to maintain intellectual and religious life. It was the spiritual and social infrastructure that allowed the besieged to marshal the psychological strength to rise up against the Nazis. After their liberation, many survivors swiftly enlisted in the armies that continued the battle against Nazi Germany.

Overall the few who emerged from the inferno hurriedly left Europe. Some launched a resolute struggle to immigrate to the Land of Israel and establish themselves in the national homeland. Many Holocaust survivors fought in Israel's War of Independence; their contribution to the consolidation of the country's Jewish presence was decisive.

Yad Vashem lauds the survivors for their strength and involvement in its educational work among members of the young generation and dedicates this book in their honor.

We thank all members of the Yad Vashem staff who in recent years have pledged themselves to the massive joint endeavor of leading Yad Vashem toward tomorrow's missions of commemoration and education.

The Editors

Remarks by the Chairman of the Yad Vashem Directorate

Holocaust remembrance is a formative experience in the collective Jewish and Israeli memory and a subject on which Israeli society has developed a broad consensus. In this respect, Yad Vashem serves as a focal point of identification and an expression of the Jewish tradition of mutual responsibility. We consider it our duty to transmit the message of Holocaust remembrance and fill it with content and depth. In this way it will retain its relevance and meaning giving rise to a continual dialogue through which our heritage, commitment to Jewish continuity, the safeguarding of basic human values, education, and imparting the lessons to generations to come will be ensured.

Fifty-one years ago Professor Ben-Zion Dinur presented the Yad Vashem Law for approval in the Knesset. Today Har Hazikaron (The Mount of Remembrance) in Jerusalem has become the center for Jewish and world Holocaust remembrance, a focal point of identification, and an important symbol in the Jewish world and Western civilization. Here we have gathered the memories, the stories, the testimonies, and the names. Here we have laid the foundations for the documentation, research, and commemoration on which Holocaust remembrance rests. And here we acknowledge the Righteous Among the Nations, who have become a universal symbol of humanity.

The survivors of the Holocaust have entrusted us with their dearest possession—their recollections and the memory of the world that was destroyed—and have made Yad Vashem the repository of their memories, their agonies, and their profound yearning to commemorate what once was.

The founders of Yad Vashem and the generations of staff, researchers, educators, public figures, and devoted volunteers have been active for more than half a century. Over the years friends from all over the world, many of them Holocaust survivors, have contributed to Yad Vashem's development and become partners in its progress. The remarkable group of Holocaust survivors who assist us in everything we do, as volunteers and as witnesses, have now been joined by members of the next generations, who are taking up the mantle of responsibility for the continuation of this vital mission.

According to the vision we are creating, the Mount of Remembrance in Jerusalem will become a place of pilgrimage for Jews and the venue for a dynamic and vital intergenerational encounter. Consequently, over the past decade we have added another layer to our edifice, making education our highest priority. Yad Vashem will be a place of contemplation, study and profound experience for young people and for educators from Israel and abroad. It will be a place that strengthens our commitment to continued Jewish existence in the spirit of the Jewish faith, values, and creative drive. In Jewish tradition, the individual, although part of a community and a nation, remains autonomous and is responsible for making the choice expressed in Deuteronomy 30:15: "See, I set before you this day: life and prosperity, death and adversity." It is each generation's duty to fulfill that personal choice, the essence of the spiritual and educational process.

Avner Shalev
Chairman of the Yad Vashem Directorate

The Establishment of Yad Vashem – The Holocaust Martyrs' and Heroes' Remembrance Authority

"And to them I will give,
in My house and within My walls,
a memorial and a name
[Yad Vashem]...
an everlasting name that
shall not be cut off."

[Isaiah 56:5]

The idea of establishing a national remembrance project to commemorate the destroyed European Jewish population was proposed even before the Holocaust had ended, when the first reports about the mass murders reached Palestine. When the war was over, the *Yishuv* institutions and the World Jewish Congress began to discuss ways to memorialize the victims of the Holocaust. Mordecai Shenhavi of Kibbutz Mishmar Ha'Emek was one of the prime initiators; he even suggested the name "Yad Vashem", after Isaiah 56:5: "I will give them in My house and within My walls a memorial and a name [Yad Vashem]… that shall not be cut off." Shenhavi's proposal to establish a central remembrance site for the annihilated Jews of Europe was accepted. In his words:

"The power of our martyred brothers' and sisters' heroism arises and bursts forth from the [scene of the] crime and the devastation. The heroism of the Jewish mother, the steadfastness of the ghetto fighters, our people's participation in the underground armies in all the occupied countries – can it be that they will remain just an oral legend? Or shall we erect a monument to Jewish heroism, one that will symbolize our people's will to live and fight and will underscore its ability to endure the most severe and bitter trials that human history has ever decreed upon a nation?"

In the summer of 1947, the Yad Vashem Directorate presented a plan for the construction of the Har Hazikaron site and, at the initiative of a special Yad Vashem committee, the first Conference on Holocaust Research was held in Jerusalem. However, the military struggle and the eruption of Israel's War of Independence curtailed this activity. In March 1948, Chaim Weizmann wrote to the Yad Vashem Directorate:

"I remember the old legend: in those terrible days when the future of the [Jewish] people is being decided, even the Jewish dead come to the

1

2

1 David Ben-Gurion arrives at a memorial ceremony at Yad Vashem, May 1959

2 Oskar Schindler plants a tree on the Avenue of the Righteous Among the Nations

synagogue to help their brethren. Thus I believe that the spirit of our six million brethren will stand at our side and strengthen our hands as the future of our community in the Land of Israel is being decided. I believe that the choice of 'Yad Vashem' as the name of this enterprise will reverberate through the hearts of all of our brethren, in our country and in all of the Diaspora, and every Jew will have a portion in this national enterprise, for there is not one of us who was not harmed by the cruel enemy."

After the State of Israel was established, initiatives were undertaken to create a central state authority that would lead the effort of preserving the memory of the Holocaust. In 1953, the Minister of Education and historian Prof. Ben-Zion Dinur, presented the *Knesset* with the Yad Vashem—State Remembrance Authority Law, and stated:

"The Yad Vashem Law, 5713-1953, is unique in that it has no precedent in any other country, since the topic with which the statute concerns itself is also unique and unparalleled in human history. Yad Vashem conveys the meaning of a place—a place and a name, a name and a place… The name also says that Israel, our land, and Jerusalem, our city, is the place for them and for their remembrance."

Laying of the Yad Vashem cornerstone, Har Hazikaron, 1954

The Holocaust Remembrance and Heroism Law—Yad Vashem, 5713-1953

1. A memorial authority, Yad Vashem, is hereby established in Jerusalem:

(1) For the six million members of the Jewish people who were doomed to tormented martyrdom, slaughter, and perdition by the Nazis and their assistants;

(2) For the families of the House of Jacob who were annihilated by the despot;

(3) For the communities, the synagogues, the movements and organizations, and the cultural, educational, religious, and charitable public institutions that were sundered and destroyed by the malefactor's scheme to obliterate the name and civilization of Israel from under the heavens;

(4) For the valor of Jews who in sanctity and purity forfeited their souls on behalf of their people;

(5) For the heroism of Jewish soldiers in the armed forces, and of underground fighters in towns and forests, who renounced their lives in battle against the Nazi tyrant and his assistants;

(6) For the heroic feats of those besieged in ghettos and the fighters who rose and ignited the flame of uprising to salvage their people's dignity;

(7) For the exalted and tenacious struggle of the Jewish masses, on the brink of devastation, for their human image and their Jewish culture;

(8) For the ceaseless efforts of the besieged to enter their homeland and for the devotion and heroism of brethren who mobilized to rescue and liberate the surviving remnant;

(9) To the Righteous Among the Nations, who risked their lives to save Jews.

2. It is the function of Yad Vashem to gather in the homeland the memory of all Jews who fell and forfeited their lives, who fought and rebelled against the Nazi enemy and its assistants, and to establish a monument and memorial to them, to the communities, and to the organizations and institutions that were destroyed due to their affiliation

with the Jewish people, and to commemorate the Righteous Among the Nations. For these purposes, Yad Vashem is empowered—

(1) To establish memorial projects at its initiative and under its management;

(2) To gather, investigate, and publish all testimony about the Holocaust and heroism and to impart its lesson to the nation;

(3) To establish in Israel and among all of Jewry the day that the Knesset has designated as Holocaust and Heroism Remembrance Day and to promote a reality of unity of memory of the heroes and victims [of the Holocaust];

(4) To bestow upon Jews who were exterminated, and those who fell in the Holocaust and in uprising, memorial citizenship of the State of Israel as a sign of their ingathering unto their nation;

(4a) To bestow honorary citizenship upon the Righteous Among the Nations and, if they have passed on, memorial citizenship of the State of Israel in appreciation of their actions;

(4b) To establish a commemorative enterprise for veterans of World War II who forfeited their lives in battle against the Nazi despot and its assistants;

(5) To authorize and guide enterprises that wish to commemorate the victims and heroes of the Holocaust, or to cooperate with such enterprises.

(6) To represent Israel in international endeavors that aim to commemorate the victims of the Nazis and those who fell in war against them;

(7) To take any other action that is necessary for the performance of its function.

2a. Victory Day

(a) The anniversary of the victory over Nazi Germany shall be marked each year in accordance with instructions that the Government shall give.

By enshrining the establishment of Yad Vashem in legislation on August 28, 1953 (as recorded in the Knesset gazette), the sovereign State of Israel honored the last will—one of many last wills and letters that Holocaust victims left behind—of Zlatke Wisniacki of Poland: "I think that someone will yet be found who will be able to report about our suffering and our bloodbath…"

According to the Yad Vashem Law, as amended in 1985, the function and powers of Yad Vashem are:

…to gather in Israel the memory of all Jews who fell and forfeited their lives, who fought and rose against the Nazi enemy and its accomplices, and to establish a memorial and a remembrance for them, for the communities, for the organizations, and for the institutions that were destroyed due to their Jewish affiliation; and to commemorate the Righteous Among the Nations…

The cornerstone for the first Yad Vashem

Laying of the Yad Vashem cornerstone, Har Hazikaron, 1954

building was laid on July 29, 1954. To mark the occasion, President Ben-Zvi delivered the following remarks:

"Our feet stand at your gates, Jerusalem, to lay the cornerstone of an enterprise whose goals may fill the heart of every Jew with holy awe. It is a great privilege and a duty of honor for every Jew, great and small, everywhere, to take part in it... *Har Hazikaron* [The Mount of Remembrance] shall serve as a symbol of the everlasting remembrance – Yad Vashem – that we have come to establish for the Holocaust and heroism of our people, in the state of the Jews, in the repository of our nation's deepest memories..."

Several entities participated in the establishment of Yad Vashem: the State of Israel, the Conference on Jewish Material Claims against Germany, and the Jewish Agency for Israel. The first two continued to subsidize the Remembrance Authority in its first decade. Israel's Ministry of

Laying of the Yad Vashem cornerstone, Har Hazikaron, 1954. The President of the State of Israel, Izhak Ben-Zvi, is speaking. Next to him: Mordechai Shenhavi and Ben-Zion Dinur

Education, Culture and Sport, the Jewish Agency, and private donors have supported Yad Vashem's day-to-day activities throughout the years.

In the Jewish year 5763 (2003), Yad Vashem marked its fiftieth anniversary. The memory of the Holocaust and Jewish heroism was shaped in Israel and around the world during those years. At the outset President Yitzhak Ben-Zvi expressed his hope:

"May it be [God's] will that we complete this edifice and augment it with large buildings that will fittingly symbolize the memory of our martyrs and heroes and the will to live of the Jewish people, now being reborn in the State of Israel..."

Since that time Yad Vashem has been building that edifice layer by layer. Its many achievements in commemoration, documentation, research, and education have earned it a worldwide reputation. Today the Mount of Remembrance contains all the elements of Holocaust remembrance: commemoration, documentation, research and education. Yad Vashem is the place where the Jewish people grapple with the Holocaust, the symbol to which all the eyes of the world turn.

The New Holocaust History Museum

In the early 1960s, Yad Vashem inaugurated its first basic historical exhibit and in 1973 established a new and large permanent exhibition at the Historical Museum. It was the first museum that attempted to cope systematically and comprehensively with presenting the history of the Holocaust and to station the Jewish point of view in the center. The exhibit, based on a chronological thematic approach, has been overhauled since then and still exists. Thus far, it has been visited by tens of millions. The Holocaust Art Museum, containing thousands of works, was established in 1982 and has hosted changing exhibits on various themes over the years.

As part of the Yad Vashem development plan that was launched in the early 1990s, a new museum complex has been built. The complex, tailored to the needs of the present and future generations, is meant to respond to the immense numbers of visitors to Yad Vashem. The complex includes a new Holocaust Historical Museum—where some 100 video screens accompany the exhibit with survivors' testimonies and original film clips including cinematic diaries that recount the Holocaust narrative—a Holocaust art museum, a pavilion for changing exhibitions, a viewing center, and a study center.

When designing the building of the new Holocaust History Museum, architect Moshe Safdie was faced with many challenges: to design a structure that would combine the story of the Holocaust while evoking an impressive experience for the visitors; and to preserve the natural landscape and maintain the prominence of the Hall of Remembrance, the focal point of commemoration at Yad Vashem since its early years.

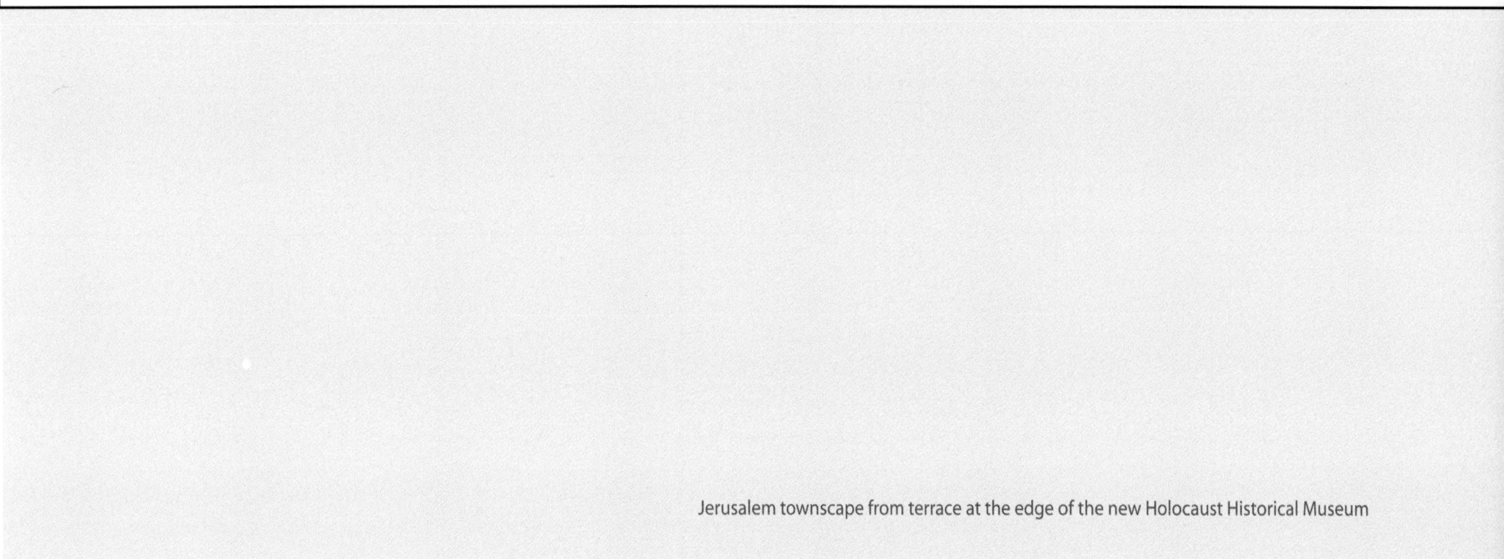

Jerusalem townscape from terrace at the edge of the new Holocaust Historical Museum

Symbolic reconstruction of Warsaw ghetto Leszno Street that includes authentic artifacts

The Museum is a prism-shaped triangular building that pierces the mountain with both ends cantilevering out into the open air. According to Safdie, the triangular shape of the building was chosen in order to support the pressure of the soil over the prism while allowing daylight to enter through the glass roof.

The entire building—floors, walls, interior, and exterior—is made of unfinished, reinforced concrete. The gently sloping floor and narrowing prism enhances the changing narrative, creating the illusion of descending deep into the mountain. As the museum nears its end, the floor begins to rise, the triangle opens up again, and the museum exits dramatically from the mountain's northern slope to a breathtaking view of Jerusalem.

The Museum's designer, Dorit Harel, created a special environment for the different focal points of the Holocaust: the use of varying space, materials and lighting to create an experience of time, place and atmosphere, with original artifacts, documents, and filmed testimonies. Inside the museum, is a 180-meter central walkway (prism) that descends deep into the mountain. The prism floor is crossed by channels containing authentic artifacts and film footage, leading the visitor through the chapters of the story on either side while maintaining visual contact with the two ends of the museum.

The Jewish World Before World War II

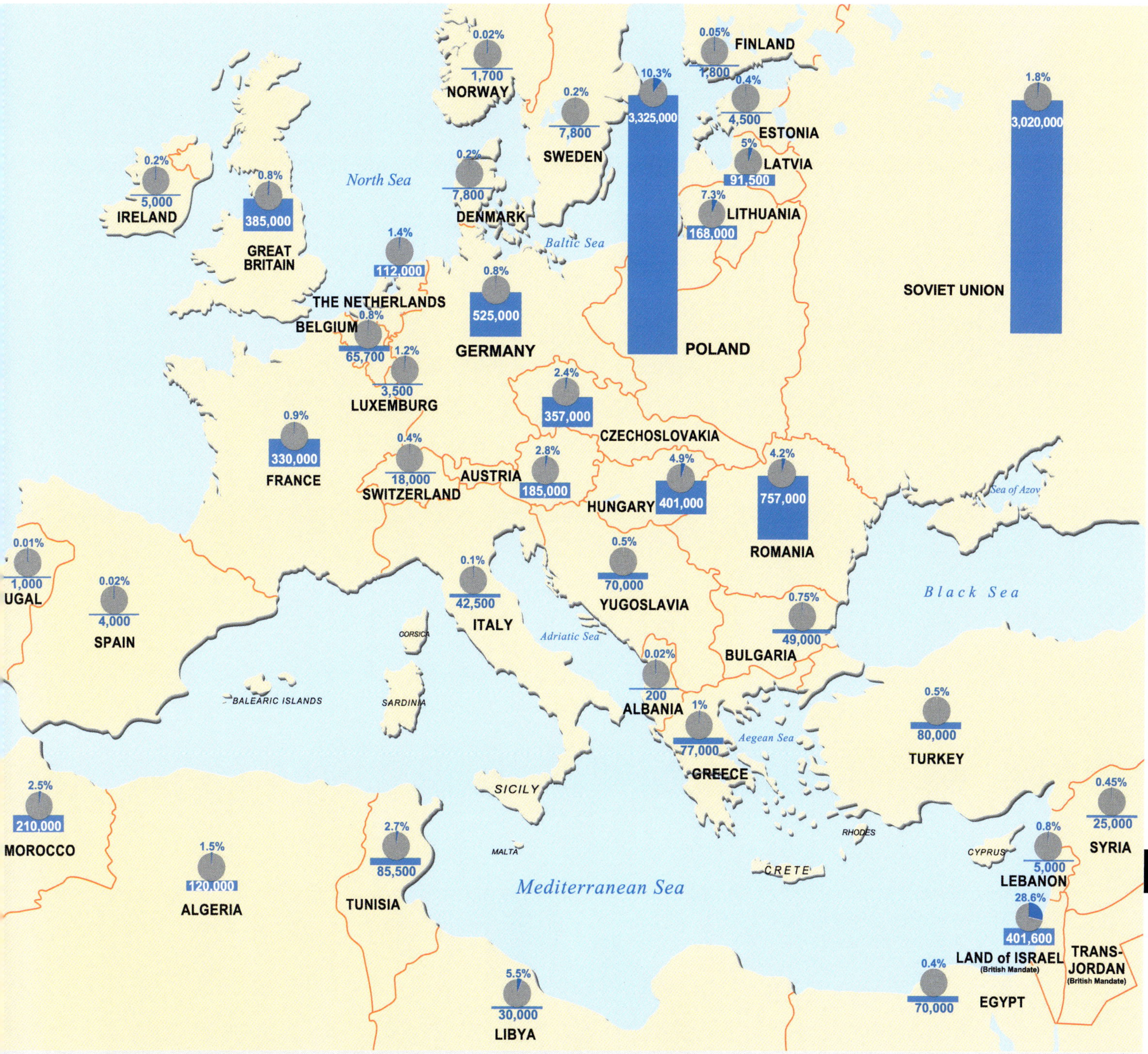

Map of Jewish communities before the Nazi rise to power

Jews lived in Europe for many centuries, often at the behest of rulers interested in benefiting from their economic skills. For generations they endured changing levels of religious hatred and were persecuted by Christianity. Even at the dawn of the Enlightenment, the nations of Europe persisted to persecute Jews, and pogroms and blood libels continued. Nevertheless, European Jewry became a dynamic and multifaceted society that contributed, in all fields of life, to the nations among which they lived, at the same time attaining impressive demographic growth.

Most East European Jews lived in the *shtetls* and villages in the Pale of Settlement. They spoke Yiddish, and their lives revolved around the strict

> **The Jewish world in Europe at that time was an exceptional vital and creative force**
>
> **Professor Salo Baron**

observance of religious laws and willing segregation from the cultural influences of their surroundings. They were also distinct in their appearance and attire. The inroads of the Enlightenment and equality in the 19th century, however, broke through the boundaries of even the most insular communities. Many young Jews left their *yeshivot* (religious schools) and homes to obtain secular education and tackle the challenges of progress. By leaving the Pale of Settlement and moving to urban centers, Jews found new economic occupations in industry, emerging, alongside a small bourgeois and intellectual stratum, as a Jewish proletariat living for the most part in poverty and deprivation.

Pogroms in 1881–1882 and 1902–1905 touched off mammoth waves of Jewish migration—along with migrations of other peoples—from East to West and, foremost, to the free countries of the United States and South America. Concurrently, Eastern European Jewish society was ensnared in a pitched battle between the old patterns of life—which the staunchly Orthodox wished to preserve—and the new ways, affirmed for the most part by the younger generation.

The Western countries—foremost

1 Prof. Ernst Simon, a Jewish soldier in the German army (seated, third from right), receives a citation of excellence for his combat service in World War I, 1916

2 The Katzenbeurg family photo, Duisburg, Germany, 1911

1

2

Germany and France—were central in the Jews' advancement. In the modern era (after the Napoleonic wars) Jews, concentrated in large cities, were given a window of opportunity to hope for equal rights. Together with this privilege, however, the new anti-Jewish current steadily gained strength. The Jews' economic progress, cultural achievements, and social ascendancy added a new dimension to their neighbors' antipathy. If they hated Jews before for daring to be different, they hated them even more now, in the modern era, for wanting to become like the majority of the population. The Jews themselves preferred to explain these manifestations as old ideas receding in the face of progress.

Despite the churning antisemitism, Jews were considered citizens who contributed perceptibly to the host state. Evidence of this is the decision of German Chancellor Otto von Bismarck to participate in the dedication of a synagogue in Berlin in 1866, as a gesture of his appreciation to the community. Due to their improved civil status, West European Jews moved into a wide range of occupations, from trade and banking, academia and the arts, to politics and the army. There seemed to be no further impediments to their progress toward becoming equal, loyal, useful, and accepted citizens in their countries of residence.

In Germany, the Jewish population was divided: some strove for total acceptance in society; they elected to assimilate and distance themselves from their people so emphatically as to change their religion. Others attempted to live in both worlds, in the sense of "a Jew in the home, a man in the street." The extensive spread of social and racial antisemitism among non-Jews, however, sounded an "early alarm" to the fragility of their lives.

At the turn of the 19th and 20th centuries, Europe developed a varied pattern regarding the Jews: in the West, they more or less flourished due to civil equality; in the East however, although there was some easing of the strictures, the fear of ongoing pogroms remained. Even as social ideas progressed however, the nationalistic tendencies of the host nations also gathered strength. These trends influenced the emergence of political parties whose nationalistic platforms challenged the existential base of European Jews. Under the influence of Europe's burgeoning national movements and the undermining of personal and collective security, the intra-Jewish debate about Jewish identity also intensified. At one extreme were those who favored total assimilation. Those who were more moderate argued that a "golden mean" should be found between loyalty to one's home society and the maintenance of Jewish traditions. At the opposite pole, urban proletarian circles and members of the Socialist camp (then in its formative phases) asserted that only a social revolution, in which the Jews and their neighbors

1

would participate together, would solve the Jewish people of its problems in society. The Jewish national movement "Zionism" stationed itself among the camps, advocating the establishment of a framework of Jewish statehood in which, at the end of the process, all Jews would set up a society that could sustain a modern Jewish way of life.

At the end of World War I, after carrying out their civic responsibility by enlisting in the warring armies, Europe's Jews believed that, in the coming era of peace, progress, and tolerance (and, foremost, after the question of national self-determination became a legitimate topic on the global agenda), they would earn protection and appreciation by dint of their overall contribution. Jewish leaders, artists, writers, and intellectuals left their imprints on European culture and higher education, particularly in Germany: Albert Einstein in physics, Sigmund Freud in psychology and Marc Chagall and Amedeo Modigliani in art. German Jews were made Nobel Prize laureates, taking pride in the honor they bestowed upon their country. They felt they had finally burst through the ghetto ramparts and become part of mainstream society. The 1920s and the 1930s, however, witnessed an eruption of radical nationalism and venomous anti-semitism. At first the Jews' economic and occupational advancement was forestalled; then they were ousted

2

1 The medal that Lily Jäger received for her service as a nurse in World War I

2 The sons of Emanuel Wertheimer of Baden, Germany. They served in the army in World War I from political life; and finally they were labeled in Germany an "inferior" race. Old and new antisemitism merged with human evil, paving the Jews' way back to the ghettos.

"The heart of the German Jewish problem [was] this: [German Jewry] was so immersed in German society that the Nazi blow came from within. Not from without, as with Polish Jewry, on whom the occupation descended, alighted. Here, there was no occupation."

Zwi Bacharach

The scenery, images and faces of Jewish life are projected on a wall 13 meters high and 11 meters wide at the entrance to the new Holocaust History Museum. Michal Rovner's video artwork takes the visitor on a journey into a world that no longer exits. The work is composed of original film clips and photographs that document the tapestry of pre-war European Jewish daily life, a dynamic and effervescent existence integrated into its social surroundings.

The artwork is composed of materials that were refurbished and blended together. The process resembled an attempt to assemble a jigsaw puzzle in which many pieces were missing and no picture was provided. The work conveys a landscape that arises from contemplation of a human society that no longer exists.

Rovner's intention was not to create a narrative film, but rather to create a kind of scroll, a quilt, a moving human landscape.

Inside the building, in the windows: old-age home in the Netherlands
Nowogrodek, Brandeis
Peto, Free-Fall Right: a shot from five towns
Middle: girls waving (from: YIVO Kolbuszowa)
Left: children playing the violin (from *Chaim*, Brautonia, Washington)

Photos courtesy of USHMM, YIVO, Beth Hatefutsoth, Steven Spielberg Film Archive, Dr. Kati Peto, Mr. Peter Forgasch, National Center for Jewish Film (Brandeis), Netherlands Filmmuseum

"The people are gone, but their traces remain..."

Ida Fink, *Traces*

On September 19, 1944, a few days before the Soviet army liberated the Klooga camp in Estonia, the Germans and their Estonian collaborators murdered more than 2,000 Jews, most of them from the Vilna ghetto. The murderers attempted to cover up all traces of the murder, but did not have enough time to burn most of the bodies. Pictures, papers and other personal effects, some of them partially burned, remained in the inmates pockets. These personal items were for them a memory and a record of their lives that had been destroyed with the Nazi occupation.

Nazi Germany and the Jews, 1933–1939

Hitler at a National Labor Day Rally, Berlin, May 1, 1934

From Traditional Hatred of Jews to Modern Antisemitism and Racism

Antisemitism had long been entrenched in Germany and other European countries, fomented by Christianity. The image of the Jew as the murderer of Jesus and the fact that Jews had rejected Christianity's embrace led to widespread hatred and suspicion. Jews in Christendom were humiliated, banished from their places of residence, forced to wear identifying marks, and confined to separate residential quarters. They were portrayed as offspring of the Devil and accused of the ritual murder of Christian children.

In the 18th and 19th centuries, antisemitism that emphasized economic, social, or political differences gained strength. A combination of racial antisemitism and social Darwinism, however, invested this traditional antisemitism with a new image and dynamic. Racial theories became prevalent in Europe and, especially, in Germany in the middle of the

Slay [the Jews] not... scatter them abroad.

Augustine, one of the Church Fathers

Christian sculpture: blindness and humiliation of Jewry contrasted with the sightedness and triumph of Christianity. Strasbourg, France, 13th century

Modern Antisemitism

Pre-war modern antisemites objected to the Jews' new status and economic achievements and were repulsed by their social involvement. They defined Jews as symbols of a threatening progress. Ethnic national movements reinforced the tendency to isolate "the Jew" and brand him as the "other." This attitude spawned two special indicators of modern antisemitism: the myth of the "Jewish conspiracy," in which Jews are accused of devising a secret plot to take over the world; and an ostensibly scientific racial theory that attributes to Jews immutable and objectionable biological traits. The new antisemitism rejected the Jews' social integration and paved the way for the pernicious vision of the Nazis.

The Protocols of the Elders of Zion

In 1903, a newspaper in Czarist Russia published a document that purported to be a secret action plan by which the Jews plotted to take over the world. Although the Russian secret police quickly proved the document to be a forgery, the Protocols were distributed across Europe. The first version in German came out in 1911, in Berlin. In 1937, a court in Switzerland declared it groundless. This finding, however, did not stave off the dissemination of the *Protocols* worldwide.

1 French edition of *The Protocols of the Elders of Zion*
2 German edition of *The Protocols of the Elders of Zion*

nineteenth century. The very term "antisemitism," which signals antipathy toward Jews not as practitioners of a different faith or holders of a separate nationality, but as members of a special race, was first coined by antisemites in Germany in the 1870s.

Political antisemitism—Jew-hatred as a factor in political life—was meant to serve as a tool in the struggle for the minds of the masses. Not until the 1930s, however, with the ascendancy of National Socialism and Adolf Hitler's accession to power in Germany, did racial antisemitism become a political instrument in the hands of the masses and, later on, official policy of a modern state. From then on the crux of Jewishness was believed to be biological uniqueness, preventing a Jew from avoiding persecution by assimilating, renouncing the customs of his tradition, or adopting a non-Jewish faith. The new racial outlook defined the German people as the finest and purest branch of the Aryan-Nordic racial trunk and labeled Jews as a subhuman race that strove to challenge the "correct" world order and deprive the "supreme race" of its position of dominance and leadership. Unless the "Aryan" race won the struggle and established its dominion, Jews would lead the world to decline and degeneration. This conviction, embraced by Hitler and his followers, had a developmental dynamic of its own. The very declaration of an uncompromising racial war later set the stage for the future "Final Solution."

1

2

The Beer Hall Putsch

In November 1923, Hitler and his supporters attempted to topple the government of Bavaria in what came to be known as the "Beer Hall Putsch." On November 8, backed by armed members of the SS, Hitler proclaimed the beginning of the national revolution. The following day a large Nazi demonstration took place in the center of Munich. The demonstrators ran up against police barriers, and a brief gun battle ensued. Hitler and his associates were placed on trial in a widely covered proceeding that gave the Nazis a propaganda victory. Hitler was sentenced to five years in prison but was released after only one year.

The Nazi Accession to Power

Hitler rose to power due to the social and political circumstances that characterized the interwar period in Germany. Many Germans could not concede their country's defeat in World War I, arguing that "backstabbing" and weakness in the rear had paralyzed and, eventually, caused the front to collapse. The Jews, they claimed, had done much to spread defeatism and thus destroy the German army. Democracy in the Weimar Republic, they argued, was a form of governance that had been imposed on Germany, unsuited to the German nature and way of life. They construed the terms of the Versailles peace treaty and the steep compensation payments it entailed as revenge by the victors and a glaring injustice. This frustration, together with intransigent resistance and warnings about the surging menace

> **No one need be surprised if among our people the personification of the devil, as the symbol of all evil, assumes the living shape of the Jew.**
>
> Adolf Hitler, *Mein Kampf*

3

4

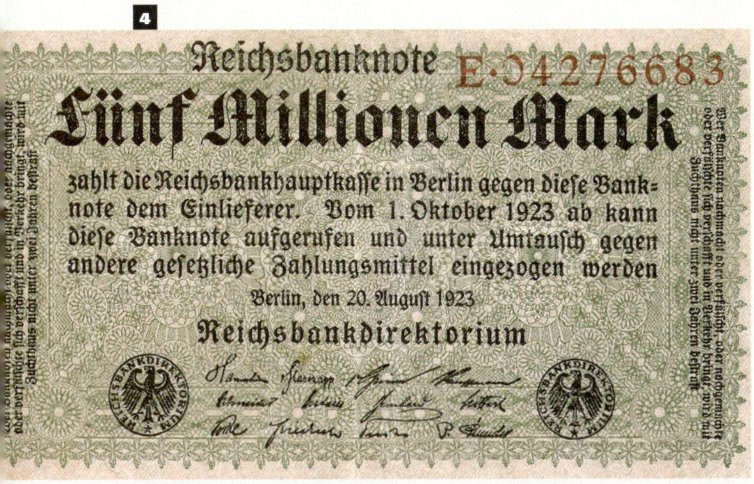

1 Cartoon depicting Mayer Amschel Rothschild as a financier who controls the global economy. Frankfurt, 1895
2 Ashtray with relief of a swine swallowing a Jew
3 Germany: the "*backstabbing*" myth, April 1924
4 Banknote and stamps issued in the Weimar Republic during the inflation era

of Communism, created fertile soil for the growth of radical right-wing groups in Germany, spawning entities such as the Nazi party.

Another catalyst of ferment and change was the economic instability that rocked Germany following WWI. In 1925, a transitory economic upturn and a promising political dialogue brought relative calm into sight. However, the severe international economic crisis that erupted in 1929, carried the instability to new heights. During his brief stay in prison, Hitler wrote his venomous book *Mein Kampf* (My Struggle), in which he expressed his ideas about racial theory and global dominion. He and his associates left no doubt about their belief in democratic freedoms as mere tools with which power might be attained. In the 1924 Reichstag elections, the

1

2

Nazi party received three percent of the vote and was represented in the parliament by fourteen delegates. In the 1928 elections, its support declined; the party was able to send only twelve delegates to the legislature. The turnaround came in 1930, the first elections held after the economic crisis began. The Nazis received 18.3 percent of the vote and sent 107 delegates to the Reichstag. In July 1932, with 230 mandates (37%), they became the largest faction in the house—an influential political force. Hitler became chancellor on January 30, 1933. President Paul von Hindenburg gave Hitler the mandate to form a government, enabling him to utilize his effective political executive power under a totalitarian regime. Hitler's use of power helped him rapidly transform the Weimar Republic's democracy into a totalitarian regime. Decisive power was concentrated in the hands of a leader who considered himself a chosen individual: a man with a mission.

1 The Reichstag building ablaze, Berlin, February 27, 1933
2 Hitler addressing the Reichstag, April 1939
3 Stein embossed with antisemitic reliefs
4 "Death to the Lie"—Nazi Party propaganda broadsheet
5 "Victory March of the Swastika," a game designed to teach children the history of the Nazi Party

3

4

5

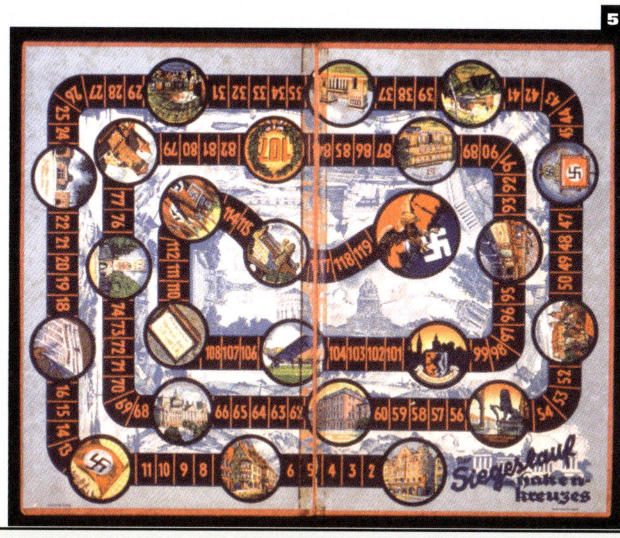

The Swastika

The symbol of the swastika is of ancient origin. It has appeared in Oriental civilizations since the fifth century, in Byzantine culture, and among North and South American Indian tribes. Today it is prevalent among Hindus and Buddhists. In 1910, the German nationalist Guido von List proposed the swastika as a universal symbol of antisemitic movements, and, in 1920, the Nazi party adopted it as its emblem. In 1935, the design of a black swastika against a red background was devised and declared the flag of Nazi Germany.

The Nazis' Anti-Jewish Policy

On March 9 1933, several weeks after Hitler assumed power, organized attacks on Jews broke out across Germany. Less than two weeks later, Dachau, the first Nazi concentration camp was opened. Situated near Munich, Dachau became a place of internment for German Jews, Communists, Socialists, and liberals—anyone whom the Reich considered its enemy. It also became the model for the network of concentration camps that would be established later by the Nazis.

In the first two years of Nazi rule, Hitler engaged in "coordination," i.e., the consolidation of Nazi influence in all areas of German life. All Germans were urged to adopt Nazi ideology and unquestioningly obey the Führer and his regime. Within a few months, democracy was obliterated in Germany, and the country became a centralized, single-party police state: the country's social institutions were reconstituted; governing mechanisms, including the judicial system, were staffed with loyalists of the regime; and the Church, wishing to assure its status and power, also capitulated to Nazi rule. In July 1933, Pope Pius XI concluded a Concordate (treaty) with Hitler, even

1

2

3

> **A country is not just what it does, it is also what it tolerates.**
>
> Kurt Tucholsky, German essayist of Jewish origin

though the Nazis had imprisoned several Church officials for protesting German terror and assaults on civilians.

In the 1930s, Germany's Jews—some 500,000 people—made up less than 1 percent of the German population. They considered themselves loyal patriots, linked to the German way of life by language and culture. They excelled in science, literature, the arts, and economic enterprise. Conversion, intermarriage, and declining birth rates, however, led some to believe that Jewish life was doomed to disappear from the German scene altogether. The paradox was that Nazi ideology stemmed from Germany and the German people, among whom Jews eagerly wanted to acculturate.

The leaders of the new German regime construed protests against their policy by world leaders as responses to Jewish incitement, and countered them by announcing a general boycott of German Jewry.

Ultimately, the boycott, preceded by countrywide propaganda, lasted only one day. On that day, April 1, 1933, vigils formed in front of Jewish-owned shops and businesses. Pro-boycott signs and demonstrations were ubiquitous, all orchestrated by members of the SA. Notably, many Germans did not submit to the campaign of defamation, choosing to shop that day at Jewish-owned establishments.

A new stage in anti-Jewish policy began in April 1933, aiming to repeal the legal and civic equality of German Jews, impose phased economic dispossession, raise a social barrier between Jews and Germans, and expedite emigration.

The first laws banished Jews from the civil services, judicial system, public medicine, and the German army (then being reconstituted.)

In 1933, ceremonial public book-

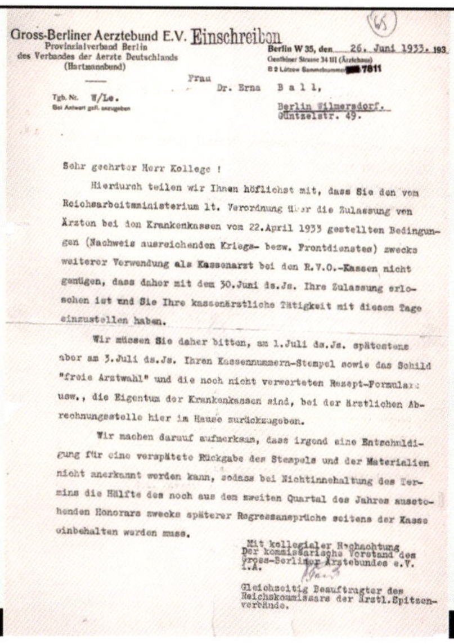

Gross-Berliner Aerztebund E.V. Einschreiben
Provinzialverband Berlin
des Verbandes der Aerzte Deutschlands
(Hartmannbund)

Berlin W 35, den 26. Juni 1933.
Genthiner Strasse 34 III (Ärztehaus)
B 2 Lützow Sammelnummer 7811

Tgb. Nr. W/Le.
Bei Antwort gefl. anzugeben

Frau
Dr. Erna Ball,
Berlin Wilmersdorf.
Güntzelstr. 49.

Sehr geehrter Herr Kollege !

Hierdurch teilen wir Ihnen höflichst mit, dass Sie den vom Reichsarbeitsministerium lt. Verordnung über die Zulassung von Ärzten bei den Krankenkassen vom 22.April 1933 gestellten Bedingungen (Nachweis ausreichenden Kriegs- bezw. Frontdienstes) zwecks weiterer Verwendung als Kassenarzt bei den R.V.O.-Kassen nicht genügen, dass daher mit dem 30.Juni ds.Js. Ihre Zulassung erloschen ist und Sie Ihre kassenärztliche Tätigkeit mit diesem Tage einzustellen haben.

Wir müssen Sie daher bitten, am 1.Juli ds.Js. spätestens aber am 3.Juli ds.Js. Ihren Kassennummern-Stempel sowie das Schild "freie Arztwahl" und die noch nicht verwerteten Rezept-Formulare usw., die Eigentum der Krankenkassen sind, bei der ärztlichen Abrechnungsstelle hier im Hause zurückzugeben.

Wir machen darauf aufmerksam, dass irgend eine Entschuldigung für eine verspätete Rückgabe des Stempels und der Materialien nicht anerkannt werden kann, sodass bei Nichtinnehaltung des Termins die Hälfte des noch aus dem zweiten Quartal des Jahres ausstehenden Honorars zwecks späterer Regressansprüche seitens der Kasse einbehalten werden muss.

Mit kollegialer Hochachtung
Der kommissarische Vorstand des
Gross-Berliner Ärztebundes e.V.
i.A.

Gleichzeitig Beauftragter des
Reichskommissars der ärztl.Spitzenverbände.

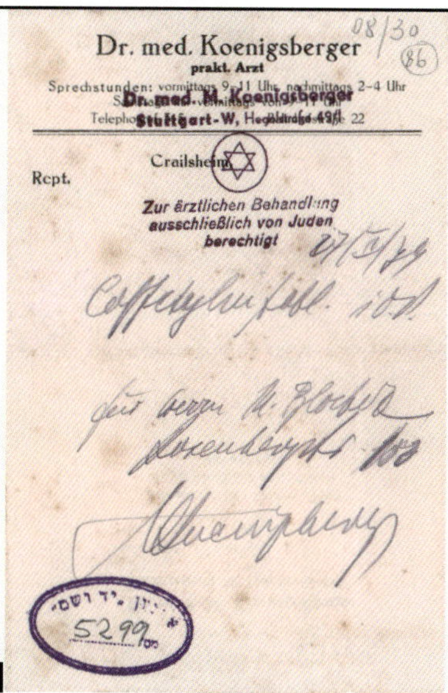

Dr. med. Koenigsberger
prakt. Arzt
Dr. med. M. Koenigsberger
Stuttgart-W, Hegelstraße 49
Rept.
Crailsheim
Zur ärztlichen Behandlung ausschließlich von Juden berechtigt

1 Political prisoners at roll call, Oranienburg concentration camp, Germany, April 1933

2 Judges pledge allegiance to Hitler, October 1936

3 The Reich Bishop, Ludwig Mueller, delivers a clenched-fist salute

4 "...We inform you that your employment permit expires on June 30 of this year and you must desist from all medical practice." Letter of dismissal received by Dr. Erne Ball on June 26, 1933, from the German Medical Association

5 Jewish doctors must mark their prescriptions with a special stamp: "Licensed to treat Jewish patients only"

"Jews Aren't Wanted Here"

Antisemitic signs posted in many locations in Germany, indicated that many Germans identified with the Nazis' racial legislation and antisemitic propaganda. The change was perceived in all fields of life: government officials disregarded enquiries by Jews, employers treated them with hostility, and co-workers and neighbors severed social relations. In schools, teachers taught Nazi racial theory. Many Jewish pupils dropped out of public schools and transferred to Jewish schools, due to the enmity they experienced. A barricade of estrangement and discrimination created a state with nearly total segregation.

1

2

3

4

burnings, a bizarre and frightening spectacle in 20th century Europe, took place around Germany. Many books were torched solely because their authors were Jews. The exclusion of Jews from German cultural life was highly visible, ousting their considerable contribution to the German press, literature, theater, and music.

"My father ... was accepted as a member of the German War Veterans Union. In late 1933, they called all the Jews and told them that they were hereby expelled because they were Jews, a disgrace to the German people, and so on. It didn't break him but it broke his belief that the Jews could fit in."

Uri Ben-Ari

Professor Hermann Zondek

Professor Hermann Zondek was director of the Municipal Hospital in Berlin. While treating his patients one day in March 1933, Professor Zondek was summoned to his room, where SS men tendered him a notice of his dismissal. His rights as a former military physician in World War I, the many awards he had received, and the fact that he was the personal physician to two former chancellors, (Stresemann and Schleicher) made no difference. Professor Zondek left Germany that very day and eventually settled in Palestine. "Only after I left Germany," he wrote, "did I understand that until 1933 the Jews had been living in a fools paradise."

The First Anti-Jewish Racial Law

A bill concerning the rehabilitation of the professional civil service was passed into law on April 7, 1933. The purpose of the legislation was to purge the civil service of officials of Jewish origin and those deemed disloyal to the regime. It was the first racial law that attempted to isolate Jews and oust them from German life. That day Victor Klemperer wrote in his diary, "Even an animal is not more deprived and persecuted [than a Jew]."

1. "Avoid Jewish Doctors and Lawyers"
2. Ticket distributed at German railroad stations: "Free ticket to Jerusalem, good for a trip from any German railroad station, non-transferable, fourth class"
3. Nazi sticker: "North Sea Spa Norderney - is Free of Jews"
4. Nazi postcard, distributed in Austria following its annexation to the Reich: "People, the Time Has Come." A Jew, a Social Democrat, and a priest shown fleeing from Nazism. Austria, July 1938

Book Burning

On May 10, 1933, a ritual "public burning of noxious Jewish writings" was organized in Opera Square, opposite the University of Berlin. Some 20,000 books by Jewish authors and non-Jews suspected of writing in a "Jewish spirit" were destroyed in the fire. Similar events took place in other German cities.

The list of banned authors included Heinrich Heine, Karl Marx, Sigmund Freud, Albert Einstein, Franz Kafka, Stefan Zweig, and Felix Mendelssohn-Bartholdy. Among the non-Jews banned were Heinrich Mann, Erich Marie Remarque, Erich Kastner, and Berthold Brecht. The works of Van Gogh, Cezanne, Picasso, Matisse, and Chagall were banished from museums.

Where books are burned, human beings are also destined to be burned.

Heinrich Heine

Germany Becomes a Racial State

A citizen of the Reich is a subject of the State who has German blood...

(Reich Citizenship Law, September 15, 1935)

The term "Nuremberg Laws" refers to a corpus of statutes first adopted by the Reichstag, whose members were guests at the party convention that took place in that city. The legislation enacted in September 1935, consisted of basic laws to which would be added executive regulations and complementary provisions. Practically speaking, they transformed Jews into second-class citizens, setting the stage for ceaseless and continually worsening persecution.

Ironically, some Jews in Germany and elsewhere greeted the Nuremberg Laws with a measure of relief. The action taken in Nuremberg, they believed, set German Jewry on a new legal footing, instead of the confusion that had prevailed beforehand. Although the legislation was severe, they claimed, it left room for Jews to exist in their own world, which had now been sealed by the strictures. Jews should organize and adjust to the new situation, they counseled.

Many Jews also still believed that they had a future in Germany because the Nazis recognized their role in trade. Indeed, the Nazi regime refrained from eradicating Jewish-owned economic enterprises for several years, especially those with links to foreign countries.

Nazi Minister of Propaganda Joseph Goebbels sought to compress cultural life into an imposed standard model. Various domains of cultural and artistic endeavor were administered by state-controlled bureaus. The regime determined what was forbidden and what was permissible, what was perceived to be good and what was unfit to be considered art, who was an artist of value and who should be banned and silenced. The regime reshaped culture and education; and teenagers were enlisted in a Nazi youth movement that trained them for future roles within the framework of the Nazi state. Jews were banned from universities; Jewish actors were dismissed from theaters; Jewish authors' works were rejected by publishers; and Jewish journalists were hard-pressed to find newspapers that would publish their writings. Famous artists and scientists played an important role in this campaign of dispossession and party labeling of

1

2

1 Members of the German Girls Association of Hamburg receive instruction in racial matters, Hamburg, 1934

2 Smoke billowing from the crematorium at the Hadamar "euthanasia" institute, Germany. Some 10,000 Germans were murdered here in 1940–1941

literature, art, and science. Some scientists and physicians were involved in the theoretical underpinnings of the racial doctrine. Over time they participated actively in crimes disguised as scientific research, including the euthanasia—"mercy killing"—of some 275,000 physically or mentally disabled Germans.

First they came for the Jews
and I did not speak out because I was
not a Jew.
Then they came for the Communists
and I did not speak out because I was
not a Communist.
Then they came for the trade unionists
and I did not speak out because I was
not a trade unionist.
Then they came for me
and there was no one left
to speak out for me.

Attributed to Martin Niemöller,
a German Protestant clergyman

The Eternal Jew

On November 8, 1937, the German Museum of Munich inaugurated the largest ever antisemitic exhibition entitled "The Eternal Jew". Joseph Goebbels and Julius Streicher gave speeches, and actors recited excerpts from Martin Luther's treatise, "On the Jews and Their Lies," and performed scenes from Shakespeare's Play *The Merchant of Venice*.

Nazi broadsheet depicting the Jew as a schemer against the purity of German blood, *Der Stürmer*, August 1938

Charlotte Salomon

Charlotte Salomon came from a family deeply rooted in the cultural and social life in Berlin. In 1935 she was allowed to enroll in the Academy for the Arts, despite being Jewish. In the aftermath of *Kristallnacht*, during which her father was arrested, her family decided to send Charlotte to the South of France. There, even after the Nazi occupation, she produced a series of hundreds of paintings entitled "Life or Theater," recounting her family's story and describing the fate of German Jewry. In 1943, she married Alexander Nagler, also a Jewish refugee. When she was four months pregnant, Charlotte and Alexander were captured and sent to Auschwitz. Neither survived.

Charlotte Salomon (1917–1943), self-portrait, 1939–1941, crayon on paper

Charlotte Salomon
(1917–1943), Landscape with the Villa l'Ermitage, 1939–1941, gouache on paper

German Jewry: An Identity in Crisis

"We were immersed in everything that was German. For example, my mother wouldn't put up with a word of Yiddish at home. Goethe, Schiller, and all the rest, [we knew] the whole thing by heart. I doubt that she'd ever heard of Bialik."

"I remember [after Kristallnacht], Mother stood, pale, and cried. What happened? I recall that she phoned non-Jewish friends. She had more non-Jewish friends than Jewish ones. No answer. Not one."

Zwi Bacharach

"I attended a Gentile elementary school and I was the only Jew, and I learned the racial theory every morning. Every morning they taught us the racial theory.... And even though I asked to be excused from this lesson, they didn't let me. Instead, I got ten whacks on my behind."

Uri Ben-Ari

Jews countered the official antisemitic policy and attacks by Nazi thugs by strengthening their inner cohesion and organizing more effectively. In September 1933, about half a year after Hitler became chancellor, the *Reichsvertretung der Deutschen Juden* (National Representation of German Jews) was established, amalgamating the main organizations of German Jewry (non-Labor Zionist and pro-assimilation circles). Jews strove to rebuild their internal lives and establish social and cultural venues for those who had been segregated from the population at large. Other circles, foremost the Zionists and youth movements, emphasized rapid emigration, occupational retraining, and promise of reestablishment under the new conditions. Broad-based action was taken to organize groups of children and teenagers under Youth Aliyah and in Zionist pioneering training facilities; special emphasis was placed on social self-help for those who had lost their sources of livelihood. After a century of struggle for equal rights, however, many German Jews had developed strong bonds with the country and its people—culturally, socially, and geographically —and considered themselves full-fledged Germans. For many, their Jewishness was only a loose religious affiliation.

I would not like to be a Jew in Germany.

Hermann Göring

In autumn 1935, a Dutch motorcyclist traveled toward Berlin and took pictures of signs: "Jews, pay attention: the way to Palestine doesn't pass here"; "The Jew is our misfortune; get out of here"; "Jews who enter this location face danger"

Der Jude ist unser Unglück
er bleibe uns vom Leibe

Non-Jewish Victims of Persecution in Germany

Aside from the Jews, the victims of Nazi persecution included members of various groups considered enemies of the Reich.

Sinti and Roma (Gypsies)

The Nazis considered Sinti and Roma a socio-racial "problem" to be expurgated from the German nation. They were subjected to special depredations; their fate was tantamount to that of Jews. Of the 44,000 Sinti and Roma who lived in the Reich, thousands were sent to concentration camps after the war began; others were concentrated in transit camps before being sent to ghettos and extermination camps during the war.

"The experience gathered in combatting the Gypsy nuisance... shows that the appropriate way to tackle the problem is to treat it as a racial matter.... Therefore, I hereby order all Gypsies... and all nomads living a Gypsy-like life to be registered by the Criminal Police of the Reich." Heinrich Himmler, head of the SS, 1938.

The Germans murdered between 90,000–150,000 Sinti and Roma.

Homosexuals

The Nazis considered homosexuality an affront to their goal of encouraging natural increase and "Aryan" family life. About 15,000 homosexuals were interned in camps, where several thousand perished due to the living conditions.

Seventh Day Adventists

Seventh Day Adventists were persecuted because of their particular faith.

1

2

The Fate of the New Christians

In the 18th century, Carolina Kaulla and her brother, Jakob, were given an official post at the court of the Duke of Württemberg. Their descendants expanded into commercial business and banking and established public institutions. They felt German; Germany was their homeland. After the Nazis came to power, most members of the family emigrated, leaving behind only those who had embraced Christianity and believed that the racial laws did not apply to them. Marguerite Kaulla, who petitioned for recognition as a Christian, was deported to the camps together with her mother, Johanna, as Jewish women. Johanna was sent to Terezin and Marguerite to Ravensbrück, where they perished.

3

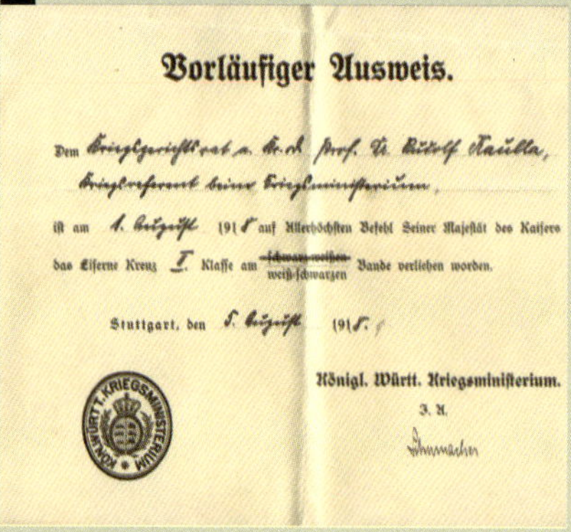

Vorläufiger Ausweis.

Dem Kriegsgerichtsrat a. [illegible] Prof. Dr. Rudolf Kaulla, Kriegsreferent beim Kriegsministerium,

ist am 1. August 1918 auf Allerhöchsten Befehl Seiner Majestät des Kaisers das Eiserne Kreuz I. Klasse am ~~schwarz-weißen~~ weiß-schwarzen Bande verliehen worden.

Stuttgart, den 5. August 1918.

Königl. Württ. Kriegsministerium.

J. A.

Schumacher

For many, the Nazi regime, with its numerous decrees, precipitated personal tragedy. Even at that early phase, however, some Jews had the foresight to realize that Nazism was not a passing phenomenon but a threat of something out of the ordinary. They also warned about the possible spread of Nazism and urged Jews to brace themselves for a period in which human dignity and sacred values would be trampled.

In the second half of the 1930s, the Nazi regime was a success story in the eyes of most Germans. The Germans were satisfied with the stabilization of their country's political system; most of them accepted the abolition of democracy and the persecution of those whom the regime considered its opponents. The country climbed out of the economic depression and rebuilt its armed forces. Hitler's foreign policy succeeded in reclaiming the Saar and Rhineland areas, in annexing Austria (*Anschluss*), and restoring national pride. The treaties with Poland, Great Britain, the Vatican, and the Soviet Union, and, especially, the successful Olympic games held in Berlin in 1936, awarded Nazi Germany international recognition. The international community continued to consider the persecution of the Jews as an internal German affair.

4

1 Racial testing of Sinti and Roma, Germany, 1933
2 Prisoners at roll call in Dachau, Germany, June 20, 1938
3 Document from World War I of Prof. Rudolf Kaulla, a descendant of Madame Kaulla
4 Postcard marking the *Anschluss*. Next to the map of the expanded Reich, the slogan, "One people, one Reich, one Führer" appears
5 The athlete Jesse Owens. After Owens defeated his German rivals, Hitler refused to shake the hand of a "member of an inferior race"
6 Inauguration of the Olympic Games in Berlin, August 1936

5

6

1938 – "The Fateful Year"

The events of 1938, which a German document termed "the Fateful Year," were part of the radicalization of the Nazis' Jewish policy. From the ouset, the Nazi regime had fomented a climate of terror by targeting various groups and individuals for overt attack. Within a few months it had obliterated democracy in Germany and transformed the country into a centralized, single-party police state. At the same time, expansionism escalated, and domestic preparations for war accelerated.

The crackdown on Jews also took on an increased ferocity viewed as part of the overall political and ideological course. An anti-Jewish campaign began that year, which included the demolition of synagogues, mass arrests, destruction and looting of shops, and registration of Jewish property for expropriation purposes. The Nazi Minister of Justice Walter Funk boasted that, by 1938, the authorities had managed to steal Jewish property worth two million marks.

On October 5, 1938, Jews' passports were invalidated, and those who needed a passport for emigration purposes were given one marked with the letter J (Jude - Jew). The idea of a special mark was the brainchild of a high-ranking Swiss official; Switzerland was one of the countries that sought to keep German Jewish citizens from entering freely.

The deportation to Zbaszyn was directly linked to a central anti-Jewish event that took place on the night of November 9–10, 1938—a pogrom known as *Kristallnacht*. This eruption of violence, blamed on a "spontanous" protest against the assassination perpetrated by Herschel Grynspan was anything but; it had been planned and implemented by the highest echelons. The signal was given by Joseph Goebbels, with Hitler's approval, and

1

2

1 Demolished businesses, Magdeburg
2 Marking of Jewish-owned businesses in Berlin, November 1938
3 Torching of a synagogue in a suburb of Berlin, 1938

the pogrom was carried out by SA stormtroopers. During the pogrom, more than 1,400 synagogues across Germany were torched; Jewish-owned shops and businesses were plundered and destroyed; Jews were later ordered to pay "compensation"; and some 30,000 Jews were arrested and taken to concentration camps. *Kristallnacht* marked the end of the period in which ostensibly constitutional methods were used to ensure social segregation, economic dispossession, and accelerated Jewish emigration. It was followed by a combination of racist acts and brutal violence, manifested mainly in the intensity and frequency of acts of unprecedented cruelty.

3

The First Mass Deportation

On October 27, 1938, Nazi Germany carried out the brutal eviction of Jews with Polish citizenship—the first mass deportation of Jews. SS men abandoned children, elderly, and the sick across the Polish border. The unfortunates, concentrated in abandoned stables near the border town of Zbaszyn, included the Grynspan family from Hannover. Mr. Grynspan sent a letter to his seventeen-year-old son Herschel, who lived in Paris, describing the hardships the family was enduring. After reading the letter, Herschel went to the German embassy and shot a low-ranking diplomat. In response to his arrest and interrogation, Herschel said, "It's not a crime to be Jewish. I'm not a dog. I have the right to live and the Jewish people has the right to exist in this world. Everywhere I am persecuted like an animal."

1

The World Closes Its Gates

Where To?

After *Kristallnacht,* Jewish emigration from Germany, Austria, and Czechoslovakia accelerated. Most countries closed their gates to Jews, who, in their desperation, attempted to reach any possible destination, including Shanghai. Domestic and external pressures induced the British government, which had closed Palestine to Jewish immigration and settlement, to admit some 10,000 children who left for Great Britain without their parents in the *"Kindertransports"*. Most of the children were received warmly by their foster families. Many never saw their parents again, as their families were later deported to the East, and murdered.

2

3

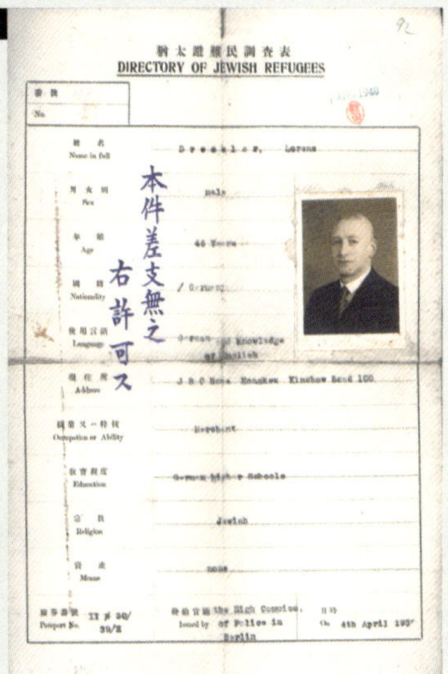

猶太避難民調査表
DIRECTORY OF JEWISH REFUGEES

No.

本件差支無之
右許可ス

Name in full	Dressler, Lorenz
Sex	male
Age	46 Years
Nationality	German
Language	German and Knowledge of English
Address	J R C Home Hongkew Kinchow Road 100
Occupation or Ability	Merchant
Education	German high-r Schools
Religion	Jewish
Means	none
Passport No.	II p 30/39/E
Issued by	the High Commissioner of Police in Berlin
On	4th April 1939

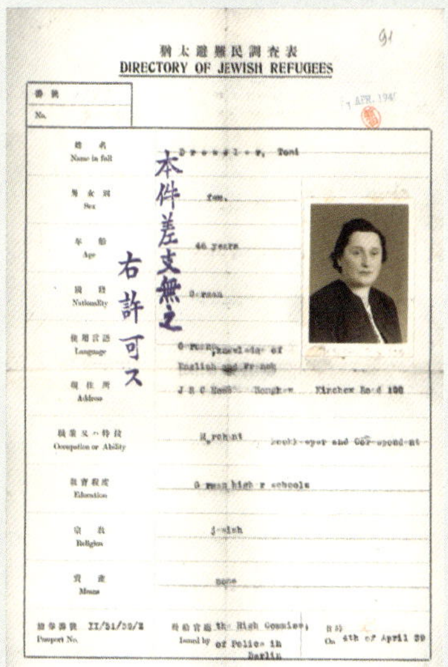

猶太避難民調査表
DIRECTORY OF JEWISH REFUGEES

No.

本件差支無之
右許可ス

Name in full	Dressler, Toni
Sex	fem.
Age	46 years
Nationality	German
Language	German, knowledge of English and French
Address	J R C Home Hongkew Kinchow Road 100
Occupation or Ability	Merchant, book-keeper and Correspondent
Education	German higher schools
Religion	jewish
Means	none
Passport No.	II/31/39/E
Issued by	the High Commissioner of Police in Berlin
On	4th of April 39

1 Torched synagogues and parchments from a Torah scroll, Germany
2 A child in the first *"Kindertransport"* to Britain, December 1938
3 The Dressler family emigrates from Germany: Two immigration visas to China, issued in 1939

The Evian Conference

As refugees attempted to emigrate from out of Germany and Austria, the American administration came under heightened pressure to examine its immigration policy. In response, President Roosevelt took the initiative of calling a conference in Evian, a French resort town on the shores of Lake Geneva. The conference, held in July 1938, was attended by representatives of thirty-two countries. All of them paid lip service to the refugees, expressed commiseration with their plight, and stated in succession that their countries could not admit any more migrants. T. W. White, Australia's delegate to the conference, claimed that, "Under the circumstances, Australia cannot do more.... As we have no real racial problem, we are not desirous of importing one."

1

2

3

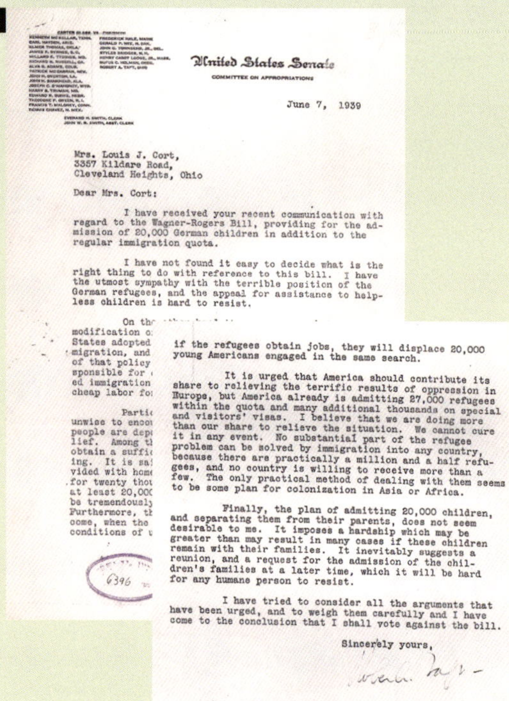

United States Senate
COMMITTEE ON APPROPRIATIONS

June 7, 1939

Mrs. Louis J. Cort,
3357 Kildare Road,
Cleveland Heights, Ohio

Dear Mrs. Cort:

I have received your recent communication with regard to the Wagner-Rogers Bill, providing for the admission of 20,000 German children in addition to the regular immigration quota.

I have not found it easy to decide what is the right thing to do with reference to this bill. I have the utmost sympathy with the terrible position of the German refugees, and the appeal for assistance to helpless children is hard to resist.

if the refugees obtain jobs, they will displace 20,000 young Americans engaged in the same search.

It is urged that America should contribute its share to relieving the terrific results of oppression in Europe, but America already is admitting 27,000 refugees within the quota and many additional thousands on special and visitors' visas. I believe that we are doing more than our share to relieve the situation. We cannot cure it in any event. No substantial part of the refugee problem can be solved by immigration into any country, because there are practically a million and a half refugees, and no country is willing to receive more than a few. The only practical method of dealing with them seems to be some plan for colonization in Asia or Africa.

Finally, the plan of admitting 20,000 children, and separating them from their parents, does not seem desirable to me. It imposes a hardship which may be greater than may result in many cases if these children remain with their families. It inevitably suggests a reunion, and a request for the admission of the children's families at a later time, which it will be hard for any humane person to resist.

I have tried to consider all the arguments that have been urged, and to weigh them carefully and I have come to the conclusion that I shall vote against the bill.

Sincerely yours,

1 Delegates to the Evian Conference
2 A cartoon published in July 1938 in *The New York Times*: "Will the Evian Conference guide him to freedom?"
3 Letter from Robert Taft, member of the US Senate Appropriations Committee, in which he explains his objection to the admission of 20,000 Jewish children from Germany, June 7, 1939
4 Passengers aboard the *St. Louis* wait at the port of Havana, Cuba, May 1939
5 The nomadic voyage of the *St. Louis*

Suicide at the Border

After Hitler came to power, one of the world's greatest literary critics, Walter Benjamin, fled to France, where he lived in poverty. When the war began, Benjamin was arrested as a German national. After his release, he decided, like many other refugees, to flee to the south and cross into Spain. He was arrested at the border. Fearing that he would be extradited, he swallowed a lethal dose of morphine.

Nowhere to Drop Anchor

In May 1939, the *St. Louis* set sail from Germany with 939 Jewish refugees aboard. Most had entrance visas for Cuba. When they reached the port of Havana, however, the Government of Cuba refused to allow them to disembark. Their attempt to enter the United States also failed because of opposition from the immigration authorities. On June 6, they were forced to head back to Germany. At the last moment the governments of Britain, Belgium, France, and the Netherlands announced their consent to receive the refugees. However, for most of the passengers, these refuges were temporary; most were subsequently murdered in the "*Final Solution*."

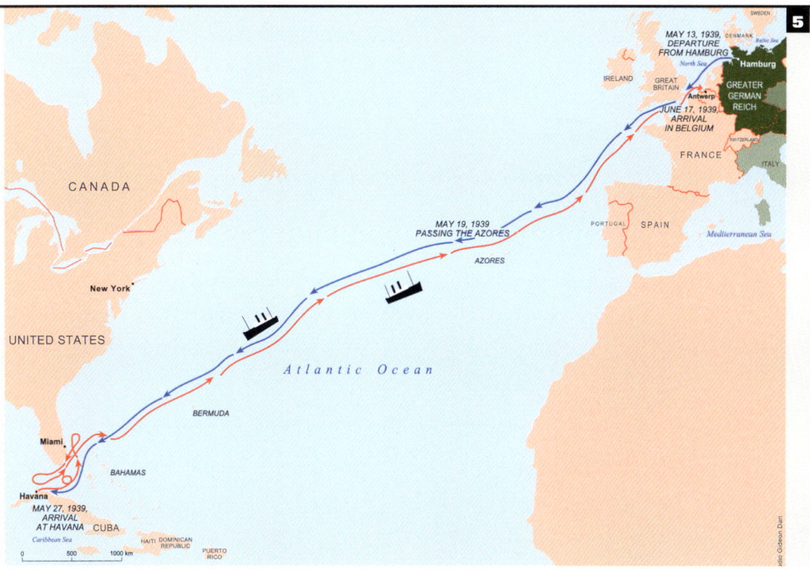

"I'm counting the days until we come out of this hell.... Everyone has only one wish: to get out of this country. And they don't hesitate to say so openly."
Hertha Nathorff, 1938

Some 78,000 Jews left Germany during 1933-1935; almost half in the first year of Nazi rule. The authorities, especially those related to the Nazi party and the police, were interested in accelarating the pace of the Jews' emigration, and were inclined to accept compromise arrangements such as the *Ha'avara* [Transfer] Agreement, a scheme that allowed emigrants to transfer goods to Palestine as part of their property. Many German Jews thus found refuge in Palestine. However, the British mandatory government in Palestine limited the number of Jews who could follow this path to survival.

Emigration surged after the racial laws were instituted; however, so did the obstacles and systematic dispossession of the Jews in a process known as "Aryanization." Overall, of the half million Jews who had been living in Germany when Hitler took power, about 300,000 managed to emigrate before the "Final Solution of the Jewish Question" began. In the late 1930s, international Jewish organizations, national associations of German Jews, and the Zionist movement played an important role in encouraging emigration. However, the severe limits imposed by various countries on the absorption of Jewish refugees prevented more Jews from emigrating from Germany (and, afterward, from other Nazi occupied areas).

The Nazis marched unopposed into Austria on March 13, 1938. Abuse of Jews became an intrinsic part of the mass enthusiasm that accompanied

1

2

3

1 Abuse of Jews in Vienna
2 Propaganda broadsheet of the Christian Socialist Party in Austria, 1920
3 Passport of a Viennese Jew
4 Attempt to obtain emigration visas, Vienna
5 The Ermann family of the Saar region. After the head of household was arrested on *Kristallnacht*, they fled to Switzerland
6 *"The Eternal Jew"* exhibition, Vienna, 1938

4

the *Anschluss* (annexation of Austria). Legislation that had taken years to draw up in Germany was duplicated in Austria immediately. Adolf Eichmann, head of the Jewish Department of the Gestapo, was sent to Vienna to establish an emigration office and organize the Jews' compulsory departure, thus purging Austria of thousands of Jews. In the aftermath of the successful "experiment" in Vienna, Eichmann became known as an expert in Jewish affairs. However, many Austrian Jews had nowhere to emigrate, and 65,000 (out of 185,000) perished.

After the fall of Czechoslovakia, Slovakia was later separated from the Czech area and became a German satellite under the rule of Catholic priest Jozef Tiso. In addition to the local Jews, Jewish refugees from Germany and Austria fell into the Nazis' clutches.

5

6

Today I will once more be a prophet: If financial international Jewry inside and outside of Germany should succeed in plunging the nations once more into a world war, then the result will not be the bolshevization of the earth, and thus the victory of Jewry, but the annihilation of the Jewish race in Europe!

Adolf Hitler, speech to the Reichstag, January 30, 1939

1

The Dictatorship Era: Europe in the 1930s

Democracies:

Britain, France, The Netherlands, Belgium, Luxembourg, Switzerland, Czechoslovakia, Denmark, Sweden, Norway, Finland

Dictatorships and Fascist Countries:

Italy, Spain, Portugal, Lithuania, Latvia, Estonia, Poland, Hungary, Romania, Austria, Yugoslavia, Bulgaria, Greece, USSR

Capitulation of the Democracies in Munich

In September 1938, Hitler demanded the German annexation of the Sudetenland (part of Czechoslovakia populated by ethnic Germans) and declared Germany's intention to take this area by force. Favoring a policy of appeasement at this time, Britain and France pressured Czechoslovakia to submit to his demands. The conference in Munich was called to debate the international crisis. Czechoslovakia, however, was not invited, and the powers in attendance decided to allow Germany to go ahead with the annexation.

After the Munich agreement was concluded, Winston Churchill warned, "Do not suppose this is the end. This is only the beginning of the reckoning."

2

3

4

There are in this part of the world [Eastern and Central Europe] 6,000,000 Jews... for whom the world is divided into places where they cannot live and places where they cannot enter.

Chaim Weizman, President of the World Zionist Organization, 1939

1 Annexation of Austria and takeover of Czechoslovakia
2 British Prime Minister Neville Chamberlain, French Premier Edward Daladier, and German Chancellor Adolf Hitler at the Munich Conference, September 1938
3 Chamberlain returns from the Munich Conference: "I believe it is peace for our time"
4 **Felix Nussbaum** (1904–1944), The Refugee, 1939, oil on canvas

The Outbreak of World War II and Anti-Jewish Violence

Felix Nussbaum (1904–1944), The Great Disaster, 1939, India ink and wash on paper

German Conquests

The beginning of World War II, on September 1, 1939, marked a new phase in German policy toward Jews. The war transformed the face of Europe and the entire world and resulted in the killing of millions of civilians of various nationalities and the evolution of a satanic scheme of genocide. Several weeks after the war began, while the Poles were still attempting to stave off the German offensive, the Soviets invaded Poland and occupied the eastern part of the country, under the terms of an agreement concluded between the Soviet Foreign Minister Molotov and his German counterpart, Ribbentrop. On September 17, when Poland was partitioned, some 1,200,000 Polish Jews came under Soviet rule. This phase lasted until June 22, 1941, when Germany invaded the USSR.

Within three weeks of the invasion of Poland, the Germans defeated Poland and divided it into three regions: The western and northern provinces of the former Polish state, including the country's second-largest city, Lodz, were annexed

> **We should take part in ruling the world and educating our people to be a master race.**
>
> Nazi Propaganda Minister Joseph Goebbels, 1936

1 Signing of the Molotov-Ribbentrop pact
2 The bombing of Warsaw
3 Removing debris in Warsaw after the bombardments, October 1939
4 Hitler and senior officers observe the army as it invades Poland, September 1939
5 The Wehrmacht in Warsaw after the surrender of Poland, September 1939
6 The Wehrmacht parades in the streets of Lodz, September 8, 1939
7 German soldiers smash a border barrier in the invasion of Poland
8 Polish prisoners await execution. Bydgoszcz, Poland, September 9, 1939. A priest is standing in the center
9 Sidney Strube (1891-1956), "Futile fight," *Daily Express*, London, 1939
10 Inhabitants of Warsaw amidst the rubble, September 1939

1

2

3

4

5

6

7

8

9

10

to the Reich; eastern districts were annexed to the Soviet Union and Lithuania. The political future of the remaining area, a salient in central Poland undefined during the initial phase of the occupation, became the *Generalgouvernement*. Approximately 1.5 million Jews were trapped in the German occupation zone in Poland. Following the onset of the war, the Germans freed themselves of many of the restraints they had maintained in peacetime. Circumstances no longer required them to bow to public opinion or political considerations. Unhesitatingly, they terrorized the Polish people, arrested its leaders and intellectual elites, and defined Poles as "hewers of wood and drawers of water," servants of the "master race."

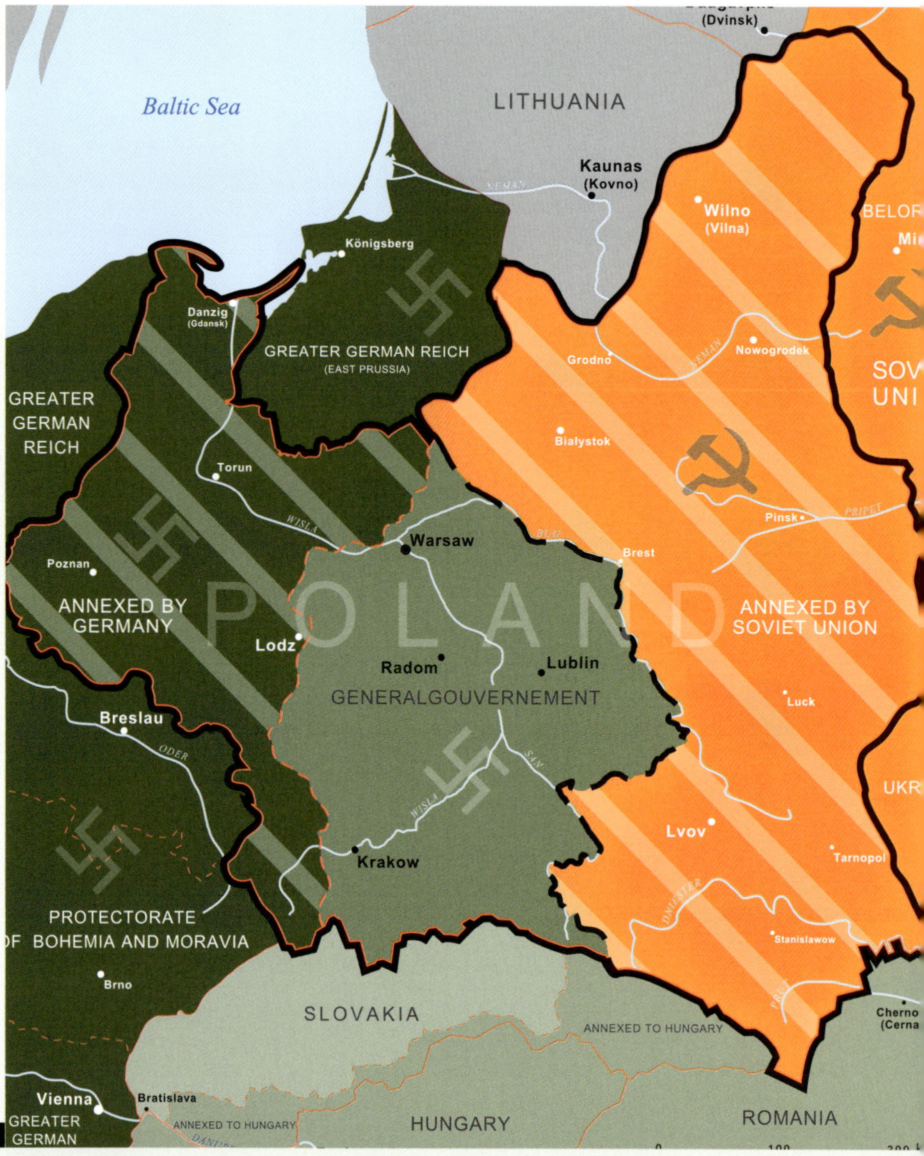

1

2

3

"Thousands of teachers, doctors, and engineers—Jews and Poles—have been taken from their homes, together with their families, and hurried to the market halls, and from there to various German jails.... Groups of prominent people are often dispatched immediately into the next world."

Dawid Szierakowiak

Before the end of September 1939, Reinhard Heydrich, chief of the Security Police, sent out a *Schnellbrief* explaining the procedures and approach that would be invoked against the Jews in the Polish occupation zones. According to the *Schnellbrief*, Jews living in towns and villages were to be transferred to larger concentrations in ghettos, and Jewish councils—Judenrat—would be established to carry out the German authorities' orders.

Heydrich's instructions distinguished between a transitional phase in solving the "Jewish problem" and the "final aim." It should not be presumed, however, that the term "Final Solution" had been defined by then or that the overall murder scheme had been planned. What existed at that time, apparently, were vague plans and a general and indefinite wish to solve the Jewish problem in some rapid and radical way. During this phase, the idea to deport the Jews from the Reich was still dominant.

As they marched into the towns of Poland, Germans preyed on Jews whom they encountered, subjecting them to humiliations and beatings, shearing the beards of the Orthodox and organizing public hangings to terrorize the population. The perpetrators were members of special SS units who accompanied the Wehrmacht. They torched synagogues and Jewish homes—some with the residents still inside—and abducted Jews from the

1 The partitioning of Poland
2 The sign states, "we Jews wanted the war." On the garbage wagon: "The Jews are our misfortune." Lodz, Poland
3 Forced labor, Wieliczka, Poland, 1939
4 SA men arrest Jews on suspicion of concealing illegal weapons, Warsaw, 1939
5 Executions of Poles, Bydgoszcz, Poland, September 1939
6 Abuse of Jewish men. In the middle: Rabbi Moshe Hagerman, Olkusz, Poland, July 31, 1940

4

5

6

street for forced labor. After being awarded enormous monetary fines for having "caused" the world war and its attendant devastation, Jewish leaders were inundated by decrees, such as the registration of a Jewish labor force and the imposition of compulsory labor. The Jews were steadily dispossessed (in "furs Aktionen," expropriation of furniture, etc.) and deprived of their sources of livelihood. Throughout the occupied areas, the Germans restored the medieval practice of requiring Jews to wear a badge of shame. The first one chosen, an armband with a Star of David was later replaced with a yellow star sewn on to their clothing.

1

2

3

1 Wehrmacht unit observes the torching of the great synagogue in Siedlce, December 24, 1939
2 Jews at forced labor
3 Execution of eleven people in front of a crowd of onlookers, Olkusz, Poland
4 Civilians give the Wehrmacht a jubilant welcome, Netherlands, May 1940
5 Anne Frank, 1940

The Fate of West European Jewry

Germany Expands Its Conquests

After completing their immensely successful military campaign in the West, the Germans tightened their grip on European Jewry. In less than two years—from the onset of their offensive against Poland in September 1939 to the beginning of the campaign against the Soviet Union in June 1941—they had managed to conquer most of Europe. Norway, Denmark, Belgium, France, the Netherlands, Yugoslavia, and Greece fell after only brief military operations. Southeastern Europe—Italy, Slovakia, Hungary, Romania, Bulgaria—willingly accepted the German dictate and was incorporated into the Nazi sphere of influence. In the vastness of continental Europe, which the Germans considered the domain of their "new order," the Jews had come under the Nazis' thumb.

The Germans employed different methods in dealing with the Jews of Western Europe. Where antisemitism lacked the intensity and popularity of the East European version and that much of the local population in Western Europe viewed the Jewish populace as an integral part of society. As a result they had to be more considerate of the local populations, and of the governments which had been left with some measure of self-rule. Italy, Hungary, Romania, and Bulgaria concluded strong alliances with Nazi Germany, although they were given a degree of freedom in their domestic affairs.

The Germans invaded the Netherlands in May 1940. Although the queen and her government fled to Britain, the bureaucracy continued to function under the occupying regime. Anti-Jewish policy in the Netherlands evolved gradually, starting with the purge of Jews from the civil service in September 1940. This was followed by the compulsory registration of Jewish-owned corporations and the registration by name of all Dutch Jews under the racial laws, thus dispossessing the Jews and restricting their movements. The Germans then decreed the establishment of the *Joodse Raad*, a Judenrat that would carry out their directives and organize internal life. From then on the policy took an increasingly radical turn. Jews

4

5

were made to wear the Star of David, and preparations for their deportation to the camps began.

1

"In the meantime, I continued to attend a Jewish school in the ordinary way, and every night children disappeared from there. Each morning the teacher opened her attendance book, counted the children, and found that there were fewer children. Then she asked someone if he knew whether he was sick or whether they'd taken him away. Mostly, the children had been taken away, so the teacher erased his name from the list of pupils and continued teaching."

Elisheva Polak, The Netherlands

When the Germans occupied France in June 1940, some 330,000 Jews were living there—half of them veteran residents, the others immigrants and refugees. France was divided into two areas of control: the north came under German military rule; in the south, an antisemitic nationalist French state was set up under Marshal Henri-Philippe Pétain. The regime there collaborated with the Germans, and it was the French police that carried out the

Between West and East

The Nazi ideology prescribed one fate for all European Jews, although the anti-Jewish policy was applied in different ways in different occupied countries.

In Eastern Europe, the Germans placed the Jews in severely congested ghettos, behind fences and walls, with the active assistance of members of the local population, cutting them off from the outside world and their sources of livelihood. The Jews there were doomed to humiliation, poverty, decline, and death.

In Western Europe, the Nazis did not ghettoize the Jews but enforced racial legislation and introduced Aryanization and discrimination. They applied the anti-Jewish policy gradually, testing the local population's state of mind. Despite these differences, the Germans' overall goal with regard to the Jews was identical.

Studio Gideon Dar

anti-Jewish actions. On October 4, 1940, the enactment of the "Jewish Statute" deprived French Jews of their civil rights. Concurrently, registration and dispossession of the Jews were also instituted. Thousands of Jews, mostly refugees and immigrants—including German Jews who had been deported from various parts of Germany—were sent to detention camps in southern France, such as Gurs, Le Milles, and Saint-Cyprien. The main detention camp was in Drancy, a short distance from Paris. In the summer of 1942, prior to the Jews' deportation, the yellow star was instituted. Between

1 Sign announcing the entrance to the Jewish quarter in Amsterdam, February, 1943

2 Partitioning of France

1941 and 1944, nearly 76,000 Jews, including many children, were sent to Auschwitz.

On May 10 1940, the Germans invaded Belgium and within three weeks defeated its armed forces. By October, local Jews had been deprived of their livelihood and possessions, placed under a nighttime curfew, and ordered to wear the yellow star in advance of their deportation.

1

2

3

4

5

6

Jacques Bielinki

A journalist and art critic who emigrated from Russia to France and wrote for Jewish daily newspapers, Bielinki attempted to bridge the gap between Jews who belonged to the French community for generations and the immigrants, with whom he had become familiar. After the occupation, he began to describe in his diary the worsening plight of the Jews of Paris. On the night of February 10,1943, Bielinki was arrested by the French police. On March 23 he was deported from Drancy to Sobibór, where he was murdered.

1. Hitler and his entourage upon the occupation of Paris, June 23,1940
2. Six year old Claret Vigder drew a picture of herself, wearing a yellow star on her dress. Paris, 1942
3. Under the sign that identifies his business as "Jewish," a Jewish merchant posts a personal advertisement: "Combat soldier, certificate no. 409150 (in World War I). Wounded in war. Totally of French origin since the 17th century"
4. Marshal Pétain thanks the French Legionnaires for joining Germany's "Crusade"
5. Fleeing to the south, France, June 1940
6. **Denise Tal** (b. 1922), The Flight to Southern France, 1940, watercolor on paper

North African Jewry

The occupation of France and the establishment of the antisemitic Vichy regime brought 415,000 North African Jews—most of the Jews on the subcontinent—into the orbit of persecution. Pétain's Nazi regime worsened the status of the Jews of Morocco, Algeria, and Tunisia, after Vichy-style antisemitic legislation was imposed in those countries. In Morocco, where Jews had civil rights, anti-Jewish laws were not formally enacted, but the French bureaucracy introduced a set of regulations, such as banning Jewish children from swimming pools and outlawing youth movements. The Jews of Algiers, who held French citizenship, were stripped of their rights, required to wear an identifying mark, and subjected to admission quotas, even in primary schools. In Libya, where the Italians had been applying racial laws since 1938, the bureaucracy stepped up its depredations, marking Jews' passports, restricting their cultural activities, and banishing thousands to concentration camps—foremost Giado—where hundreds died of starvation and disease.

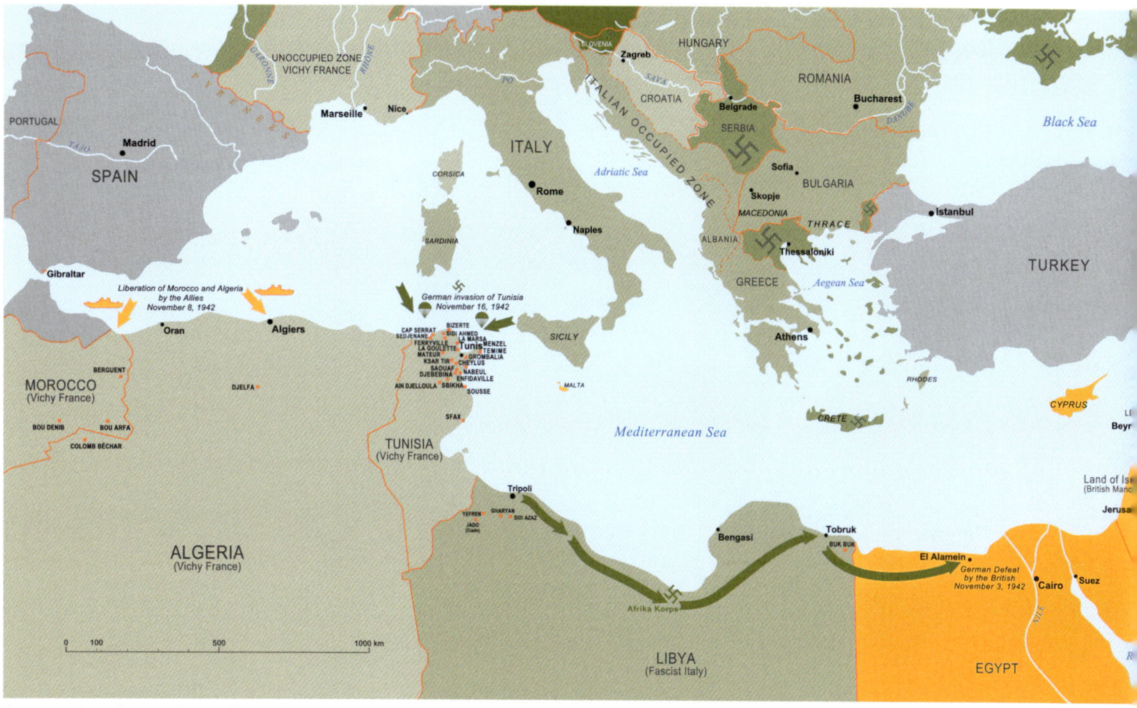

Germany invades northern Africa

This was a painful, surprising betrayal by a culture on which I had pinned all my hopes, to which I had devoted all of my admiration, my heartfelt ardor. A betrayal that I may have partly been anticipating, but here it has been confirmed with such brutality... All of Europe has turned into a monster.

Albert Memmi, *The Pillar of Salt*

Felix Nussbaum (1904–1944), View from the Studio with Gloves, 1940, gouache on paper

"All at once on that day, lots of Germans circulated in the streets with tanks.... We didn't know much about them and we also didn't know a thing about what was going on in Europe."

Shoshan Cohen

"The Italian Government took us to Giado.... We got to the concentration camp and they divided us up... 25 families in each building—with one blanket per family. It was very hard, crowded, typhus. Whoever got sick at night, was found dead in the morning. Every day, seven or eight died."

Chai Zuaretz

Approximately 13,000 Jews with foreign nationality were sent to concentration camps in Europe. When the Allies liberated Northern Africa (1942), the Jews of that part of the world were spared the fate of their brethren in Europe.

"We were in Tripoli and one day they told us that we had to get ready, they're taking us to Italy, they don't know where.... We'd lived there for three years.... Suddenly a truck came with two Germans, and whomever they found in the street, just like that, on the spot, they began to yell 'Raus, raus'.... We arrived safely, they put us in Bergen-Belsen.... They put all the families in one room.... We thought we'd never get out of there.... No one believed that we'd leave Bergen-Belsen."

Linda Tayar

1 Tunisian Jews being led to forced labor, December 1942
2 Tunisian Jews wearing badge of shame, 1943
3 **Raphael Uzan** (b. 1922), The German Entry into Nabeul, December 1942, acrylic and India ink on paper

The Case of Tunisia

When France fell to the Germans in 1940, the French colonies were forced to operate under the policies of the Vichy Government. In November 1942, after the Allies invaded Morocco and Algeria, the Wehrmacht entered Tunisia, along with a SS unit tasked with applying the anti-Jewish policy there. After pausing briefly to consolidate their affairs, the Germans began to expropriate the Jews' belongings and mobilized many Jews for the construction of fortifications. The Jews' main contact with the Germans took place in the capital, but in other communities as well, such as Djerba, they were also mistreated. But the overriding hardship was forced labor. The Jews of the capital were forced to establish a local Judenrat, which was ordered to select 5,000–6,000 Jews, some of whom were sent to labor camps. In early May 1943, military developments forced the Germans to retreat.

3

The Nazis Threaten the Mediterranean

Hajj Amin al-Husayni, the Mufti of Jerusalem, expressed support of the Nazi regime as early as 1933. In October 1939, he fled to Iraq, where he was central in organizing the pro-Nazi insurrection in April 1941. After the insurrection was quashed, he exiled himself to Germany and served the Axis countries in their war against the Allies. Husayni disseminated venomous anti-Jewish propaganda and tried to persuade the Axis powers to extend the extermination plans to the Middle East and northern Africa. In spring 1943 he mobilized and organized Bosnian Muslim units in Croatia that fought under SS auspices in Bosnia and Hungary.

The Jews of Iraq

In 1934, under the influence of the German ambassador, the Iraqi nationalist government enacted anti-Jewish laws and, in 1936, pogroms took place. In April 1941 a pro-German government was appointed, which did not prevent attacks against Jews. When British forces occupied Baghdad in May 1941, riots broke out in which 179 Jews were killed and hundreds injured. Although the new government restored order, relations between Muslims and Jews remained tense. Some Iraqi Jews chose to emigrate to China, settling in Shanghai.

The Ghettos

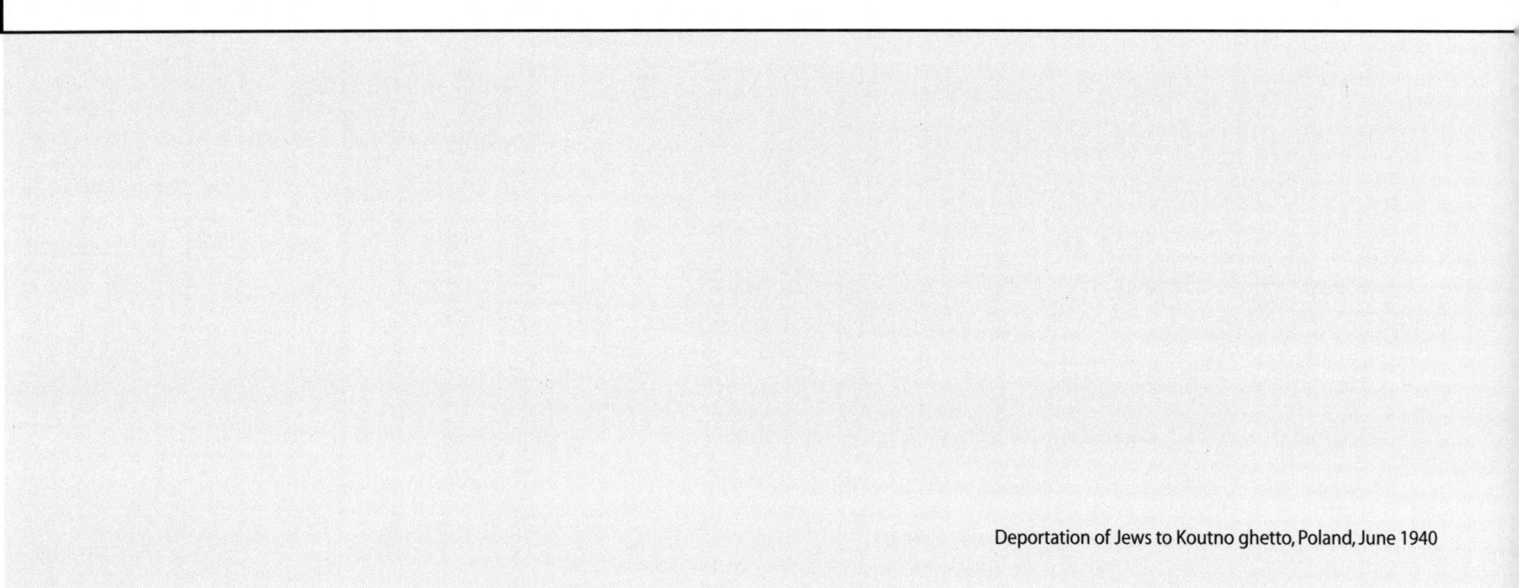

Deportation of Jews to Koutno ghetto, Poland, June 1940

> **The creation of the ghetto is, of course, only an interim measure.... The final aim must in any case be to totally cauterize this plague spot.**
>
> From Friedrich Übelhör's order to ghettoize the Jews of Lodz

Before the first year of the occupation was over, the Jews living in the German-controlled part of Poland had been interned in sealed ghettos, mostly in the worst slum quarters, without electricity or basic hygienic conditions. A large, hermetically sealed ghetto was set up in Lodz. The largest of all, however, was formed in the autumn of 1940, in Warsaw, where nearly half a million Jews were concentrated for some time.

Jews from scores of towns and villages near the cities were taken to the large ghettos, only exacerbating the hardships and starvation. Ghettoized Jews were given half of the food rations

The Yellow Star

The yellow star was the badge of shame that Nazi Germany forced Jews to wear on their clothing to make them easier to identify. The badge of shame was pioneered by the Muslims, who in the eighth century required non-Muslims to establish themselves as different by means of their clothing. In Europe, Christians imposed the compulsory wearing of a badge of shame pursuant to a decision to this effect by the Catholic Church in the thirteenth century. The mark usually included a yellow pointed hat.

Nazi Germany reinstated the badge-of-shame requirement at the recommendation of Reinhard Heydrich, who proposed it in a discussion that took place in the aftermath of *Kristallnacht*. Indeed, after the occupation of Poland, orders requiring Jews to wear an identifying mark were issued. There was no ab initio decision about the shape and color of the mark (in the *Generalgouvernement*, Jews wore a white armband with a blue Star of David), but an order of November 14, 1939 mandated the wearing of a "Jewish yellow" armband. In December, a directive requiring Jews to affix identical patches to their chests and backs was added.

In September 1941, two years after the mark-of-shame requirement was imposed on the Jews of Poland, a directive ordering all Jews in the Reich-occupied territories to affix a "Jewish star" to their clothing was declared. The yellow star now became part of the preparations for the Final Solution. The satellite states also introduced the marking of Jews—a step toward the deportation of the Jews to the east.

1 Children in Lodz ghetto
2 Lublin ghetto

allotted to Poles, which were meager to begin with. Hunger and disease in the ghettos caused escalating mortality, which the hard-pressed Judenrat could not alleviate. The corpses of Jews who had starved to death became common sights in the ghetto streets. Despite the inhuman conditions and the fight for survival, a focused effort was made in the ghettos to sanctify life and respond to the public's needs—an immense psychological strain for people whose physical strength was dwindling.

The German authorities attained several goals by establishing the ghettos: they concentrated the Jews under conditions of severe congestion and close supervision, deprived them of their property, exploited their labor, isolated them from the rest of the world, made them vulnerable and unprepared at crucial moments, and incited the local population against the Jews, whom they resented anyway. After mass killings, the Germans also established ghettos in the Soviet areas that they occupied, even though they intended to leave the Jews in these ghettos for a only very short time. The Germans occupied Hungary in March 1944, and by June of that year had already begun transporting the country's Jews to Auschwitz. At that time they proclaimed the establishment of a ghetto in Budapest and confined the Jews in this city to special buildings marked with Stars of

1

2

1 Children and teenagers at a key workshop, Lodz ghetto
2 Wooden bridge over the main street of Lodz connects the two parts of the ghetto
3 Map of ghettos

SOVIET UNION
Moscow
SWEDEN
Baltic Sea
LATVIA
Riga
Daugavpils (Dvinsk)
Panevezys
LITHUANIA
Kaunas (Kovno)
Wilno (Vilna)
BELORUSSIA
Minsk
Grodno
Baranowicze
Lomza
Bialystok
Slonim
Plonsk
Plock
Warsaw
Pruzana
Pinsk
Siedlce
Brzesc Litewski (Brest)
Lukow
Lodz
Otwock
Tomaszow Maz.
Radom
Zdunska Wola
Piotrkow-Tryb.
Radomsko
Wolanow
Zwolen
Opole
Lublin
Kowel
Czestochowa
Konskie
Szydlowiec
Kielce
Ostrowiec
Terezin (Theresienstadt)
Bedzin
Chmielnik
Luck
Slavuta
Krzemieniec
Sosnowiec
Tarnow
Rzeszow
Izyaslav
Prague
Krakow
Przemysl
Lvov
Tarnopol
Khmelnicki
Berdichev
Sanok
Nowy Sacz
Drohobycz
Stryj
Brzezany
Yarmolintsy
Stanislawow
Kamenets-Podolskiy
Kolomyja
Obodovka
Mogilev-Podolskiy
Bershad
PROTECTORATE OF BOHEMIA AND MORAVIA
SLOVAKIA
Bratislava
Vienna
Uzhorod
Mukacevo
Satoraljaujhely
Berehovo
Chust
Sevlus
Tacovo
Nyiregyhaza
Debrecen
Budapest
HUNGARY
UKRAINE
Kiev
Kharkov
Donetsk (Stalino)
TRANSNISTRIA
Odessa
Sea of Azov
CRIMEA
Zagreb
CROATIA
ROMANIA
Bucharest
Belgrade
SERBIA
Black Sea
Adriatic Sea
Sofia
BULGARIA
MACEDONIA
THRACE
Istanbul
TURKEY
Thessaloniki
Aegean Sea
100 200 300 400 500 km
Studio Gideon Dan

3

David. In all, the Germans established more than 1,000 ghettos in Central and Eastern Europe.

"The Jews ... shall be concentrated in a sealed ghetto.... Guard units shall be posted... and the streets shall be closed by barriers and other obstacles....The harshest measures are to be taken against the Jews.... After the preparatory works are completed and sufficient guard forces are allocated, the ghetto shall be established in one go on the date that I shall determine."

From Friedrich Übelhör's order to ghettoize the Jews of Lodz

Lodz Ghetto

The Lodz (Litzmannstadt) ghetto, established in May 1940, was the second-largest ghetto in the German-occupied areas and the one that was most severely insulated from its surroundings and from other ghettos. Some 164,000 Jews were interned there, along with three additional groups: tens of thousands of Jews from the district, other Jews from the Reich, and Sinti and Roma. The ghetto, although intended to be a temporary transit facility, lasted for more than four years after the interests of local Nazis led to a decision to exploit the Jewish labor force.

"Seizures for forced labor don't stop.They are almost always accompanied by beatings and sadistic acts. A lot of Jewish men are leaving the city.Trains to Warsaw are terribly overloaded with everyone heading to Warsaw and Russia.... Every day here is worse....Decree follows decree, and life becomes harder and harder."

"...A student from the German gymnasium [high school] ran up to me with a big stick in his hand and shouted:'Come work!'... He took me to a square where over a dozen Jews were already at work picking up leaves.... I have never been so humiliated in my life as when I looked through the gate to the square and saw the happy, smiling faces of passersby laughing at our misfortune."

Dawid Sierakowiak, Lodz ghetto

In the spring of 1940, the Lodz ghetto was sealed from the rest of the world by a wooden fence surrounded by additional barbed-wire fences. The Jews were packed into the ghetto with no electricity or water. Disease and starvation rapidly diminished their numbers.

"Not the bridge, not the barbed wire, Not even the gate is the symbol of the ghetto....The symbol of the ghetto is the pot...."

Yosef Zelkowicz, Lodz ghetto

3

4

1 "Legend of the Prince"—an illustrated story recited at theater sessions for children at the sewing workshop in the Lodz ghetto. The purpose of the theater was to raise the morale of children who had to work in ghetto factories in order to avoid deportation to extermination
2 Outside the public kitchen, Lodz ghetto
3 **Hirsch Zvi Szylis** (1909–1987), Street in the Lodz Ghetto, 1942, oil crayon on cardboard
4 Ghettoization of the Jews of Lodz, 1940

Mordechai Chaim Rumkowski, the domineering, controversial chairman of the Lodz Judenrat, believed that labor would give the Jews an opportunity to go on living and the hope to survive. Thus, he established a multifaceted system in which the Jews of the ghetto worked for the Germans, including "Ressorts" (workshops) that employed even young children. The Germans, however, regarded the ghetto's output merely as a pause in the task at hand—extermination.

"In the ghetto there are no children, but small Jews...small Jews aged ten and over who already work… Such a child has no breakfast before he goes to work…. He has to work at the Ressort for a few hours before he receives some thin soup…."

Yosef Zelkowicz, Lodz ghetto

Ghetto Housing

A typical residential building in the ghetto had three or four multi-storey divisions and a central courtyard, with some 1,000 tenants. After the occupation began, the Jews established a self-help organization that ran house committees in most buildings (more than 2,000). These committees helped and protected the tenants, especially the needy and the refugees. They were assisted by volunteers, and set up soup kitchens and children's corners, arranged financial aid, and organized cultural and educational activities.

Warsaw Ghetto

The Jews of Warsaw were ghettoized on November 16, 1940. Although a third of the city's population was Jewish, the ghetto stood on just 2.4 percent of the town's area. Masses of refugees who had been transported to Warsaw brought the ghetto population to 500,000. Surrounded by walls that they built with their own hands and under strict and violent guard, the Jews of Warsaw were cut off from the outside world. Within the ghetto their lives oscillated between a desperate struggle for survival and death from disease or starvation.

1

3

1 Ghettoization of the Jews of Warsaw, 1940
2 Jewish self-help in Warsaw—shelter for refugees in a synagogue
3 Building the ghetto wall in Warsaw

1

2

1 Section of the Warsaw ghetto wall at Krochmalna Street, filmed from the Polish side, October 15, 1941

2 Bodies in mass grave, Warsaw ghetto, September 1941

3 **Moshe Rynecki** (1881–1943), Refugees, 1939, watercolor on paper

3

The crowded ghetto became a focal point of epidemics and mass mortality, which the Jewish community institutions, foremost the Judenrat and the welfare organizations, were helpless to combat. More than 80,000 Jews died in the ghetto.

When the first deportation orders were received, Adam Czerniaków, chairman of the Judenrat, refused to prepare the lists of persons slated for deportation and, instead, committed suicide (July 23,1942). *Aktionen* against the Jews did not cease; some 360,000 Jews from the ghetto were murdered in the Treblinka death camp.

The ghetto Jews' struggle was manifested primarily at the existential level. At this point in time they disregarded many of the Germans' decrees and engaged in rampant smuggling of food into the ghetto.

"The wagon-driver from Moranovska, Mr. Eizenstadt, carried different products on his cart. He would bring textiles to Naleveki and Gensha, leather to Katchenska, and tin to Gzibowska. Later, when the deportations came, he brought wardrobes, beds, sofas, tables and every door belonging to the Jewish people.

Today is 23 November 1941. Mr Eizenstadt, 42, is carrying something for the first time that he never thought he would carry: his is carrying the body of his wife who died in a basement apartment from exhaustion and hunger. For three days he ran in vain between different institutions to obtain the 20 zloty needed to pay for her burial. Now with his only son Yosele, aged 7, he will bring his wife to the cemetery"

From the "Oneg Shabbat" Archives

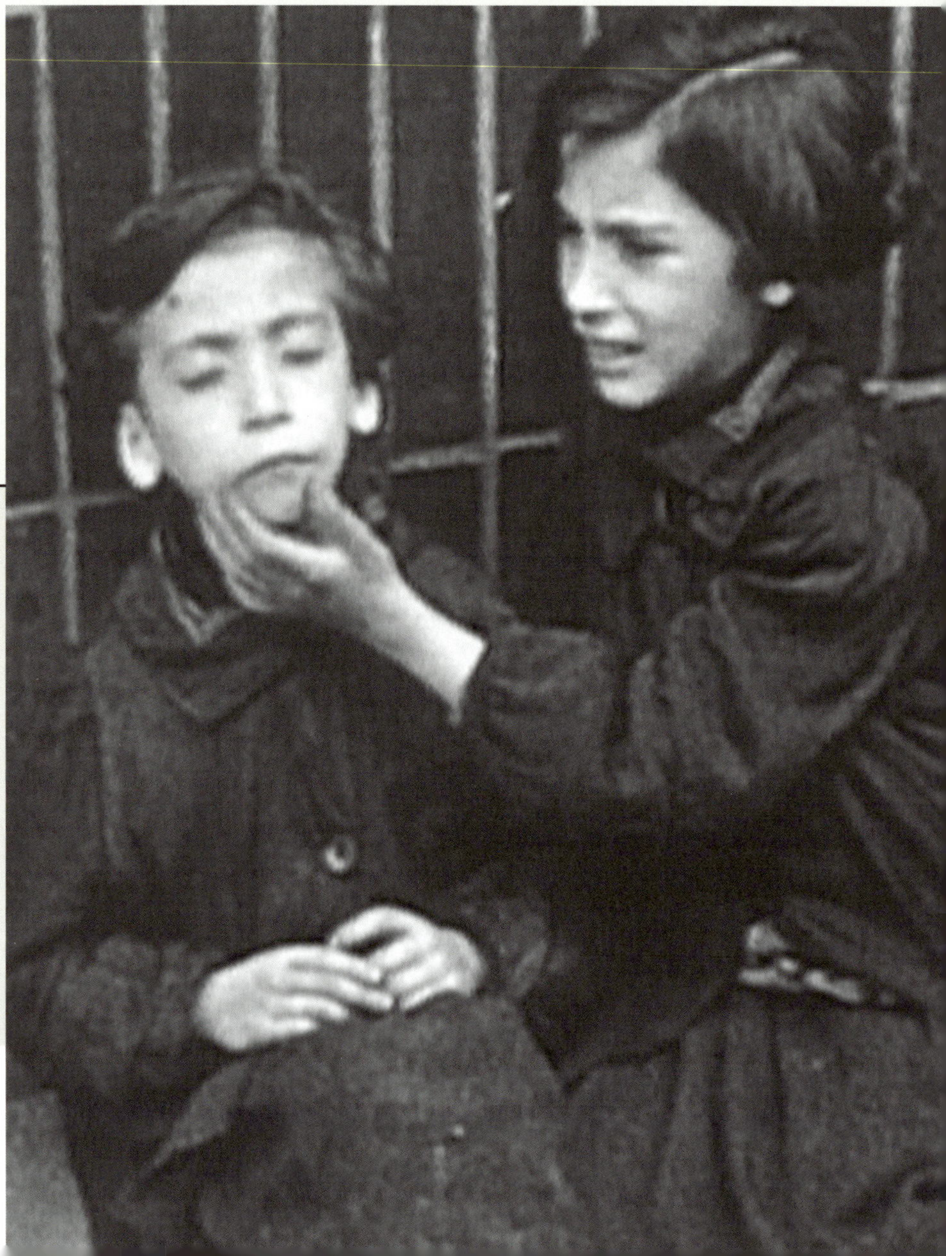

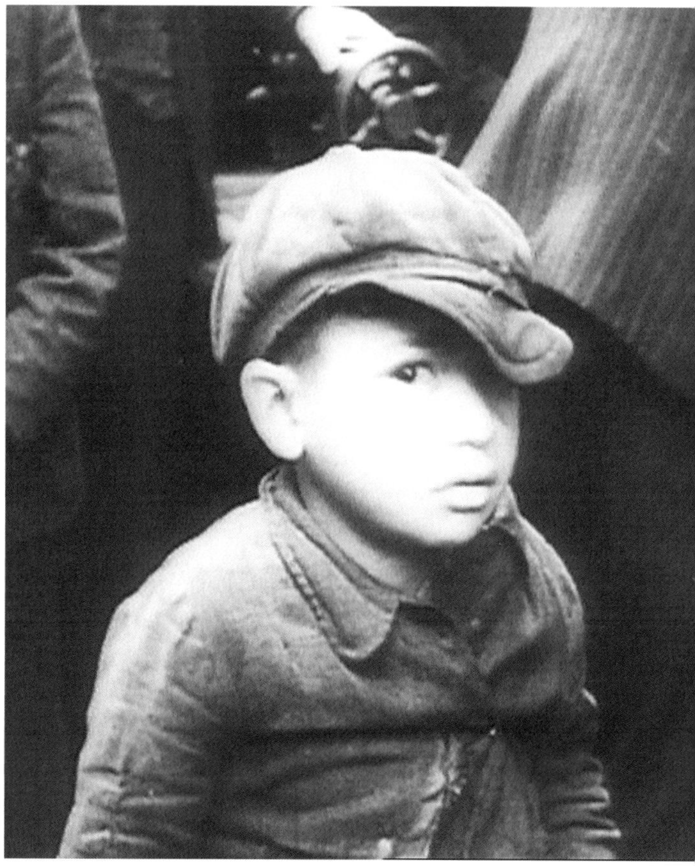

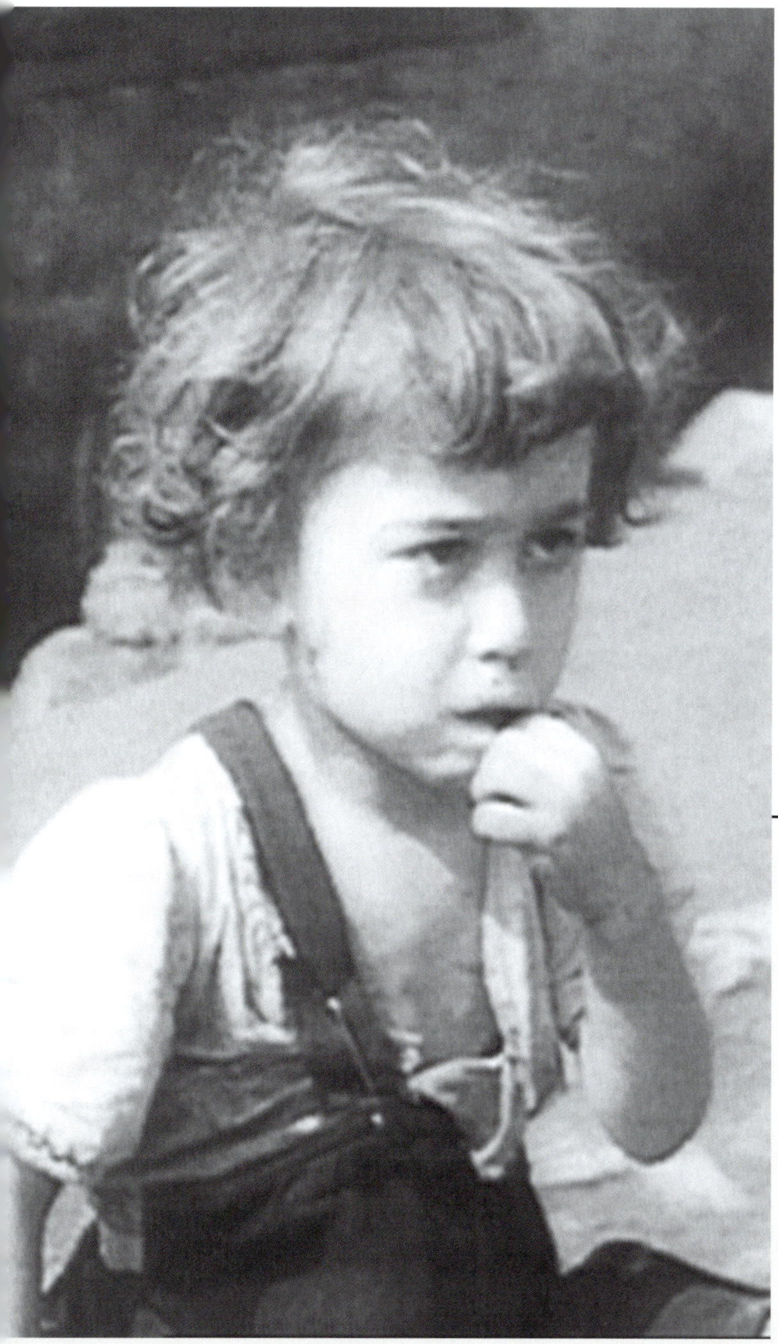

"The Jews were convinced that things could not get worse. The truth is that every stage, ultimately, was something worse and more terrible. This developmental dynamic is the very essence of terror."

Israel Gutman

"They saw every time paupers in the streets asking for charity, who would die from starvation or cold. They would cover them as the [Jewish] tradition requires, with a newspaper if no rags were available, and placed stones on [the covers] so the wind would not blow them away."

Zimra Kaminski

"It's hard to imagine what it is for a young boy to come home and there's nothing to eat. Not that you don't know about; nothing."

Yosef Czerny

Although forbidden to make a living except in the service of the Germans, the ghetto inhabitants continued to work secretly in clandestine factories. Political parties and, especially, youth movements regrouped in the

underground. Surreptitiously, they began to distribute newspapers, which created a sense of routine, established credibility, and provided information about developments on the front. These newspapers were all the more important as the occupation authorities had banned free press, and Jews were not allowed to listen to the radio.

Religious and educational activities, banned by the Germans, resumed in secret. Teachers circulated from house to house and taught children; adults furtively set up religious study centers. A network of underground schools

"Oneg Shabbat"

When the Germans occupied Poland, the historian and public activist Dr. Emanuel Ringelblum realized that the Jews were facing an unprecedented reality. Ringelblum began to document the events as they unfolded. Concurrently, he established an underground archive named "*Oneg Shabbat*," gathering documents, personal diaries, and studies that documented the life and the destruction of Polish Jewry, especially that of Warsaw. In order to gather the materials and organize the writing, he surreptitiously mobilized people of all public affiliations and political persuasions. Their writings create a multifaceted picture of events in the ghetto. The collection was placed in hiding; a portion was found at the end of the war. Ringelblum and most members of the archive staff were murdered.

Parts of the archive were concealed in the ghetto during the "great deportation," in a hiding place at Borochov School, 68 Nowolipki Street. Searches in the ruins of the school in 1946 and 1950 uncovered ten crates and two milk pitchers containing material from the archives. The rest has not been recovered.

Rachel Auerbach

Before the war Rachel Auerbach had belonged to a group of Yiddish writers in Warsaw. After the occupation began and the Jews of Warsaw came under increasing distress and hunger, Dr. Emanuel Ringelblum asked her to run a soup kitchen for the destitute residing at 40 Leszno St. Auerbach remained active in literature, keeping a diary and serving as a member of the documentation staff of the underground "*Oneg Shabbat*" archive. In March 1943, she escaped from the ghetto, went into hiding under a false identity, and survived the war.

On February 13, 1942, Rachel Auerbach, manager of the soup kitchen at 40 Leszno St., wrote, "The only thing that may come of our work is that the whole ghetto won't die in one stroke."

was formed; lectures on cultural and political themes were held; concerts and theatrical productions were performed regularly; and underground archives were established.

The scourge of starvation caused the network of soup kitchens to expand at the initiative of the Jewish self-help organization, supported by the American Jewish Joint Distribution Committee. In 1941, however—the year of the great distress—the relief funds ran out, and mass starvation ensued. Apart from serving tens of thousands of meager portions of food, mostly consisting of a bowl of soup, the public kitchen served as an underground meeting place for cultural and political activity. Children's kitchens also served as clandestine classrooms.

The Little Smuggler

Over the wall, through holes, and past the guard,
Through the wires, ruins and fences,
Plucky, hungry and determined
I sneak through, dart like a cat...
And if the hand of destiny
Should seize me in the game,
That's a common trick of life.
You, mother, do not wait up for me...
And only one request
Will stiffen on my lips:
Who, mother mine, who
Will bring your bread tomorrow?

The poet Henryka Lazowert, murdered in Treblinka

1

Culture Without Frontiers

The ghetto ramparts did not stifle the inhabitants' cultural efforts. The population of the Warsaw ghetto—hundreds of thousands strong—included scientists, intellectuals, and artists of various kinds, who remained active despite the harsh living conditions. The Nazi occupation and the Jews' ghettoization also prompted artists to articulate the crisis that had engulfed their world. Some of the trapped ghetto public yearned for cultural life. Books, scholarship, music, and theater provided them with a refuge from the surrounding reality and allowed them to recall their prior lives.

2

3

Kovno Ghetto

The day after the German invasion of the Soviet Union, even before the Germans had entered Kovno, the Lithuanians began to riot and murder thousands of Jews, encouraged by the Germans. As the Germans entered Lithuania and its capital, Kovno, Jews were murdered, raped, dispossessed, and abused by their Lithuanian neighbors.

On August 15, 1941, the gates of the Kovno ghetto were sealed, and 20,000 Jews were interned by order of the Germans in the slum suburb of Slobodka (Wiliampole). The turning point in ghetto life took place on October 28, 1941, when the Germans rounded up the entire ghetto population and carried out a brutal selection. More than 9,000 inhabitants were led to the Ninth Fort (one of a set of fortresses near the town) and murdered.

During the first two years of the occupation, the ghetto was repeatedly downscaled and its inhabitants put to forced labor. The Ältestenrat (as the Judenrat in Kovno was known), chaired by Dr. Elchanan Elkes, tried to establish a set of workshops to employ ghetto inhabitants, pointing out to the Germans the Jews' productive value. Nevertheless the *Aktionen* and murders did not cease. During the ghetto's existence, the Ältestenrat also worked to spare the children. In the summer of 1943, however, the ghetto became a concentration camp. Several months later it absorbed a severe blow, as some 1,200 babies, children, and elderly were murdered and many young people were sent to labor camps in Estonia. In July 1944, as the Red Army was about to liberate the city, the Kovno ghetto was liquidated; those who remained were sent to Stutthof, Dachau, and Auschwitz-Birkenau.

1 Jewish refugees in Warsaw—song hour at the boys' home
2 Selling books in the ghetto
3 Entrance to the Eldorado Theater, Warsaw ghetto, 1941
4 Barbed-wire fence near the Varniu Street entrance to the Kovno ghetto
5-6 Moving to the ghetto

4

5

6

The Documenters

Sensing their impending demise and aware that they were witnesses to an unprecedented occurrence in Jewish history, the Jews of Kovno mobilized to document their lives in the ghetto. Some of these activities were organized by the Ältestenrat; others were initiated by private individuals. A graphics workshop produced underground albums that documented the decrees. The Brit Zion youth movement prepared an almanac. Even the ghetto police produced a written account of their history. Poems and diaries, clandestinely written, were gathered and preserved. Painters reenacted scenes and produced portraits; the photographer Zvi Kadushin recorded ghetto sights on film. Fearing that nothing from the ghetto would survive except for this documented testimony, part of the collection was smuggled out and placed in hiding. Most of it was found after the liberation.

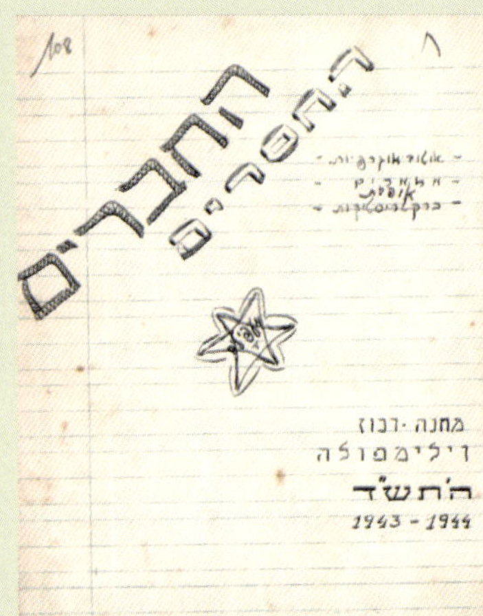

"We, the young [members] of the Brit Zion organization, have decided to record our history in a book. If we survive, this book will serve us as a memento of our Zionist work in the ghetto. If it is our fate to die, however, then this book of ours will be a monument to all the sacred work that we did."

Zvi Kadushin was an amateur photographer before the war. With the German invasion and the start of the pogroms against the Jews of Kovno, the photographs became testimony, and Kadushin wandered around the ghetto, taking pictures from beneath his coat.

1 Lithuanian militiamen lead Jews to the Seventh Fort, June-July 1941
2 Moving to the small ghetto
3 Girls in classroom, Kovno ghetto
4 **Jacob Lifschitz** (1903–1945), Krisciukaicio Street, Slobodka, 1942, India ink on paper

4

Terezin Ghetto

In 1941 the Nazis established a ghetto in Terezin (Theresienstadt), a garrison town in northwestern Czechoslovakia, where they interned the Jews of Bohemia and Moravia, elderly Jews, persons of "special merit" in the Reich, and several thousand Jews from the Netherlands and Denmark. Although in practice the ghetto, run by the SS, served as a transit camp for Jews en route to extermination camps, it was also presented as a "model Jewish settlement" for propaganda purposes.

Internal life in Terezin was administered by the Ältestenrat (Judenrat) headed by Jacob Edelstein. Despite severe congestion, food shortages, and compulsory labor, the extensive educational and cultural activities in the ghetto reflected the prisoners' will to live and their need for distraction

1

2

3

4

5

6

from their plight. In June 1944, the Nazis exploited a Red Cross visit to the ghetto to create the false impression of a vibrant community. Of more than 155,000 Jews who passed through Terezin until its liberation in April 1945, 35,440 died in the ghetto, and 88,000 were sent to extermination.

7

1 Bunks in the ghetto
2 A burial process, photographed secretly by the Czech gendarme, Karl Slava, who served as a guard in the Terezin ghetto, January 1942
3 Banknote from Terezin ghetto, 100 Krone
4 Places from which Jews were deported to Terezin ghetto
5 Savings book in a bank that operated in the ghetto
6 Deportation from Hanau, Germany
7 A transport from the Netherlands with 870 Jews aboard reaches Terezin ghetto. January 20, 1944
8 1944 calendar, prepared in Terezin ghetto by Asher Berlinger
9 **Eli Lichtblau** (b. 1911), Studying Hebrew, 1943, Watercolor and India ink on paper

8

9

Jan Burka (b. 1924), Portrait of Mrs. Erna Ingus (b. 1866), sanguine on paper

The Elderly

Thousands of unaccompanied elderly people were transported to the Terezin ghetto from all over the Reich. For lack of space, the Ältestenrat had to house them in lofts or out in the open. Some worked, but most were ill, without the strength even to stand in the lengthy queues for food. Despite attempts to establish nursing institutions for them, and assistance from young people, many of them died.

Charlotte Buresova (1904–1983), The Visit, 1942–1945, ink, wash, pencil, and gouache on paper

ALMA SARA SCHWARZ
VII 719

The Lives of Children and Teenagers in Terezin

Encouraged by the Ältestenrat, the ghetto inhabitants made special efforts to provide children with reasonable lives under the harsh conditions that had been imposed. Young children lived with their mothers or in residences for infants, toddlers, and children; teenagers were housed in separate residences for boys and girls. Although prohibited, study was an important part of the children's lives. The task was given to the finest teachers and instructors and was accompanied by comprehensive cultural enrichment.

Of some 8,000 children and teenagers who were sent from Terezin to the extermination camps, 474 survived. Freddy (Frantishek) Hirsch was born in Germany, and, as a young man was a member of the Young Maccabi movement. He was one of the most revered instructors in the ghetto. When the racial laws first came into effect, he moved to Prague, where he worked as a sports instructor. One of the first to be sent to Theresienstadt, he devoted himself to caring for youth. In September 1943, he was sent to Auschwitz-Birkenau.

Monopoly game, made by the graphics workshop in Terezin ghetto to inform children about ghetto life

Dolls made in Terezin ghetto by Alice Randt, a deportee from Germany

Doll made in Terezin ghetto by Pauline Klauber

Petr Ginz (1928–1944), Rooftops and Towers of Prague, 1939–1940(?), gouache and India ink on paper

The Final Solution

Marcel Janco (1895–1984), Under the Boot of the Nazi Oppressor, 1940, India ink on paper

Aktion in Ivangorod, Ukraine, 1942

1941—The Invasion of the Soviet Union and Mass Murder

The last phase of the Nazis' plan to "solve the Jewish problem" began with Operation Barbarossa, the massive military invasion of the Soviet Union (June 22, 1941), intended to wind up the war by the winter. The invasion, in violation of the agreement concluded between the two countries' foreign ministers, Molotov and Ribbentrop, had long been in the planning. To carry it out, the Germans prepared units of Ukrainian, Lithuanian, Latvian, and Belorussian nationalist and oppositionist collaborators. In the course of this murderous onslaught, which lasted almost until the end of the war (May 9, 1945), Jews in the occupied Soviet territories were pursued and slaughtered.

Hitler considered the invasion of the USSR as the beginning of his plan to provide the German nation with "living space" (Lebensraum) and an opportunity to destroy Communism, which he loathed. For this reason he instructed his military commanders to subject Kommissars (political officers who accompanied the Red Army) and

1

2

3

intellectuals to harsh treatment. Under his inspiration, the "Kommissars Order" set forth the rules for treatment of these officials and for Jews in the Soviet territories.

Operation Barbarossa was a turning point in World War II and in the fate of the Jews. The deployment of Einsatzgruppen (operation divisions) behind the eastern front marked the beginning of a satanic plan geared to the steady, unrelenting annihilation of all Jews in the German sphere of control and influence. Millions of Soviet civilians also fell victim to the Nazis' blood lust.

1 Aerial photograph of an air raid on Bialystok, July 1941
2 Propaganda manifestos distributed by the Germans in the Ukraine
3 German column during the invasion of the Soviet Union, July 1941

Four Einsatzgruppen—A, B, C, and D—operated behind the corps that took part in the campaign against the USSR. The units were made up of SS, police, and auxiliaries mobilized from the local population. Their official task was to purge the occupied territories of hostile local elements. However, as stated by Otto Ollendorf, the commander of one of these formations which murdered 90,000 Jews, Reinhard Heydrich had issued a verbal order to kill every last Jew.

1 German soldiers arrest Jews, Jasionowka, Poland, June 28, 1941
2 Ukrainian volunteers in Lvov enlist in the Waffen-SS
3 A Ukrainian village ablaze

1

Studio Gideon Dan

1 Murder routes of the Einsatzgruppen

2 Execution of Soviet inhabitants, Kraigonev, 1941

2

1

Commander of the Security Police (SD)

Berlin, July 6, 1941

30 copies

Copy No 18

Secret Reich Matter!

Report No. 14 on Operational Activity in the Soviet Union

Location: Tarnopol

On July 5, Ukrainians rounded up approximately 70 Jews and eliminated them with bursts of gunfire. Twenty additional Jews were beaten to death in the street by military forces and Ukrainians….

2

Einsatzgruppe C, commanded by Dr. Emil Otto Rasch, was made up of some 1,000 men and operated in the Ukraine. Under its auspices, the Ukrainians massacred and abused the Jewish townspeople of Lvov. As the front advanced, they moved eastward, murdering Jewish men in towns and villages along the route of its advance—Tarnopol, Dobromyl, Sambor, Vinnitsa, Zhitomir, Belaya Tserkov, Bugoslav, Babi Yar, Uman, and Lubny— aided by Ukrainians. Afterward, the killing of women and children began, and the murders became systematic and total. Hundreds of thousands of Jews were shot to death, and their corpses were hurled into pits and ravines.

1 Execution of Soviet inhabitants, Kraigonev, 1941
2 Murder of Jews in Tarnopol, Ukraine
3–5 Murder and abuse of Jews of Lvov by Ukrainians, June 30–July 3, 1941
6 A Jew and his son near the market square, during an *Aktion*, Uman
7 Jewish men in Zhitomir, August 7, 1941

3

4

5

6

7

2

1

3

4

5

1 Murder of women and children, Misocz, Ukraine
2 Einsatzgruppe soldier murders a Jew, Vinnitsa, Ukraine, July 1941
3–4 Murder of Jews, Kovno, June 1941
5 Murder of the Jews of Liepaja, Latvia, December 15–17, 1941

1

2

3

4

1–4 Murder of the Jews of Liepaja, Latvia, December 15-17, 1941

Babi Yar

At a meeting of army commanders and the commander of Einsatzgruppe C, a decision was made to murder all Jews in Kiev in response to acts of sabotage that had been carried out in the area. The Germans posted notices ordering Jews to report on September 29, 1941, for "resettlement." That morning a Sonderkommando unit of Einsatzgruppe C arrived and led the Jews toward the Jewish cemetery on the outskirts of town. On that day and the next, the soldiers in this formation murdered 33,771 Jews. Babi Yar became a killing ground for Sinti and Roma and Soviet prisoners of war as well.

1 German police supervise local inhabitants as they exhume corpses.
2–3 Belongings of murder victims at Babi Yar

1

2

3

Who Planned and Perpetrated These Murders?

The planners and perpetrators of the "Final Solution" were Germans and Austrians, abetted by members of the occupied peoples—foremost from the Baltic countries—who did their bidding. Most of the murderers belonged to the SS, an organization commanded mainly by men in their thirties. Two-thirds of them had attended university; about half held doctoral degrees in law, economics, political science, or philosophy. By enlisting for service in the SS, they expressed their belief that they were the elite of the Aryan race, driven by the sense of a historical mission to implement the ideology and shape the new world order in the Nazi image. Their willing enlistment in the eradication of Jews was prompted largely by this ideology.

"All the Roads... Lead to Ponary"

From July 1941 to July 1944, tens of thousands of Jews were murdered and buried in a forest about 10 kilometers south of Vilna. The victims were led from Vilna and its vicinity to pits, shot by Germans and Lithuanians, and thrown in. Only a few survived the massacres, and only a few among them managed to elude the local population. In total, more than 70,000 people, nearly all of them Jews, were murdered at Ponary.

"On September 1 [1941], the entire Jewish quarter [of Vilna] was surrounded and several thousand people were taken from their apartments straight to Ponary.... For days on end, we heard barrages of machine-gun fire from that direction, usually preceded by a single gunshot."

Aryeh Wilner (Yorek), a Hashomer Hazair leader in Warsaw who perished in the Warsaw Ghetto Uprising

Perforated spoon found at the killing site in Ponary

Ponary
Softly, softly! Let's be silent!
Graves are growing here.
They were sown by our tormentors,
Green they grow, and fair.
Toward Ponary run roads aplenty,
From Ponary not one.
Father's disappeared, and with him
All our joy is gone.

Lyrics: Shmerl Kaczerginski, poet and partisan
Music: Alek Wolkowyski (Alexander Tamir) aged 11, Vilna ghetto, April 1943

1

"Toward evening, we reached a place called Ponary. Then we saw the pits. The pits had already been prepared. Obviously we knew we weren't staying there, that we weren't workers. They went past us with dogs, moved us to the middle and surrounded us, stood next to us with the dogs, and told us to undress and to put our things in one place. Everyone decided to undress. I undressed, but not all the way. That's enough, they said. I kept a dress and shoes on. My grandmother and aunt, who were with me, had to undress all the way. Then they took ten women, ordered all ten women to walk to the pit and stand next to the pit. The automatic [weapons] that's a killing machine were already there, with those who were sitting there. We had to stand, ten women, next to the pit. They shot them and they fell. I was almost one of the last ones. Then I reached the pit, they shot at us, and I fell. I fell—the pit was already full. I fell at the edge, where there were already lots of people, and I was right on the top, at the edge. Then I looked and I saw everything. I turned over somehow and sat down on the dead people. They hit lots of people but missed some. For that reason, there was crying in the pit all the time, and everyone, it was just horrific, unendurable. There was crying, they asked for mercy, and the Nazis came afterwards and heard people still alive, then they came and shot them. Seven. I was seven years old."

Dina Beitler

In April 1941, the Germans occupied Serbia, part of Yugoslavia. A Communist-led popular uprising broke out in July, and the Germans responded with a brutal crackdown. The local German administration, aware that it was Berlin's policy to eradicate the Jews, executed Jewish men who were interned in camps on the pretext that the Jews were Communists and, therefore, had incited the rebellion. Most of the murders took place in September–December 1941. About 8,000 women and children were gathered at the Sajmiste camp, near Belgrade, and murdered in March–May 1942, in a gas van.

After Yugoslavia was partitioned in April 1941, parts of the country were controlled by Hungary, Italy, Bulgaria, Germany, and independent Croatia, under the leadership of the Fascist leader Ante Pavelic, head of the Ustasa party. Pavelic's administration, operating under Hitler's patronage, embarked on the liquidation of hundreds of thousands of Serbs and opponents

1 The partisan Shmerke Kaczerginski of Vilna found this photograph in Ponary and identified Benyamin and Rjvka Aharonovitch of Vilna; their two children; Rjvka's father, Liba Gilinsky; and Binyamin's father. Binyamin was abducted around the time the Germans entered Vilna and his traces vanished. Rjvka remained with her children in Vilna and was evidently sent with them to Ponary. Chana Levin Gilinsky, Rjvka's sister-in-law, was sent to Ponary from Swienciany ghetto on the night of April 4-5, 1943, and took the photo with her.

2 Order of the day from Hitler to his soldiers on the eastern front, October 2, 1941

2

Soldaten der Ostfront!

Erfüllt von tiefster Sorge für das Dasein und die Zukunft unseres Volkes habe ich mich am 22. Juni entschlossen, den Appell an Euch zu richten, dem drohenden Angriff eines Gegners noch in letzter Stunde zuvorzukommen. Es war die Absicht der Machthaber des Kremls — wie wir es heute wissen — nicht nur Deutschland, sondern ganz Europa zu vernichten.

Zwei Erkenntnisse, Kameraden, werdet Ihr unterdes gewonnen haben:

1. Dieser Gegner hatte sich für seinen Angriff militärisch in einem so enormen Ausmaße gerüstet, daß auch die stärksten Befürchtungen noch übertroffen worden sind.

2. Gnade Gott unserem Volk und der ganzen europäischen Welt, wenn dieser barbarische Feind seine Zehntausende an Panzern vor uns in Bewegung hätte setzen können.

Ganz Europa wäre verloren gewesen. Denn dieser Feind besteht nicht aus Soldaten, sondern zum großen Teil nur aus Bestien.

Nun, meine Kameraden, habt Ihr selbst mit eigenen Augen das „Paradies der Arbeiter und der Bauern" persönlich kennengelernt. In einem Lande, das durch seine Weite und Fruchtbarkeit die ganze Welt ernähren könnte, herrscht eine Armut, wie sie für uns Deutsche unvorstellbar ist. Dies ist das Ergebnis einer nunmehr bald 25jährigen jüdischen Herrschaft, die als Bolschewismus im tiefsten Grund nur der allergemeinsten Form des Kapitalismus gleicht.

Die Träger dieses Systems sind aber auch in beiden Fällen die gleichen: Juden und nur Juden.

Soldaten!

Als ich Euch am 22. Juni gerufen habe, um die furchtbar drohende Gefahr von unserer Heimat abzuwenden, seid Ihr der größten militärischen Macht aller Zeiten entgegengetreten. In aber knapp 3 Monaten ist es, dank Eurer Tapferkeit, meine Kameraden, gelungen, diesem Gegner eine Panzerbrigade nach der anderen zu zerschlagen, zahllose Divisionen auszulöschen, ungezählte Gefangene zu machen, endlose Räume zu besetzen, — nicht leere, sondern jene Räume, von denen dieser Gegner lebt und aus denen seine gigantische Kriegsindustrie mit Rohstoffen aller Art versorgt wird.

Denn dieser Kampf wird — vielleicht zum ersten Mal — von allen Nationen Europas als eine gemeinsame Aktion zur Rettung des wertvollsten Kulturkontinents angesehen.

Gewaltig ist aber auch die Arbeit, die hinter Eurer gigantischen Front geleistet wurde.

Fast 2000 Brücken von über 12 m Länge sind gebaut worden;

405 Eisenbahnbrücken wurden hergestellt;

25 500 km Eisenbahnen sind wieder in Betrieb genommen;

Ja: Über 15 000 km Bahnen sind bereits auf die allgemeine europäische Spurweite umgenagelt.

An Tausenden von Kilometern Straßen wird gearbeitet.

Große Gebiete sind schon in die zivile Verwaltung übernommen. Dort wird das Leben schnellstens wieder nach vernünftigen Gesetzen in Gang gebracht. Ungeheuere Lager an Verpflegung, Treibstoff und Munition aber liegen bereit!

Dieses größte Ergebnis eines Kampfes wurde dabei erreicht mit Opfern, deren Zahl — bei aller Schwere für die einzelnen Kameraden und ihre Angehörigen — im gesamten noch nicht 5 vH. derjenigen des Weltkrieges beträgt.

Was ihr, meine Kameraden, und was die mit uns verbündeten tapferen Soldaten an Leistungen, an Tapferkeit, an Heldentum, an Entbehrungen und Anstrengungen in diesen kaum dreieinhalb Monaten hinter Euch haben, weiß keiner besser als derjenige, der einst selbst als Soldat im vergangenen Krieg seine Pflicht erfüllte.

In diesen 3½ Monaten, meine Soldaten, ist nun aber endlich die Voraussetzung geschaffen worden zu dem letzten gewaltigen Hieb, der noch vor dem Einbruch des Winters diesen Gegner zerschmettern soll. Alle Vorbereitungen sind - soweit sie Menschen meistern können - nunmehr fertig. Planmäßig ist dieses Mal Schritt um Schritt vorbereitet

1

2

1 The Nazi takeover reaches its climax

2 **Gerson Apfel** (1922–1999), Heading towards Jasenovac 1941, Etching

Report on the Execution of Jews on October 9 and October 11, 1941

The Order: On October 8, 1941, an order to execute 2,200 Jews in the Belgrade camp was issued.

Implementation: After thorough examination of the locations and appropriate preparations, the first executions were carried out on October 9.

At 5:30 [a.m.], the first prisoners were led out of the Belgrade camp.

The people were issued with shovels and other tools to create the impression that they were being taken out for labor. Valuables and other objects were collected under supervision and were taken... to the security police [the SD].

We employed the prisoners at a distance of about eight kilometers from the execution site and they were taken from there as needed. The execution was implemented by rifle fire at a twelve-meter range. Five riflemen were posted for each doomed person... Two riflemen were made available to the doctor, and where necessary and at his command they killed the person by shooting him in the head.

On October 9, 180 people were shot. It all ended at 18:30. There were no special events. The unit returned to the camp with a sense of satisfaction.

Serbia, report by Lieppe, the commander of the operation

of the regime. The Fascist regime's orders and decrees also affected Jews, and the deportation of the Jews of Zagreb to concentration camps began in June 1941. The Jews of Bosnia, Herzegovina, and Sarajevo were deported during August. Most of the deportees were murdered a short time later. The Jasenovac camp, established south of Zagreb in August 1941, became the largest concentration camp in the country and a central murder site. In addition to some 25,000 Jews, hundreds of thousands of Serbs, thousands of Sinti and Roma, and opponents of the regimes were murdered there. The camp was liquidated in late April 1945.

Romania, a dutiful ally of Nazi Germany, had a Jewish population of about 757,000 before World War II. Extreme antisemitic tendencies, long evident in the country, escalated on the eve of the war. The Romanian dictator Ion Antonescu was among the few leaders from the axis states that Hitler coopted into his murderous plans. With the German invasion of the USSR in the summer of 1941, Antonescu ordered the murder of the Jews in Bessarabia and Bukovina. The killings were carried out by the army, gendarmerie and local Romanian population, with the cooperation of the Wehrmacht and Einsatzgruppe D. The Jews that remained alive in these areas were cruelly transported to an area between the Dneister

The Pogrom in Jassy

The massacre of the Jews of Jassy began on June 27, 1941. Romanian soldiers, police, and civilians broke into Jewish homes and arrested thousands. Those not arrested were forced to march through the city streets. The weak were shot along the way; the others were dispossessed. All were led to the railroad station and packed into cattle cars. With neither water nor food, many died during the eight-day trip. The slaughter in Jassy claimed the lives of at least 15,000 Jews. Later on, when the Romanian administration realized that the war would not end well for them, and after the Allies had issued them with stern warnings, the Romanians, deterred, called off the slaughter.

1

2

Gerta the Doll

When the Modval family was deported from their home in Transnistria, eight-year-old Eva took along her beloved doll. On the way the members of the family were separated, and Eva watched as her father wrapped a white kerchief around her mother's neck and told her, "You will be my beloved forever." Eva and her mother were imprisoned, but Eva's father, who was taken to a different prison, managed to arrange refuge for them at the Romanian embassy in Budapest, to which they were removed. After the war they discovered that Eva's father had been killed while attempting to escape.

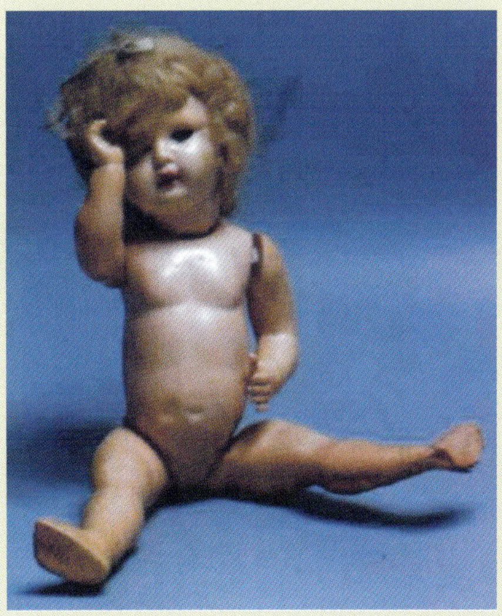

3

1 Deportation of Jews from Briceva (Bessarabia) to Transnistria
2 Murder sites on Romanian soil
3 Lists by Binyamin Hauer, 1941–1944, document the fate of the Jews of Mogilev, Transnistria. The lists were produced in Hebrew and German on the backs of labels affixed to jars of jam

and Bug rivers, which Hitler gave to Romania, known as Transnistria. There the Romanians continued their mass murder of the Jews in the killing fields of Bogdanovka, Domanevka and Akhmetchetka. In all, some 400,000 Jews were murdered in the regions under Romanian rule, including the Jews of Transnistria.

"After my mother was murdered, I was deported together with my father to Transnistria. We have spent many weeks on a penal trek of sorts.... For days we have been slogging along roads deep in mud, a lengthy convoy surrounded by Romanian and Ukrainian soldiers who flog and shoot at us. Father holds my hand tight; my feet no longer touch the ground. But the sound of the water slices at my legs and my hips. It's dark all around; apart from Father's hand I don't feel a thing. Truth to tell, I don't feel his hand either, since my hand is already partly numb. If I move just a little I'll surely drown. Even Father won't be able to pull me out. Lots of children have already drowned this way. I fall asleep, still clutching his hand. But not for long. While the sky is still dark, the soldiers light up the convoy with sniping and gunfire. Father holds my hand and tugs me. The mud is deep and I can't feel the bottom. I'm still half asleep and tremendously afraid. 'It hurts,' I call out. Father hears my call and answers at once, 'Make it easier for me, make it easier.'"

Aharon Appelfeld

1

2

Bogdanovka

Bogdanovka, an extermination site that the Romanians established in October 1941 near the Bug River in Transnistria, received some 54,000 Jewish deportees from Odessa and Bessarabia. Due to cases of typhus, the Romanian district governor decided to murder all the camp internees. Soldiers, police, Volksdeutsche (ethnic Germans), and Ukrainians took part in the massacre (December 21, 1941). About 5,000 people were concentrated in two barns and burned alive. The others were taken to a nearby forest, pushed to the edge of a ravine, ordered to undress, and shot. The murders continued for four days; thousands froze to death while waiting for their turn to be gunned down. The operation resumed on December 28, as another 11,000 Jews were shot. The perpetrators then cremated the bodies to cover up what they had done.

1 **Arnold Daghani** (1909–1985), Szulek (Shalom), a Jewish Youth in the Bershad Ghetto, 1943, gouache on paper

2 **Arnold Daghani** (1909–1985), Semmel the Tinsmith, Bershad Ghetto, 1943, gouache on paper

"...So what was there? Romanian soldiers stood there with rifles, eight soldiers, a convoy of people. They took eight people—children, women, men— eight people, stood them up on the edge of the pit where there was a fire at the bottom. And they killed them, a real barrage. There were mountains of clothes that they took off the people..."

Esther Gelbelman

The Wannsee Conference

I have been authorized by the Reichsmarshal [Hermann Göring] to make all the necessary preparations... for the Final Solution of the Jewish Question in Europe.... I therefore invite you to the conference, immediately followed by breakfast....Heil Hitler Reinhard Heydrich

On July 31, 1941, shortly after the invasion of the Soviet Union, the Nazi Reichsmarshal Hermann Göring instructed Reinhard Heydrich, head of the RSHA, "to make all the necessary preparations... for the Final Solution of the Jewish Question in the German sphere of influence in Europe." On January 20, 1942, a crucial meeting, only of 90 minutes, was held in Wannsee (a suburb of Berlin), chaired by Reinhard Heydrich, with the participation of sixteen officials and representatives of the main Reich authorities. At this meeting, the RSHA coordinated the extermination plans vis-à-vis the relevant ministries and authorities. Heydrich spoke about the inclusion of 11,000,000 Jews in the Nazi program for the "Final Solution to the Jewish Question."

The minutes of the Wannsee Conference record that: "Due to the war, the emigration plan has been replaced with deportation of the Jews to the east, in accordance with the Führer's will. The senior officials were invited... to coordinate the methods."

The commander of Auschwitz-Birkenau, Rudolf Höss, stated in his autobiography that in 1941 (no exact date given) he was summoned to Berlin, where Himmler informed him that the Führer had issued an order to solve the "Jewish Question" for good, and that the order was to be implemented by the SS. "The existing extermination places in the East are unsuited to a large scale, long-term action. I have designated Auschwitz for this purpose," Himmler said.

I order the resettlement of the Jewish population in the General gouvernement to be performed and completed by December 31, 1942.

Heinrich Himmler, July 19, 1942

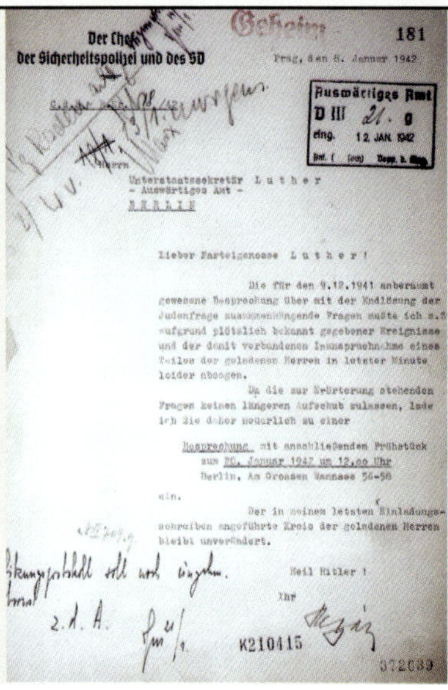

Der Chef der Sicherheitspolizei und des SD

Geheim

181

Prag, den 8. Januar 1942

Auswärtiges Amt
D III 21. g
eing. 12. JAN. 1942

Herrn
Unterstaatssekretär Luther
- Auswärtiges Amt -
BERLIN

Lieber Parteigenosse Luther!

Die für den 9.12.1941 anberaumt gewesene Besprechung über mit der Endlösung der Judenfrage zusammenhängende Fragen mußte ich s.Zt. aufgrund plötzlich bekannt gegebener Ereignisse und der damit verbundenen Inanspruchnahme eines Teiles der geladenen Herren in letzter Minute leider absagen.

Da die zur Erörterung stehenden Fragen keinen längeren Aufschub zulassen, lade ich Sie daher neuerlich zu einer

Besprechung mit anschließendem Frühstück am 20. Januar 1942 um 12.00 Uhr Berlin, Am Grossen Wannsee 56-58

ein.

Der in meinem letzten Einladungsschreiben angeführte Kreis der geladenen Herren bleibt unverändert.

Heil Hitler!
Ihr

K210415

372039

Land	Zahl
A. Altreich	131.800
Ostmark	43.700
Ostgebiete	420.000
Generalgouvernement	2.284.000
Bialystok	400.000
Protektorat Böhmen und Mähren	74.200
Estland - judenfrei -	
Lettland	3.500
Litauen	34.000
Belgien	43.000
Dänemark	5.600
Frankreich / Besetztes Gebiet	165.000
Unbesetztes Gebiet	700.000
Griechenland	69.600
Niederlande	160.800
Norwegen	1.300
B. Bulgarien	48.000
England	330.000
Finnland	2.300
Irland	4.000
Italien einschl. Sardinien	58.000
Albanien	200
Kroatien	40.000
Portugal	3.000
Rumänien einschl. Bessarabien	342.000
Schweden	8.000
Schweiz	18.000
Serbien	10.000
Slowakei	88.000
Spanien	6.000
Türkei (europ. Teil)	55.500
Ungarn	742.800
UdSSR	5.000.000
Ukraine 2.994.684	
Weißrußland ausschl. Bialystok 446.484	
Zusammen: über	11.000.000

Page from the minutes of the Wannsee conference, noting the number of Jews included in the Final Solution scheme

The Death Camps

Written in Pencil in the Sealed Railway Car

Here in this carload
I am Eve
With Abel my son
If you see my older son
Cain, son of man
Tell him that I . . .

Dan Pagis

There is no document in our possession that indicates specifically by whom, at what time, and in what way it was decided to embark on the total extermination of the Jews. Many scholars believe that such an order was never issued in to writing; instead, it was given orally, by Hitler, or with his knowledge, in the summer of 1941. Immediately following the invasion, the mass murder of men, women and children began, but in November 1941, the German policy toward Jews took a fateful turn. Mass murder by gunfire failed to meet the Nazis' expectations and was taking a cumulative toll on the German soldiers' performance. By then, too, the Nazi leadership realized that the Blitzkrieg had not gone well, that the war against the Soviet Union would not end quickly, and that killing by gunfire was not efficient enough and failed to achieve its goal. As a result, a decision was made in November or December to shift to planned, organized industrial murder. The Wannsee Conference, therefore, was a consequence of Hitler's wish to obliterate the Jewish people, coupled with developments in the Soviet territories. Mass deportations from the ghettos to deportation camps — beginning with Chelmno death camp — began in December 1941, and peaked in the summer and autumn of 1942. Entire communities were obliterated, the *Aktionen* lasting many days. Ceaselessly, the trains of the Reich thundered eastward, carrying masses of Jews to their deaths.

Chelmno—Murder by Gas Vans

"I am a Jew from the next world. The whole Jewish nation is being murdered. I myself buried a whole city of Jews...at Chelmno. They're killing everyone with gas in the forest and burying them in a mass grave."

Jacob Grojanowski (Shlamek Feiner), who escaped from the Chelmno camp and gave testimony in Warsaw in February 1942. He was murdered in Belzec.

Chelmno was the first extermination camp that the Germans established on Polish soil. Murder operations began there on December 8, 1941, and continued intermittently until January 1945. The Jews of the Lodz ghetto and the vicinity were murdered in Chelmno by means of gas vans. When

1

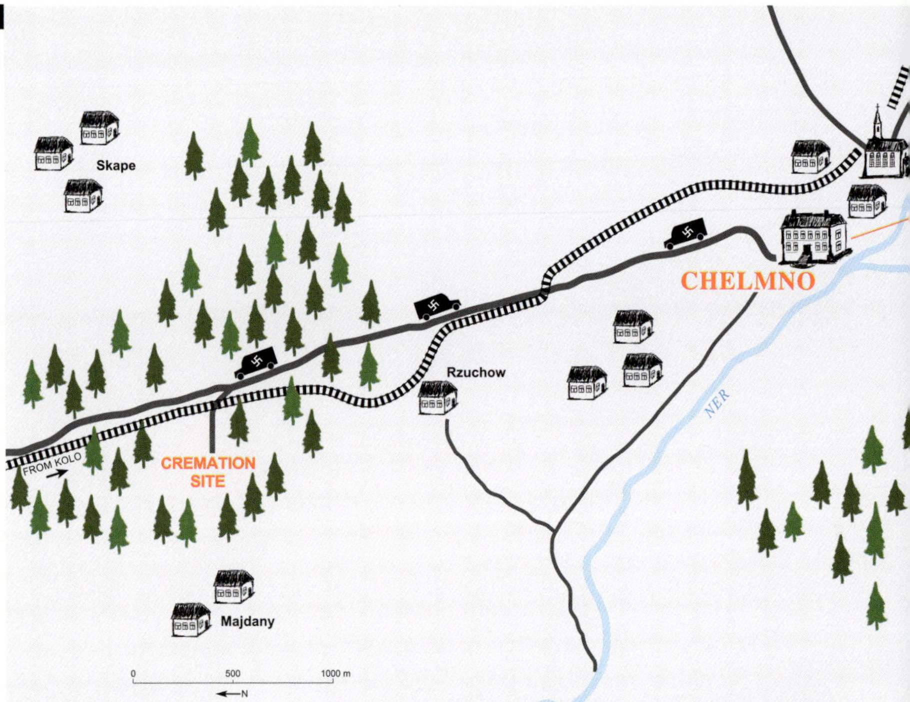

2

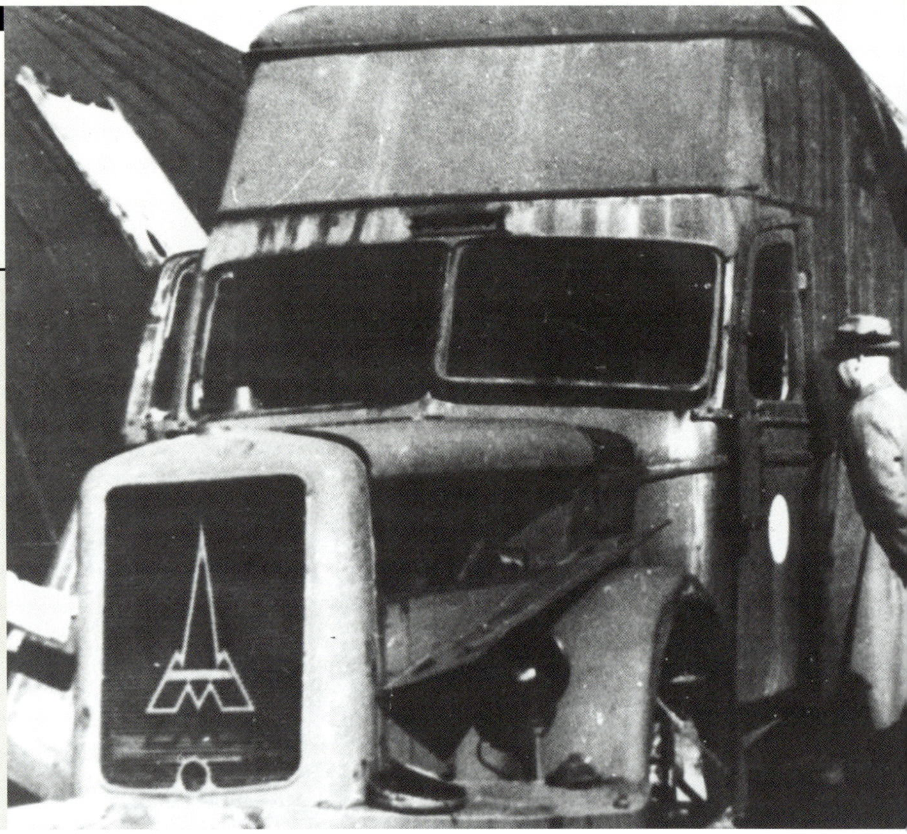

1 Murder of Jews in gas vans. Chelmno
2 Gas van used to murder Jews in Chelmno
3 Shackles worn by Jewish forced laborers in the extermination camp Chelmno
4–5 Belongings of murdered people, found on the grounds of the Chelmno extermination camp

the deportees reached the camp, they were ordered to undress, stripped of their belongings, and tricked into boarding a van whose exhaust pipe was actually connected to its interior. After the doors were closed, the van began to drive toward a designated burial place in a nearby forest. Nobody survived. By using three gas vans, nearly 300,000 Jews and 5,000 Sinti and Roma were murdered in Chelmno. Only three Jews survived this death camp.

"When we reached Chelmno, the older people said, 'What a lovely place. It'll be good for us here'... I stayed in the Hauskommando, we built a barracks; that's where I was.... There was a big tent, Jews sat there and did the selection. How do I know my mother reached Chelmno? There were lots of files there, a mountain of files. Once I found a file with pictures of my mother and all the documents. I said right then,...'My mother.' He said: 'Yes. But she's in heaven.'... It wasn't just my mother. I went through thousands of mothers there.

"... When they opened the doors [of the van], you saw everyone torn apart, everyone. They'd wanted to live so they clawed at each other. It was ghastly. When the van got to the crematorium, two people went in, the crematorium was already lit and there was a grid of rails there. They put a layer of wood on top, set it on fire, then a layer of people, a layer of wood.

"That's how it was for two whole days, two whole days, but they took out the gold teeth... and I'd sit and take out the gold... when I was in Chelmno, thirteen years old."

Shimon Srebrenik

3

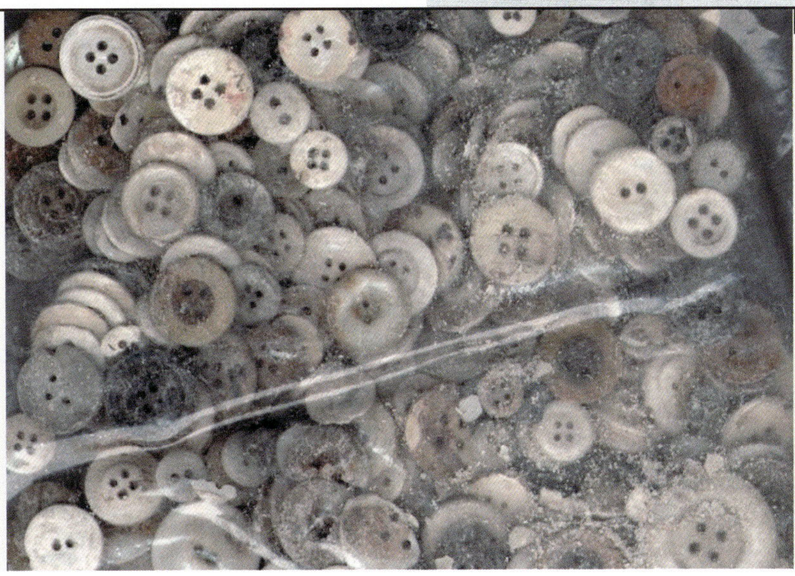

4

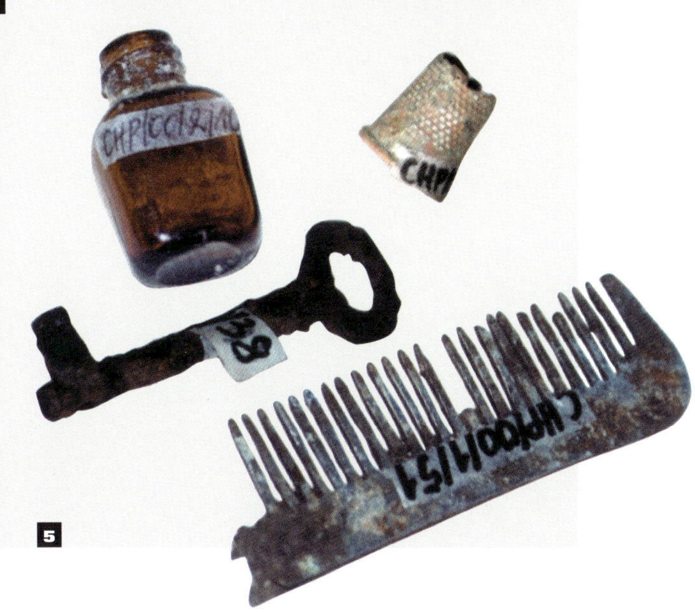

5

"For four weeks now they've been removing people from Kolo.... and all the towns in the county. Despite all efforts, I knew nothing about what was happening to them. But this week a few refugees escaped from there and said that they were killing everyone, Heaven forbid, gassing them to death en masse and burying them in a pit.... Don't sit there with your arms folded. Don't be silent."

Rabbi Jakub Sylman, rabbi of Grabów, in a warning letter to the Jews of Lodz on January 19, 1942. He did not survive.

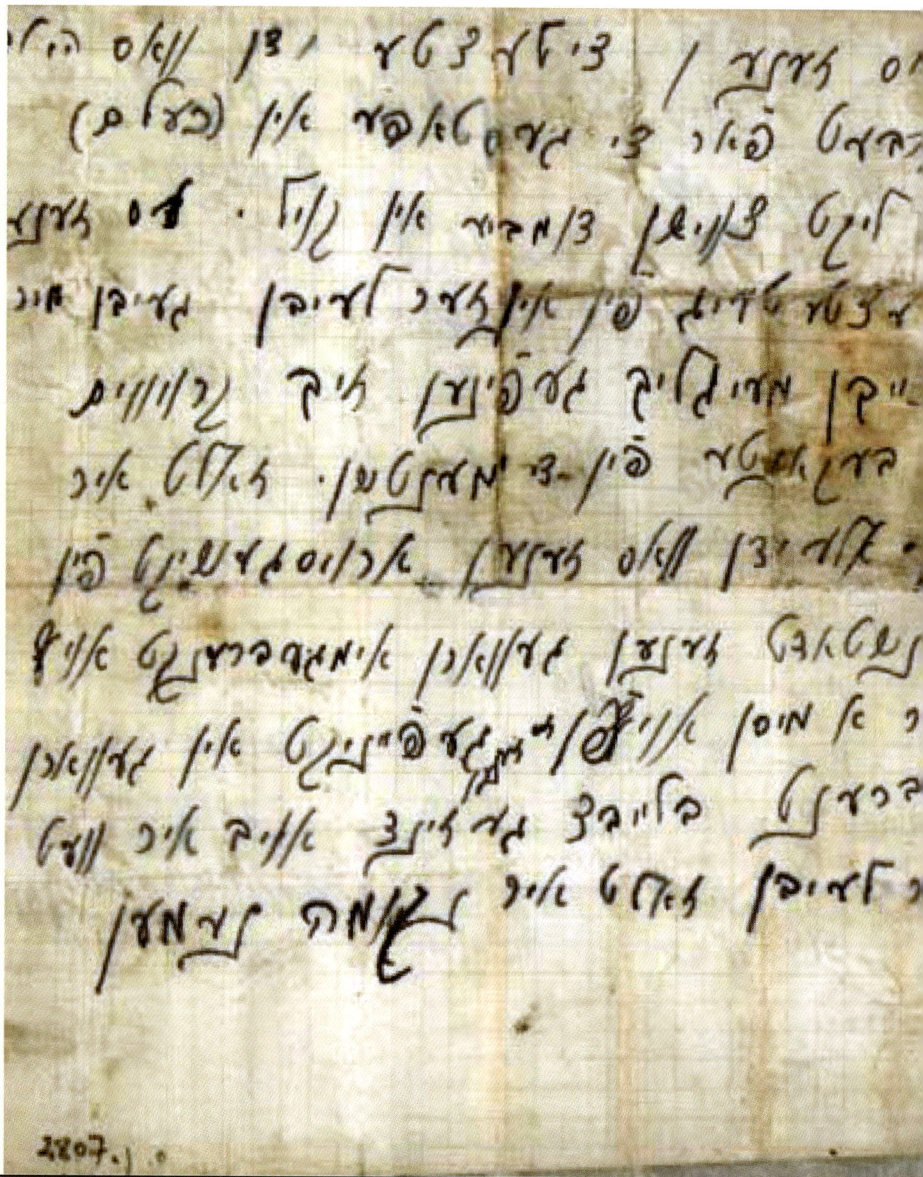

1

Operation Reinhard

In March 1942, after the action guidelines were worked out at the Wannsee Conference, the Germans began to construct three extermination camps at the eastern boundary of the *Generalgouvernement*, not far from main railroad lines: Belzec (established in March 1942, this camp functioned until December of that year; in the spring of 1943, the cremation of bodies began in order to cover up the traces of the murders committed); Sobibór (May 1942–October 1943); and Treblinka (July 1942–August 1943). The Nazis' purpose in building these camps was to carry out the systematic murder of European Jewry as part of the "Final Solution."

Permanent gas chambers were constructed in these camps. Each camp had a small staff of about thirty Germans aided by Ukrainians. The murder operation in these camps was eventually code-named "Operation Reinhard," after Reinhard Heydrich, who was killed by members of the Czech resistance in May 1942.

The extermination operation was headed by the SS and police leader in the Lublin area, Odilio Globocnik.

No selections were performed in these camps. As the deportation trains arrived, the victims—men, women, and children—were sent directly to the gas chambers. Appoximately 1,700,000 Jews were murdered in these three extermination camps, and most of the victims were from Poland.

2

"They pushed us along with beatings and I saw piles, piles of suitcases, clothing, duffle bags. Right away they divided us

3

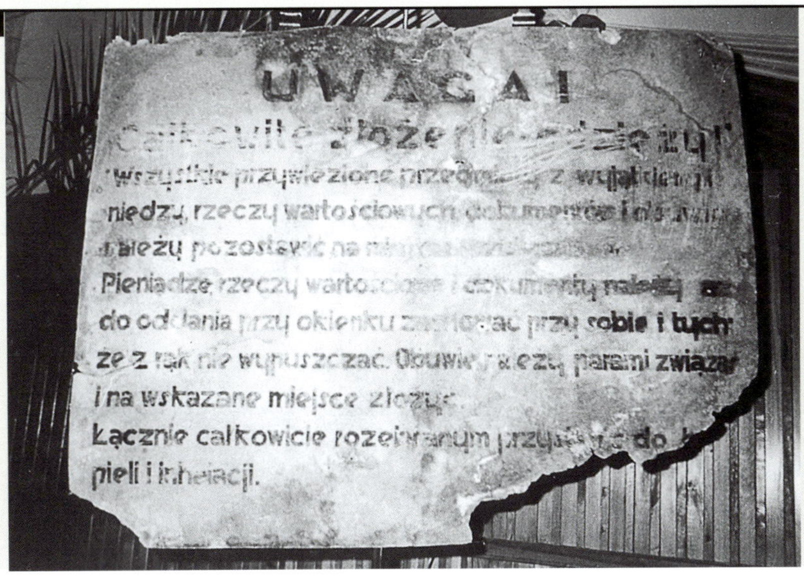

1 Belongings strewn on the floor of the synagogue in Kolo, where Jews were concentrated before being sent to the Chelmno camp
2 Sign at the railroad station of Treblinka village
3 Sign at the Belzec extermination camp. The purpose was to deceive the victims.

1
Danzig
(Gdansk)
EAST PRUSSIA
GREATER
GERMAN
REICH
NEMAN
Treblinka
WISLA
Warsaw
BUG
PRIPET
WARTA
Chelmno
Lodz
Radom
Lublin
Sobibor
Majdanek
GENERALGOUVERNEMENT
ODER
SAN
WISLA
Auschwitz
Birkenau
Belzec
Krakow
Lvov
DNIESTER
SLOVAKIA
0
100
200 km
HUNGARY

into one group to sort the clothes. I didn't know where I was any more.... There were people who were dealing with sorting these things, sorting entire piles.... I was in Treblinka for eleven months and spent most of the time in the compound where the gas chambers, the pits, and the crematoria were. Most of the time I was there in that compound, in hell, as we called it.... My job was to remove asphyxiated bodies from the gas chambers...."

Eliahu Rosenberg

"Jews and only Jews came [to Belzec].... They were ordered to undress, leaving their belongings in the yard.... An instant later, the little ones were torn away from their mothers, the old and the sick were thrown onto stretchers, men and little girls prodded with rifle butts further and further towards the fenced-in path leading straight to the chambers.... I could tell precisely at which moment everyone understood what was awaiting them.... "We dragged [from the gas chambers] the bodies of people who had still been alive a little while before; we used leather straps to drag them to the huge, waiting mass graves, and the orchestra played all the time. It played from morning to evening...."

Testimony of Rudolph Reder, the only survivor of Belzec

"The women were herded into the barrack [on the left side].... They were ordered to undress and then they were forced out of the barrack on the run... into a narrow passageway with a barbed-wire fence on both sides... towards the building where the gas chambers were located. After a few minutes, we heard terrible screams, but we could see nothing because the trees in the forest blocked our view...."

Testimony of Avraham Krzepicki, member of Hanoar Hazioni in the "Oneg Shabbat" archives. He managed to escape from Treblinka and return to the ghetto, where he gave detailed testimony about the murder operation. He was killed in 1944.

The transports from the ghettos were part of a complex operation that involved intricate logistics and the cooperation of the military and civilian authorities. The Reich railroad administration, for example, placed its rolling stock at the disposal of the perpetrators. The transports spanned all of Europe and were camouflaged in complex ways. The order to begin an *Aktion* was handed to the Judenrat

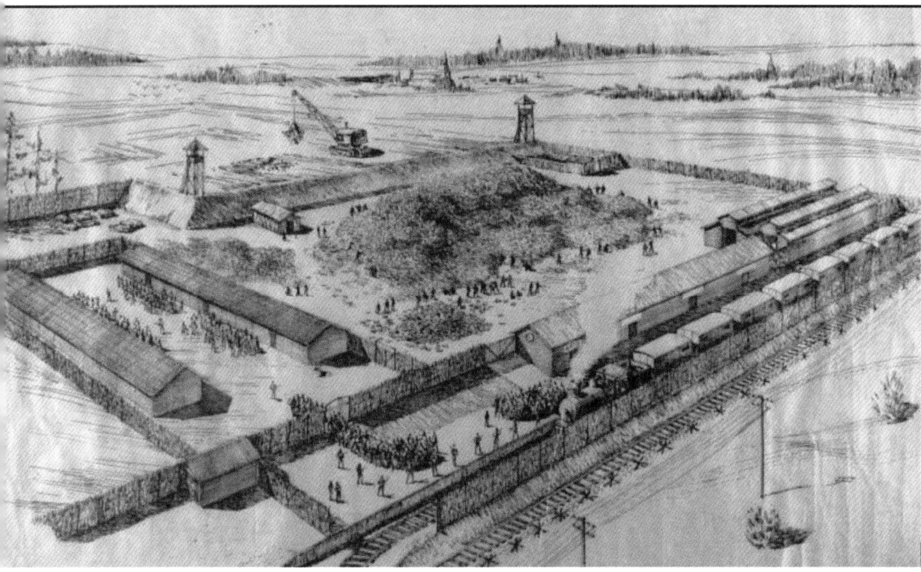

2

1 The extermination camps—Chelmno, Belzec, Sobibor, Treblinka, Majdanek, and Auschwitz-Birkenau

2 **Samuel Willenberg** (b. 1923), View Towards Treblinka, india ink on tracing paper

without warning, often at times of Jewish festivals, when the victims' guard was down. Implementation was entrusted to the local police; the Jewish Order Service was also required to take part. The Jews were ordered to gather at a designated assembly point, usually near a railroad station, and to bring only a few belongings. During the *Aktion*, anyone who failed to report as ordered or to march fast enough was shot. At the railroad station the deportees were packed into unventilated freight cars and the cars were sealed from the outside. The trip lasted for days and claimed many victims, who died of thirst and starvation.

1

1 Deportation of Jews from Lublin
2 Deportation of the Jews of Ioaninna, Greece, March 1944
3 *Aktion* in Siedlce, August 22, 1942

2

3

Aktion in Siedlce, August 22, 1942

Women and children during the deportation of the Jews of Szydlowiec (Kielce district) and the vicinity to Treblinka

1

2

3

1 Jews from Siedlce being placed aboard a deportation train
2 "When they were all put aboard, screaming burst forth from all the cars: 'Water,' we pleaded. 'My gold ring for water.'" Siedlce
3 "When they began to load them into the cattle cars, we saw terrifying scenes."

Transports and Extermination in the Death Camps

Mendel Grossman takes pictures of the deportation of Jews from the Lodz ghetto. The Judenrat employed photographers to document ghetto life

The Liquidation of the Ghettos

Deportations from the Lodz Ghetto

Transports from Lodz to the Chelmno extermination camp began in January 1942. The chairman of the Lodz Judenrat, Rumkowski, was ordered to prepare lists of candidates for deportation and to organize the roundup. By then his attempts to reduce the number of deportees had failed. Between January and May, 55,000 Jews and 5,000 Sinti and Roma were removed from the ghetto. In September, 20,000 persons were sent to death in another week-long deportation *Aktion* that had apparently been organized by the Germans themselves.

The Note

Rachel Böhm, deported from the Lodz ghetto to Auschwitz-Birkenau in 1944, concealed a note in a crevice on the wall of her freight car. She wrote the note at the behest of youth-movement members who worked at the railroad station and noticed that the cars were returning to the ghetto a short time after their departure. They asked deportees to hide notes in order to inform those who remained about the destination of the deportations. One of Rachel's comrades found Rachel's note, on which she marked down the route of the trip, the time of their arrival, and the deportees' state of mind. Rachel Böhm was murdered in Auschwitz-Birkenau shortly before the camp was liberated. **"I'm writing another note in case you don't find the earlier one. I'm listing the stations.... The trip is excellent. We are continuing to sing our song .... Auschwitz, 10:30. It's 12:00. Big barracks. We don't know the name of the station. Men and women are separated. There are children here, too. Old people also. They look good. NILI. [An acronym for "God will not betray the Jews"] Be strong and courageous. Rachel."**

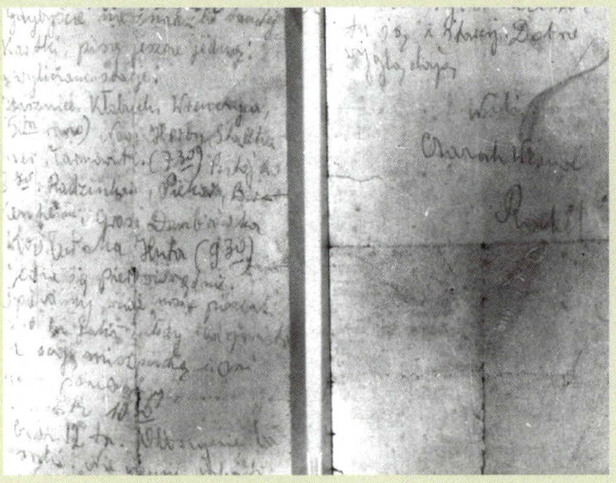

The Children's Selection

"...The ghetto has been struck a hard blow. They demand what is most dear to it—children and old people. Yesterday, in the course of the day, I was given the order to send away more than 20,000 Jews from the ghetto. I was not privileged to have a child of my own and therefore devoted my best years to children.... I never imagined that my own hands would be forced to make this sacrifice on the altar. In my old age I am forced to stretch out my hands and to beg: 'Brothers and sisters, give them to me!—Fathers and mothers, give me your children.' I must carry out this difficult and bloody operation; I must cut off limbs in order to save the body! I must take away children, and if I do not, others too will be taken, God forbid...."

Mordechai Chaim Rumkowski to the ghetto inhabitants, September 4, 1942

Liquidation of the Krakow Ghetto

The Kraków ghetto was established over a two-year period, from March 1941 to March 1943, interning some 20,000 Jews. The ghetto was liquidated in three deportation *Aktionen*. The deportees were rounded up in a square that became a center of crisis and terror. Some 15,000 Jews were sent to extermination camps, most to Belzec and a smaller number to Auschwitz-Birkenau. All the deportations were conducted violently, and many Jews were murdered in the streets. In the last *Aktion*, some 2,000 Jews were taken to the Plaszow concentration camp, a short distance from town.

Our Town is Burning

Our town is burning, brothers, burning
Our poor little town is burning
Angry winds are fanning higher
The leaping tongues of flame and fire,
The evil winds are roaring!
Our whole town burns!
And you stand looking with folded arms
And shake your heads.
You stand looking on, with folded arms

While the fire spreads!
Lyrics and music: Mordechai Gebirtig

In March 1936, three Jews were murdered and dozens injured in a pogrom in the town of Przytyk. The incident stunned the Jews of Poland and inspired Mordechai Gebirtig to write this poem, which was later sung by ghetto fighters and partisans. Gebirtig was murdered in the Krakow ghetto.

1

1 **Josef Bau** (1920–2002), The "Magnificent" Gate, c. 1950, ink on paper

2 Photos from a German officer's album document the deportation from the Krakow ghetto

2

Deportation from the Krakow ghetto

> **With particular joy I have learned from your notice that for 14 days now a train has been traveling every day to Treblinka with 5,000 members of the chosen people....**
>
> **Karl Wolff, chief of staff to SS Chief Heinrich Himmler, August 13, 1942**

On July 22, 1942, on the eve of the Ninth of Av in the jewish calendar, the Germans began the "great deportation" from the Warsaw ghetto. By the time it ended on September 21, some 260,000 ghetto inhabitants had been uprooted and deported to the Treblinka extermination camp. The first to go were the refugees, the sick, and the homeless. By order of the Germans, the city streets were cordoned off, and the Jewish Order Service forcibly removed the inhabitants from the buildings. They were then led to the Umschlagplatz (deportation square), where they were packed into freight trains. Ten days into the deportation, the Germans escalated the level of terror in the ghetto and murdered an increasing number of persons in the streets. In the final phase of the deportation, the remaining Jews were transferred to a small number of streets, where a brutal selection was performed.

"It began when I woke up in the morning. There was a mass of people in the room and they'd already told [us]. We went out, too—a mass of people went out and there were notices in Polish and German that a station called the Umschlagplatz had been opened. Umschlagplatz is German for a transit station of sorts."

Halina Birnbaum

Jews who had managed to obtain forged papers lived in hiding outside the ghetto, on the "Aryan" side of Warsaw and in smaller localities nearby.

"Shabbat, August 1, 1942
The sword is dealing death without and terror is doing so within [paraphrasing Deut.32:35]. The eleventh day of the *Aktion*, which is steadily gaining in horror and cruelty. Germans go and empty out houses and half-streets.... Horrific panic and terror.... It's a ghastly sight: [people] carrying bundles with pillows and cushions.... There's no escape, no refuge. They abduct and abduct relentlessly.... Mothers lose their children... They place

The Song of the Murdered Jewish People

Empty train cars!
You were just full, and now you are empty again.
What did you do with the Jews?
What has happened to them?
Ten thousand counted and sealed—and here you are again!
O tell me you empty train cars,
tell me where you have been.

Yitzhak Katzenelson, October 26, 1943.
A poet and educator, when the uprising began, he found a hideout together with his son, but both were captured and deported to the Vittel camp in France. In April 1944, they were transported to Auschwitz, where they were murdered.

a weak old woman aboard the bus. The tragedies cannot be described in words. "My world has gone dark: Lova was taken during the curfew at 30 Genshe [St.] … Maybe she'll survive? And if not, God forbid? I went to the Umschlagplatz…. I haven't the words to describe the crisis I'm going through. I should have followed her, that is, [I should] have gone to death, but [I haven't] the strength to take that step. Ora—and her tragedy, a girl who needed a mother so badly. And how she loved her…"

Avraham Levin, From the Notebook of the Teacher from Yehudiya. Levin died in the January 1943 *Aktion*.

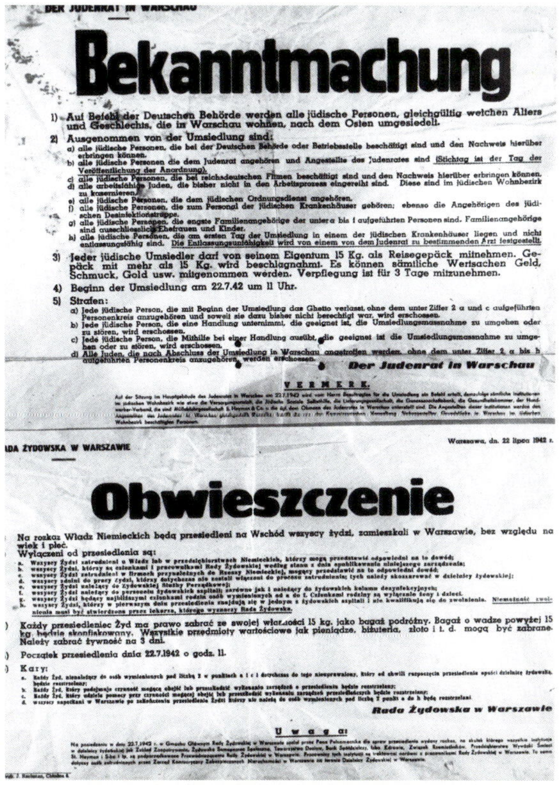

DER JUDENRAT IN WARSCHAU

Bekanntmachung

1) Auf Befehl der Deutschen Behörde werden alle jüdische Personen, gleichgültig welchen Alters und Geschlechts, die in Warschau wohnen, nach dem Osten umgesiedelt.

2) Ausgenommen von der Umsiedlung sind:
a) alle jüdische Personen, die bei der Deutschen Behörde oder Betriebsstelle beschäftigt sind und den Nachweis hierüber erbringen können.
b) alle jüdische Personen die dem Judenrat angehören und Angestellte des Judenrates sind (Stichtag ist der Tag der Veröffentlichung der Anordnung).
c) alle jüdische Personen, die bei reichsdeutschen Firmen beschäftigt sind und den Nachweis hierüber erbringen können.
d) alle arbeitsfähige Juden, die bisher nicht in den Arbeitsprozess eingereiht sind. Diese sind im jüdischen Wohnbezirk zu kasernieren.
e) alle jüdische Personen, die dem jüdischen Ordnungsdienst angehören.
f) alle jüdische Personen, die zum Personal der jüdischen Krankenhäuser gehören; ebenso die Angehörigen der jüdischen Desinfektionstruppe.
g) alle jüdische Personen, die engste Familienangehörige der unter a bis f aufgeführten Personen sind. Familienangehörige sind ausschliesslich Ehefrauen und Kinder.
h) alle jüdische Personen, die am ersten Tag der Umsiedlung in einem der jüdischen Krankenhäuser liegen und nicht entlassungsfähig sind. Die Entlassungsunfähigkeit wird von einem von dem Judenrat zu bestimmenden Arzt festgestellt.

3) Jeder jüdische Umsiedler darf von seinem Eigentum 15 Kg. als Reisegepäck mitnehmen. Gepäck mit mehr als 15 Kg. wird beschlagnahmt. Es können sämtliche Wertsachen Geld, Schmuck, Gold usw. mitgenommen werden. Verpflegung ist für 3 Tage mitzunehmen.

4) Beginn der Umsiedlung am 22.7.42 um 11 Uhr.

5) Strafen:
a) Jede jüdische Person, die mit Beginn der Umsiedlung das Ghetto verlässt, ohne dem unter Ziffer 2 a und c aufgeführten Personenkreis anzugehören und soweit sie dazu bisher nicht berechtigt war, wird erschossen.
b) Jede jüdische Person, die eine Handlung unternimmt, die geeignet ist, die Umsiedlungsmassnahme zu umgehen oder zu stören, wird erschossen.
c) Jede jüdische Person, die Mithilfe bei einer Handlung ausübt, die geeignet ist die Umsiedlungsmassnahme zu umgehen oder zu stören, wird erschossen.
d) Alle Juden, die nach Abschluss der Umsiedlung in Warschau angetroffen werden, ohne dem unter Ziffer 2, a bis h aufgeführten Personenkreis anzugehören, werden erschossen.

Der Judenrat in Warschau

VERMERK.

[illegible]

RADA ŻYDOWSKA W WARSZAWIE

Warszawa, dn. 22 lipca 1942 r.

Obwieszczenie

Na rozkaz Władz Niemieckich będą przesiedleni na Wschód wszyscy żydzi, zamieszkali w Warszawie, bez względu na wiek i płeć.

Wyłączeni od przesiedlenia są:

[illegible]

Każdy przesiedleniec Żyd ma prawo zabrać ze swojej własności 15 kg. jako bagaż podróżny. Bagaż o wadze powyżej 15 kg. będzie skonfiskowany. Wszystkie przedmioty wartościowe jak pieniądze, biżuteria, złoto i t. d. mogą być zabrane. Należy zabrać żywność na 3 dni.

Początek przesiedlenia dnia 22.7.1942 o godz. 11.

Kary:

[illegible]

Rada Żydowska w Warszawie

Uwaga:

[illegible]

The order to resettle the Jews of the Warsaw ghetto, July 22, 1942

Janusz Korczak (Henryk Goldszmit)

Janusz Korczak was a celebrated teacher, physician, and writer in Poland. His educational philosophy called for the protection of children's dignity and insisted that adults treat children fairly and lovingly. In the Warsaw ghetto, he ran an orphanage where he attempted to insulate the children from the harsh reality and continue to offer them a normal life. On August 6, 1942, in the midst of the great *Aktion*, the Germans led the children of the orphanage to the Umschlagplatz and from there to Treblinka. **"The orphanage children [walked] four abreast in a line behind Korczak. His eyes were lifted to heaven…. It was not a march to the cars but rather an organized, mute protest against the murderousness!"**

Marila Spatt and her thirteen-year-old daughter Inka were interned in the Warsaw ghetto without Inka's father, the banker Emil Spatt, whom the Germans had shot to death. Marila and Inka, together with Inka's cousin, Baszia Bergman, were smuggled out of the ghetto through a courthouse on Leszno St. with the assistance of a Polish woman, who concealed them in her home.

After the hideout was discovered, Marila, her daughter, and niece decided to seek shelter in Rawka, a town in the Carpathian area. She and her daughter were caught on their way to the hideout and executed. Baszia reached the town but evidently committed suicide.

Warsaw

Tuesday. I dont remember the date. I know its July. My nerves are fraying.

Im still in Warsaw and Im also working in the factory. In Warsaw, **hell** is continuing. In Warsaw, the **pogrom** is continuing. The victims are endless. The deportations continue non-stop. 200,000 people have already been deported from Warsaw and its almost sure that no one will be spared. Today is Tuesday. Im very nervous as I write this letter. Im always glancing into the yard to see if the gendarmes have come or whether people came in. Our postal services are working. If your letter is returned to you, youll know that Ive been deported or that Im not among the living. If it isnt returned, then youll know that I received it. It seems to me that few days remain for me to live in Warsaw, but if I survive, Ill try to get in touch with you. Dont despair, my little one, because it cant be any other way. I already gave one letter to someone but I dont know whether he sent it. In that letter, I described everything to you. Im sure that if you were in Warsaw, youd would get a job as a hairdresser at the factory. I dont have the stamina for it and I cant do it because Im afraid to go into the street. Little Yaakov and his whole family have already been deported. Elisha has almost certainly been deported, too. Yaakov was already in the car but Solek, a policeman, saved him. I dont know what to do: to go there myself or to wait for the ghastly death. In Warsaw, its becoming more and more crowded. They check your passes. You can get a pass only at 5:00 a.m. As for food, a kilo of potatoes costs 25 zloty. One cucumber costs 5 zloty. I drink boiled water. What can I tell you? People race from street to street because the houses are being taken for the use of factories. They havent yet taken our house on Dzielna Street. I dont go there at all. The house on Franciszkanska Street is still empty but they can take it at any time . When I work at the factory, I earn enough money to buy four cucumbers a day. And whats going to happen later? Dont be amazed about my haphazard writing. I cant concentrate and Im in a rush. Im standing and looking into the yard to see whether people are running there. Dont budge from where you're staying with the girl and don't dare go out. Heaven forbid. I have one request: stay alive. Maybe well see each other again some time. Maybe, but I strongly doubt it. Dont cry, my little one. Im kissing you a thousand times. If you have a little time during the day, put Lilke on your lap and tell her that her father loves her more than [he loves] life. If you do that, itll be much, much easier for me. If only we could see each other one more time. In my heart of hearts, I want it so badly. Afterwards, Ill be able to die. I wont regret losing my life.

And maybe, when I go to that unknown place, maybe I'll be lucky to find a job and have a slice of bread. Just now I got word that they're going to take the house on Franciszkanska Street. I don't know if it's true. If it is, I'll voluntarily report for deportation tomorrow morning. I'll take my warm underwear, summer clothes, and all the hairdressing equipment, and leave everything else to its fate. Imagine my emotions. Every little thing that we had was dear to us and well kept. For what purpose have I been put to such suffering? And now, where am I going? Where? Where? If I knew where so be it. But here they send you to an unknown place where they make you into fat or fertilizer. It's a good thing that you didn't see how skinny I've become. For the last time, stay healthy for me. You are my two beloved souls and apart from you I have no one on earth. I have a request of you: if there was a dark corner in our lives, forgive me. It was out of pleasure. I loved only you; apart from you and the girl I never saw anyone.

A thousand kisses. You can write a letter even though no letter to [address] has reached us. Czernowitz, Soviet Union, 2 Sebastopolskaya Street. I'm taking one of your letters with me on the way because you must have the second letter. If I find things difficult, I'll throw my things away, but not that.

Kisses, kisses, and kisses, for you and for Lilah. Don't cry.

Maks Bromberg

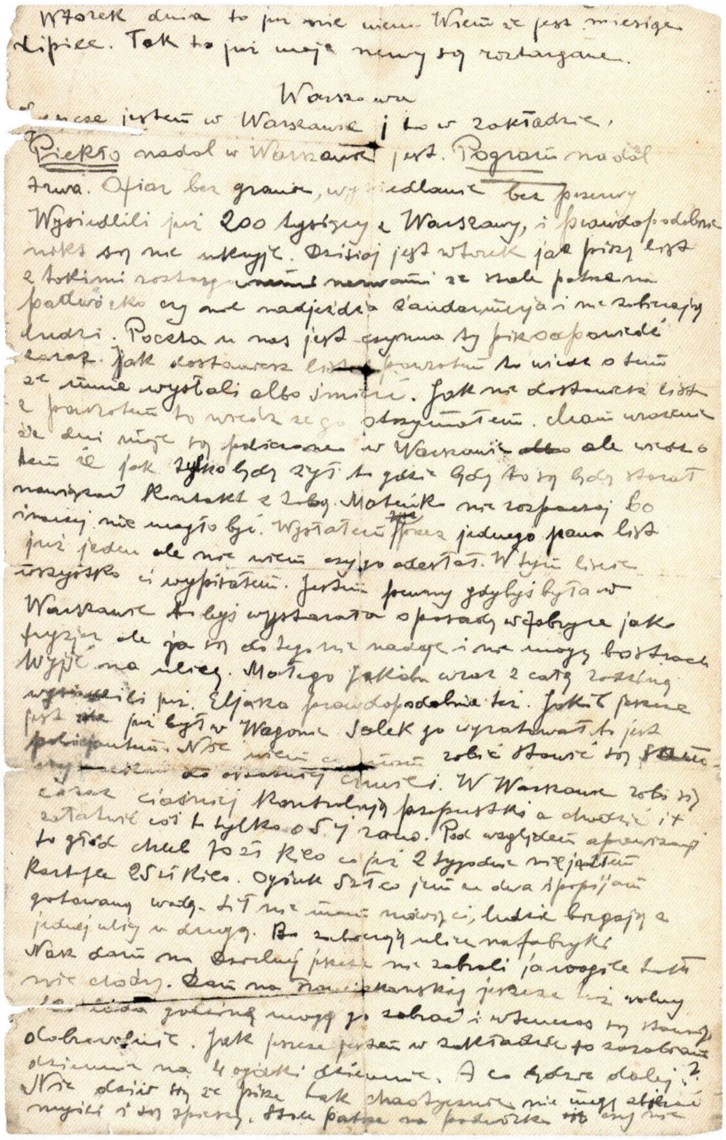
Wtorek dnia to już nie wiem. Wiem że jest miesiąc Lipiec. Tak to już moje nerwy są rozstrojone.

Warszawa

Jeszcze jestem w Warszawie i to w zakładzie.
Piekło nadal w Warszawie jest. Pogrom nadal trwa. Ofiar bez granic, wysiedlanie bez przerwy. Wysiedlili już 200 tysięcy z Warszawy, i prawdopodobnie [illegible]

Deception and Realization

"Tomorrow we'll already be heading to the unknown; if it is our fate to live, very well, and if not ..."

Plonsk, December 1942

"My landlords were sent away... in what direction, and where to? What should I do with the boy?"

Sosnowiec, May 1942

"During the first weeks of the deportation *Aktion* in Warsaw, the city was full of greetings from Warsaw Jews who had been deported.... They were lies! All the trains [full] of Warsaw Jews went to Treblinka...."

Zalman Friedrich, September 1942

"...I saw signs... saying 'From here you're going to Bialystok,' 'From here you're going to Przemysl,' 'From here to the Ukraine,' that we'd come there to be in transit. All we had to do was obey the Germans' orders. We'd enter a room with showers, we'd undress, we'd leave our things separately. We'd bathe and come out and get new clothes and we'd go, you, that is, you'd take a train to wherever you want....Cars would come and pick you up...."

Eliahu Rosenberg

The murder machine, powerfully set in motion throughout Europe, made use of various ruses and deceptions. Polish Jews were told about the transport of "special unemployed elements" to the East for labor; Jews in the West were told that they would be resettled in the East. The Germans first deported the weak (the poor, the refugees, the foreigners) and gave the others the false impression that the operation had nothing to do with them. After the first deportation, however, the next phases followed, until all were exterminated.

The Jews' response to the defective scheme was a consequence of several factors. During the years preceding the extermination operation, the Nazis had done everything possible to drain Jews of their physical strength, numb their will, deprive them of their human dignity, destroy their ability to organize, and cut them off from the outside world. Indeed, systematic starvation and looming death had diminished the endurance of the ghettoized masses and their ability to gather their strength. By now the Jews concerned themselves with immediate matters only—rescue of family members,

1

2

3

4

5

6

7

1-2 Deportation of the Jews of Bielfield to Riga, Germany, December 1941

3-5 Deportation of the Jews of Stropkov to Zilina, Slovakia, May 1942

6 *Aktion* in the Vilna ghetto

7 Jews in the Warsaw ghetto Umschlagplatz, 1943

obtaining some bread, and sustaining the body, which yearned for warmth and nutrition. The Holocaust splintered into innumerable personal disasters and a state of helplessness. The murder machine struck towns and cities without forewarning. The *Aktionen*, which lasted several days or weeks, dealt the Jews a shock that thwarted any possibility of organizing large-scale self-defense of any kind. The rumors about the death camps were usually greeted with disbelief, as ordinary logic and the human mind refused to grasp the very possibility of what was rumored. Thus, Nazi Germany managed to mislead the masses until, literally, the last moment.

Let Us Not Go Like Sheep to the Slaughter!

Information about the mass murder of Jews in Ponary and an encounter with an injured girl who had escaped the bloodbath prompted Abba Kovner, a leader of the the *Hashomer Hatzair* youth movement and the Vilna ghetto resistance, to realize that the plot being perpetrated against the Jews was systematic murder. At a rally of Zionist pioneering youth in the Vilna ghetto, Kovner read out a broadsheet that he had written: "Hitler is scheming to annihilate all of European Jewry... Let us not go like sheep to the slaughter!" In the summer of 1943, as the ghetto was being liquidated, Kovner led a group of resistance members to the Rudniki forests. There, as commander of the "Avenger" Jewish Partisan Unit, he continued to fight the Germans.

Itzik Wittenberg, first commander of the FPO in the Vilna ghetto

Jewish youth, do not be led astray. Of the 80,000 Jews in the "Jerusalem of Lithuania" [Vilna], only 20,000 remain. Before our eyes they tore from us our parents, our brothers and sisters. Where are the hundreds of men who were taken away for labor by the Lithuanian "snatchers"? Where are the naked women and children who were taken from us in the night of terror of the "provocation"?

Where are the Jews [who were taken away on] the Day of Atonement?

Where are our brothers from the second ghetto?

None of those who were taken away from the ghetto has ever come back.

All the roads of the Gestapo lead to Ponary.

And Ponary is Death!

You who hesitate! Cast aside all illusions. Your children, your husbands, and your wives are no longer alive.

Ponary is not a camp—they were all shot there.

Hitler is scheming to annihilate all of European Jewry. The Jews of Lithuania were tasked to be the first in line.

Let us not go like sheep to the slaughter!

It is true that we are weak and defenseless, but resistance is the only response to the enemy!...

Resist! To the last breath.

Abba Kovner, Vilna ghetto, January 1, 1942

Abba Kovner

From the beginning of the war, youth organizations sent out liaisons (mostly young girls) to maintain contact with other Jewish population centers. This is how information about the Germans' murderous *Aktionen* became known. The ghettos buzzed with rumors about the murder of Jews. Most inhabitants, however, found the vague information difficult to absorb, especially in view of the unprecedented nature of the events described. However, resistance groups obtained reliable information about the murders by means of couriers and liaisons outside the ghettos. As the information accumulated, they finally realized that a terrifying campaign of systematic murder, unknown in human history, was being perpetrated. However, even after the members of the resistance became aware that this was so, only after deportation *Aktionen* from the ghettos did they organize to fight back. The war of self-defense was carried out on three levels: armed uprisings in ghettos and camps; escape and smuggling of Jews from towns and ghettos to the forests for partisan warfare; and hiding by individuals in various secret places, rescue actions, and rescue of children.

Couriers in the Service of the Resistance

"These heroic girls… who travel back and forth to cities and towns in Poland, equipped with Aryan papers as Poles or Ukrainians….Every day they face great dangers. They rely on their Aryan facial features and the kerchiefs around their heads. They assume the most difficult missions and fulfill them… without a trace of hesitation. When it is necessary to travel and to smuggle… underground publications, documents, money … When comrades from Vilna, Lublin or other cities need to be rescued—they accept their missions….They were the first to bring the news of the tragedy of Vilna….How many times have they faced death?"

From the diary of Emanuel Ringelblum, May 19, 1942

1

2

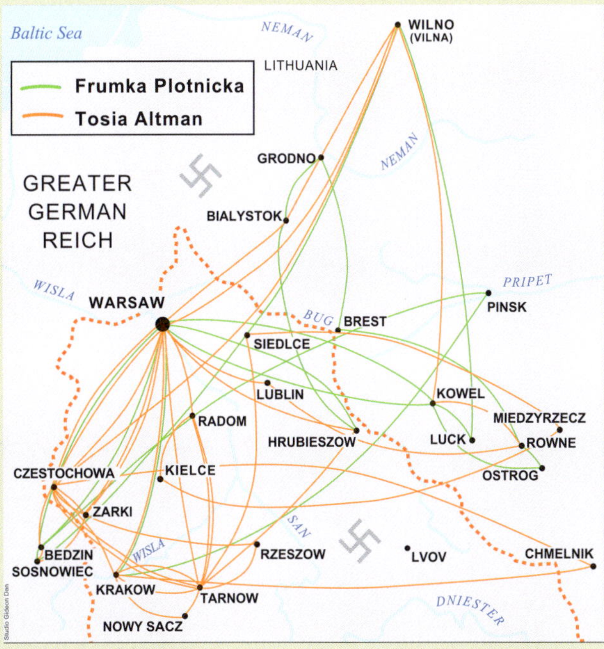

1 Three women couriers from the Dror movement. Bialystok, early 1942. Right: Lonka Kozibrodska, Bella Chazan, Tema Schneiderman

2 Route taken by two women couriers

The Warsaw Ghetto Uprising

The preeminent feat in the underground struggle was the Warsaw Ghetto Uprising, organized in April 1943 under the leadership of Mordechai Anielewicz, commander of the Jewish Fighting Organization (SFO; ZOB—Zydowska Organizacja Bojowa). The Jewish Military Union (ZZW—Zydowski Zwiazek Wojskowy) under Pawel Frenkiel, staffed from the ranks of the Betar movement, also took part in the fighting. On January 18, 1943, the Germans launched an *Aktion*. The underground leadership, believing it to be the onset of the final deportation, ordered its forces to respond by force of arms. The resistance stopped the *Aktion*, and the incident marked a turning point for most of the ghetto population, which from then on prepared for mass resistance.

"Today I am still alive! Tomorrow I don't know.... As I write this, there are no more Jews in Warsaw. I would still like to see my beloved wife and my two children.... I doubt that I'll ever see them. I am going through difficult days. I would still like to live.... I feel that the end is approaching."

From the last testament of
Sewek Kalnierzyk

The final *Aktion* began on April 19, 1943, the eve of Passover 5703. The fighting groups and ghetto inhabitants barricaded themselves in bunkers and hideouts, their demonstrations of resistance taking the Germans by surprise. The ZOB scattered its positions throughout the ghetto; the ZZW did most of its fighting at Muranowska Square, impeding the Germans' attempts to break in. In response, the Germans began systematically to burn down the buildings, turning the ghetto into a firetrap. The Jews fought valiantly for a month until the Germans took over the focal points of resistance. It was the first popular uprising in a city in Nazi-occupied Europe.

"It is impossible to put into words what we have been through. What happened exceeded our boldest dreams. The Germans fled twice from the ghetto.... "My life's dream has come true. Self-defense in the ghetto has become a fact. Armed Jewish resistance and revenge are actually happening. I have witnessed the glorious and heroic combat of the Jewish fighters."

Mordechai Anielewicz,
Warsaw ghetto, April 23, 1943

Mordechai Anielewicz

German documentation of the repression of the Warsaw Ghetto Uprising. Jürgen Stroop prepared an album titled, "The Jewish Residential Quarter in Warsaw Is No More"

Synagogue on Tlomackie Street, Warsaw. The destruction of the synagogue symbolized the Nazi victory over the Jews

Resistance in the Ghettos

The Warsaw Ghetto Uprising, which was a popular revolt, became an example for Jews in other ghettos and camps. The uprisings that followed, however, were smaller in scope because of their isolation, a shortage of arms,and hostile surroundings.

In Krakow, underground organizations became active from the establishment of the ghetto. The most conspicuous were affiliated with the Akiva and *Hashomer Hatzair* youth movements. In October 1942, the Jewish Fighting Organization was created, and a decision was made to carry the fighting to the "Aryan" side of town. Hela Schuepper, a member of the JFO, was sent to Warsaw to obtain arms. She returned with handguns and explosives procured from the Communist resistance. The JFO carried out a series of operations, the most famous of which was the attack on the Cyganeria Café. The Poles could not believe that a group of Jews had dared to execute this act; according to rumors, the feat had been perpetrated by Soviet parachutists.

Dolek Liebskind

"At the last Oneg Shabbat, Dolek Liebskind said,'This is the last time we'll meet together.We are doomed to death, but we have to record three lines in Jewish history: that Jewish youth stood up and fought for national dignity.'"

Yehuda Poldek-Maimon

"Before Dolek's hideout was discovered, the hideout of comrades who had taken part in an operation and returned from it was discovered. Then, even after all of them were caught, they came to Dolek's hideout, too. It was the hideout of the command center; weapons, money, and uniforms that we used were kept there. When it was attacked, two of our comrades, Dolek and Yehuda Tannenbaum, were there. They were attacked and they defended themselves. They exchanged gunfire and shot

Inseparable Lovers

Shimshon and Gusta (Justina) Dranger vowed that if either were arrested the other would commit suicide. Shimshon, a leading personality in the Akiva youth movement and the Hehalutz Halohem (Fighting Pioneer) resistance in the Krakow ghetto, was arrested in January 1943. Several days later, Gusta turned herself in to the Gestapo. In prison, she recorded the exploits of the Krakow resistance in a diary that she kept on pieces of toilet paper. On April 29, 1943, the Drangers escaped to the forests and enlisted for warfare. On November 8, Shimshon was captured and Gusta turned herself in again. Both were murdered.

Underground organization and locations of ghetto uprisings

Germans, too. Only then did both of them commit suicide. They killed themselves with the last rounds in their handguns. But the resistance did not stop.

"On Christmas Eve, groups of ours approached a German café called Cyganeria, a café of Nazi officers, and threw a bomb that blew up. Dozens of Germans were killed or wounded."

Rivka Schpiner Libeskind

"We didn't go out to win a victory by force of arms; victory wasn't ours to win. We went out to defend the spirit. The enemy did not kill our spirit. Death is neither defeat nor disgrace. And the violent force that defeats a handful of rebels is not a force that triumphed."

The He-chalutz Halochem manifesto, August 1943

An uprising broke out in the Bialystok ghetto in August 1943. On August 15, the Germans entered the ghetto and began the liquidation *Aktion*. The underground urged the inhabitants of the ghetto to resist; but they did not respond. The uprising was brief; all members of the resistance were killed.

"We knew no one would survive but Mordechai realized that he couldn't deprive people of all hope. Therefore, he said back then, at the rally, that anyone who remains alive after the uprising has to make every effort to reach the forest and fight there."

Bronka Klibanski

Massive *Aktionen* took place in Vilna in September 1943; those captured were taken to Ponary and murdered. In one of these *Aktionen*, the deportation *Aktion* to Estonia (September 1 and September 4, 1943), the underground United Partisan Organization (FPO—Fareynegte Partizaner Organizatsye), believing that the final liquidation was at hand, urged the ghetto inhabitants not to report for deportation but instead to

Josef Glazman

Josef Glazman had been a member of the *Betar* movement from early youth. In November 1941, he was deputy commander of the Jewish police in the Vilna ghetto and a founding member of the United Partisan Organization (FPO). He was named deputy commander of the FPO engaging also in educational activity. Due to his activity in the underground, Glazman did not hesitate to clash with Jacob Gens, the commander of the ghetto police and the de facto head of the ghetto. On July 24, 1943, Glazman and a group of comrades left the ghetto to join the partisans. He established a partisan unit in the Narocz forest and was killed in a clash with a German force.

begin an uprising. During the last deportation from Vilna, the members of the resistance headed to the forests to continue fighting.

Uprisings were attempted in additional ghettos, such as Lvov. Surviving fighters from Bialystok and Vilna managed to reach the forests and establish partisan units that continued to fight the Germans.

The uprisings broke out belatedly and were very small in scale for a number of reasons: non-Jewish resistance organizations seldom helped the Jews to organize; their weapons were scanty; and the Nazis *Aktionen* usually took the Jews by surprise, making it impossible to organize and instigate a full-fledged uprising. The fighters knew they could neither survive nor defeat the bitter enemy by means of their warfare. They were aware, however, that their fighting would be important from the human and national perspectives, and was meant to express human solidarity and exalted values.

Mordechai Tenenbaum Tamaroff

Mordechai Tenenbaum was a leading figure in the *Dror* pioneering youth movement in Poland. A progenitor of the idea of fighting in the ghetto, he was sent by the Jewish Fighting Organization in Warsaw to the Bialystok ghetto to establish a resistance organization there. Aware that the Jews' fate had been sealed, Tenenbaum acted doggedly to organize an uprising and struggle against the Germans. He documented the resistance activity in his personal diary and in an underground archive that he established. Tenenbaum was killed in an attempted uprising by the resistance during the ghetto liquidation *Aktion* in August 1943.

Deportations from Western and Central Europe Continue

By September 1939, when World War II began, only about half of the 500,000 Jews who had lived in Germany remained there. Most of them were elderly. The closure of most Jewish organizations in Germany after the *Kristallnacht* pogrom dealt a fatal blow to the community's social and cultural infrastructure. Those Jews who remained were rendered almost penniless. Many had to leave their homes and concentrated in Jewish houses. In 1940, thousands of Jews were deported to Poland and France. By October 1941, Jews in Germany were obliged to wear a yellow star, and deportations to ghettos and extermination sites in the East began.

1

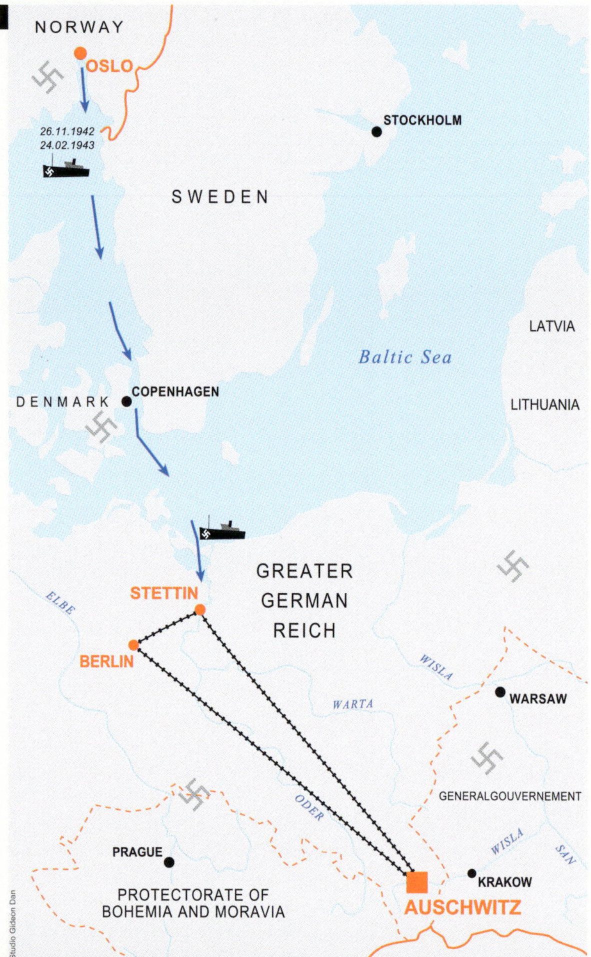

2

3

1 Deportation from Norway
2 Deportation of the Jews of Plzen to Terezin ghetto, January 16–26, 1942
3 Deportation of the Jews of Oslo, autumn 1942
4 Deportation of the Jews of Hanau to Majdanek and Sobibor. Germany, May, 1942
5 En route to the concentration point, ahead of deportation. Amsterdam, Netherlands, May 1943

1

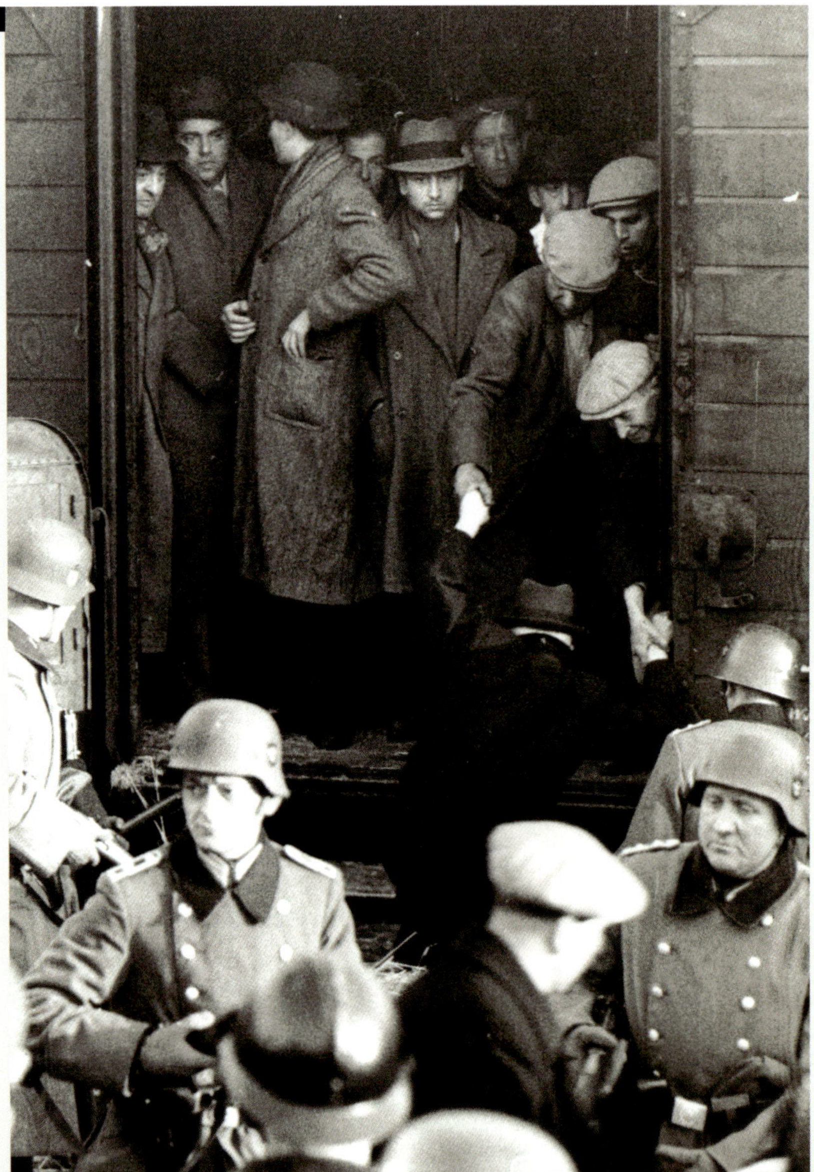

In Spring 1942, after the Wannsee Conference, the Nazis began to deport the Jews of Central and Western Europe to extermination camps. The deportations operation was run by the Jewish Affairs Department of the SS, commanded by Adolf Eichmann. The procedure was similar in most locations, geared to misleading the victims. Under German command, the deportations were carried out by the local police, such as the Dutch, French, and Belgian forces. The transports to the extermination camps embarked from transit camps like Westerbork, Drancy and Mechelen.

The deportation of the remaining Jews in Germany, Austria, and the Protectorate resumed in 1941. The deportation began in September with

2

1 Deportation of the Jews of Marseilles to Compiegne and thence to Drancy, January 1943
2 **Jacob Barosin** (1906–2001), Transport from Gurs to Germany, 1943, pencil on paper
3 Deportation of Jews from Westerbork to Auschwitz-Birkenau
4 Local police in Hollerich, Luxembourg, deport citizens. September 19, 1942
5 Members of the Ustasi militia supervise the deportation of Croatian Jews to concentration camps around the country, June-August 1941

a transport to the Lodz ghetto and was followed by transports to the Soviet territories and Terezin.

As they set out to implement their anti-Jewish policy in Western Europe, the Germans acted cautiously, resorting to deceptions and ruses. It was not easy to uncover Jews in this part of the continent; most were indistinguishable from the rest of the population in their appearance and way of life. In some Western countries, civilians treated the Nazi policy as that of an invading occupier and, in some cases, overtly identified with the persecuted Jews. The Germans deported Jews via transit camps and usually entrusted implementation to the local bureaucracy and police. In Belgium, the concentration of Jews began in July 1942 at the Malines

3

4

5

(Mechelen) transit camp. "Asocial elements" and foreign nationals were rounded up first; they were deported to Auschwitz in August. The concentration for deportation of Jews who held Belgian citizenship was suspended for a year due to the intervention of Queen Mother Elizabeth and Cardinal Van Roey. In September 1943, however, deportations to Auschwitz included Belgian-born Jews as well. The deportations continued even after the Allied landing in Normandy; one of those in the last transport was the German-born painter Felix Nussbaum.

In Italy, the dictator, Benito Mussolini, prevented the deportation of Jews despite Hitler's demands. Jews in parts of Albania, Croatia, Greece, and southern France were relatively safe due to Italian control of these locations.

Collaborative regimes (such as Croatia and Slovakia) were headed by leaders who were pleased to cooperate with Germany to solve their "Jewish Question." Slovakia, a Nazi satellite state, expressed no opposition to the program of deportations to the east. Slovakian Jews were the first to reach Majdanek and Auschwitz despite courageous attempts by Jewish leaders to save them. During 1942, 58,000 Slovakian Jews were sent to the extermination camps. The deportations were halted late that year but resumed at the end of the Slovakian uprising (August 1944). Most Jews in Serbia were murdered within the borders of the country.

1

2

3

4

1 Transit camp in Mechelen, Belgium
2 Slovakian Jews being loaded aboard deportation trains
3 **Osias Hofstatter** (1905–1994), Deportation from Brussels, 1953, gouache, India ink, and pencil on paper
4 Jews captured attempting to cross into Switzerland are loaded aboard deportation trucks opposite the prison in Varese (near Milan), Italy

The Fate of the Jews of Thrace and Macedonia

On March 4, 1943, the Bulgarian authorities, which had annexed Thrace from Greece and Macedonia from Yugoslavia, arrested all the Jews in these districts and sent them to two detention camps. Shortly afterwards, the Thracian Jews were transported in cattle cars with a Bulgarian police escort to the port town of Lom on the Danube River and handed over to the Germans. The Jews were loaded onto four small boats and arrived in Vienna ten days later. From there, they were sent to extermination at the Treblinka camp. The Jews of Macedonia were deported to Treblinka by land. In all, 11,370 Jews were deported.

1

The Accordion

After Macedonia was occupied, Shabtai Shemi handed over the accordion he had received from his parents for his bar mitzvah to a Muslim friend and fled with his sister, Gita, to relatives in Greece. He and Gita were deported from Greece to Birkenau along with the rest of the Jews there. From Birkenau, they reached Bergen-Belsen in the death marches. Shabtai died two days after being liberated. Gita survived, returned to Macedonia, and reclaimed the accordion.

1 Deportation of the Jews of Salonika to Auschwitz
2 Abuse of Jews in Salonika during "The Black Saturday," July 1942

2

The Jews in Croatia were murdered or deported to the East with the active assistance of some local inhabitants. Only in the Italian-controlled part of Croatia, as noted, did Italian officials thwart the turnover of Jews to the Nazis. Greece was divided into three occupation zones: a Bulgarian occupation zone–western Thrace, eastern Macedonia, and the Aegean islands of Thesos and Samothraki; a German occupation zone–a strip of eastern Thrace, central and eastern Macedonia, including Salonika, and the island of Crete; an Italian occupation zone–central Greece, including Athens, the Peloponnisos, part of the western coast, and the Ionian islands, including Corfu.

The Jews of Greece were deported in several phases. The expulsion from Thrace and Macedonia in March 1943 was followed in March–May by deportations from Salonika and the vicinity, which were under German occupation. The Jews of Salonika were demeaned, marked, dispossessed, and—ahead of the deportation—briefly ghettoized. In March–April 1943 and in the summer of 1944, Jews living in the areas that Germany seized after the surrender of Italy were deported. Nearly 60,000 Greek Jews perished, most in Auschwitz-Birkenau.

Deportation of Jews from Dhidhimotikhon, Greece

The Liquidation of Hungarian Jewry

The Hungarian Jewish community, the last in continental Europe, lived in relative safety until the Germans occupied the country (March 19 1944)—notwithstanding antisemitic legislation and the mobilization of 100,000 Jewish men for military labor brigades, in which most of them died. The Fascist elements in Hungary enjoyed broad popular support and the Horthy Government concluded an alliance with Nazi Germany. When Hungary joined the war against the Allies, nearly 20,000 Jews from Kamenets-Podolski who held Polish or Soviet citizenship were turned over to the Germans and deported to their deaths. The extermination phase in Hungary began later, after the Nazi invasion. Adolf Eichmann and his staff went into action and transports to Auschwitz began in a now routine manner. In just eight weeks, some 437,000 Jews—most from peripheral towns—were sent to Auschwitz-Birkenau in railroad cars. After October 1944, when the Arrow Cross party came to power, thousands of Jews from Budapest were murdered on the banks of the Danube and tens of thousands were marched hundreds of miles towards the Austrian border. In all, some 565,000 Hungarian Jews were murdered.

1 Broadsheet demanding a "Jew-free Hungary"
2 German soldiers at the royal palace in Budapest on the day of the invasion of Hungary, March 19, 1944
3 Hungarian Jews perform forced labor on the eastern front, Ukraine, winter 1942–1943

1

2

3

1

2

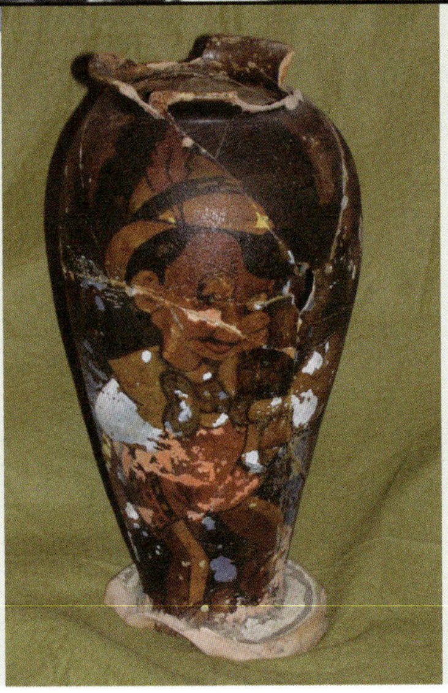

3

1 Jewish family in the Budapest ghetto, 1944
2 Container of personal effects, buried in the soil in Novi Sad
3 Deportation of Hungarian Jews, 1944
4 Transport of Jews from Koszeg to extermination in Auschwitz-Birkenau, 1944
5 Deportation from Budapest
6 Deportation of the Jews of Nagy Bereszna, Hungary

4

5

6

Despoiling the Jews

Despoiling the Jews was an integral part of Nazi policy. Property and possessions of European Jewry that had been part of their economic and cultural life for hundreds of years were systematically plundered. With their rise to power, the Nazis banished Jews from economic life with rising momentum and, in 1938, established the dispossession of the Jews in law. When the war began, the Nazis applied these policies of dispossession and theft to the occupied territories. They confiscated all types of property—homes, real estate, factories, businesses, and artistic and cultural treasures. In Eastern Europe, the plundering continued in the ghettos. When the Jews were sent to death camps, the local population took control of their homes and property. Trains carrying victims' valuables regularly left the death camps for Germany.

The Auschwitz-Birkenau Concentration and Extermination Camp

Samuel Bak (b. 1933), Thou Shalt Not Kill, 1978, oil on canvas

Time there is not like it is here on earth.... The inhabitants of this [other] planet had no names, they had no parents nor did they have children.... They breathed according to different laws of nature, they did not live—nor did they die—according to the laws of this world. Their name was the number

K. Tzetnik (Yechiel De-Nur)

1 Selection on the "ramp" in Birkenau
2 **Zinovii Tolkatchev** (1903–1977), Birkenau Landscape, 1945, pencil on paper
3 Canisters that contained Zyklon B, Majdanek
4 Selection on the "ramp" in Birkenau

4

Auschwitz-Birkenau, the largest of the concentration and extermination camps established on Polish soil, served concurrently as a labor camp and as a center for the rapid extermination of Jews. Chosen as the central location for the annihilation of the "undesirables," it was equipped with several extermination facilities and crematoria. Extermination was carried out by means of Zyklon B gas, a substance that had previously been tested on Russian prisoners. In October 1941, another camp, Birkenau (Auschwitz II), was established three kilometers from Auschwitz. Exterminations in the four gas chambers of the new camp began in March 1942. By November 1942, the camp had become a mass killing factory, receiving transports from all over Europe. Most of those brought to the camp were Jews. Nearly all were sent at once to the gas chambers; only a small proportion were selected for labor in the camp itself, labor in munitions plants at satellite camps, or the "medical" experiments of Dr. Josef Mengele and his staff. In the Spring and Summer 1944, the rate of extermination was increased as the Jews of Hungary and the Lodz ghetto were brought to the camp.

The process of selection and killing was carefully planned and organized. When a train stopped at the platform, veteran prisoners received the victims and gathered their belongings in several barracks in an area known as "Kanada." The arrivals were lined up in two columns— men and boys in one, women and girls in the other—and SS physicians performed a selection. The criterion was the appearance of the prisoners, whose fate, for labor or for death, was determined at will. Most were sent immediately to the gas chambers. Before they entered, they were told that they were about to be disinfected and ordered to undress. Rushed and pressed together in fear amidst the chaos, Jews were gassed in locked rooms, murdered in a span of a few minutes. After the victims were dead, their gold teeth were extracted and women's hair was shorn. The bodies were hauled to the crematorium furnaces for incineration. Bones were pulverized and ashes were scattered in the fields. Repeat selections took place several times during the day in roll calls. Inmates who had become weak or ill were separated from the ranks and sent to the gas chambers. A brutal regimen based on a set of punishments and torture was invoked in the camp. Few managed to survive. In Auschwitz-Birkenau, more than 1.1 million Jews, 70,000 Poles, 25,000 Sinti and some 15,000 prisoners of war from the USSR and other countries were murdered.

"... My sister tells me,'I see they're separating people at the front of the column. First they separate men from women and then they split them up more."Let's stay together,' she says.'You take little Harry.' She puts a kerchief on my head and begins to pound me so I'll be red and not pale and not so scared.'You walk with your boy and my daughter, and we'll walk together so they won't separate us.'Then we reached Mengele; at that time we didn't know it was Mengele...

"The four of us managed to get past Mengele. I was happy that he didn't separate us but then I suddenly felt a hand on my shoulder, turning me around. It was Mengele. He was really handsome, like a movie actor, I can't tell you how beautiful this human being was, how well groomed he was, how he looked, how handsome his facial features were.... My sister said to me in Hungarian, quietly,'Tell them you're nineteen years old.' He looks at me and hypnotizes me the way they hypnotize a snake. I simply can't get a word out of my mouth. I don't say a thing, and then he says, 'What are you doing

1

2

1 Unloading belongings of prisoners taken to Auschwitz-Birkenau, "Kanada" barracks
2 Selection on the "ramp" in Birkenau

here?' and gives me a kick, and I flew to the right. I was separated from the little boy, I dropped his hand and he stayed in that big crowd, Harry, and he screamed, 'Miri, Mommy, Rita, where are you? What happened? Where are you?' He stayed all by himself in that big crowd, and all I can hope is that they died together in the crematorium."

Rita Weiss

This transport was one of many that reached the Auschwitz-Birkenau station. Its arrival was unique, however, because SS photographers documented it in many detailed pictures. Unlike the millions who were murdered in the death camps, a large portion of those appearing in this album have been identified and have recovered their names and visages. Thus, the album had become a human and historical document of exceptional interest and importance.

The original album was found after the war by Lili Jacob, who had been in the transport.

"Thus in an instant, our women, our parents, our children disappeared. We saw them for a short while, as an obscure mass at the other end of the platform. Then we saw nothing more."

Primo Levi

In addition to their tremendous efforts to live in such appalling conditions, some death-camp prisoners displayed astonishing heroism by launching uprisings. In August 1943, the uprising in Treblinka broke out. Groups of prisoners who had been put to work burning bodies and sorting the many victims' belongings killed some of their commanders and guards, took over the armory, and set the gas chambers and the camp barracks ablaze. The uprising brought the murders in Treblinka to an end. In Sobibor, prisoners rose up and several managed to escape. In Auschwitz-Birkenau, a group of prisoners blew up one of the murder facilities.

1

2

The Ovitz Family

Shimshon Eizik Ovitz and his wife, of Marmarossziget, Transylvania, had ten children, seven of whom were dwarfs. Before the war, they studied music, established a band called Lilliput, and performed in Eastern Europe. In 1944, they were deported to Auschwitz and became the objects of medical experiments at the hands of Dr. Josef Mengele. After liberation, they returned to their hometown, found the tiny musical instruments that they had concealed before the deportation, and established a new band.

3

1. **Yehuda Bacon** (b. 1929), In Memory of the Czech Transport to the Gas Chambers, 1945, pencil on paper
2. Crematorium IV in Birkenau, blown up and set afire by members of the Sonderkommando on October 7, 1944
3. Door for removal of ashes. Corpse incineration facility at a crematorium in Birkenau
4. Corpse incineration furnaces at Crematorium III, Birkenau
5. Chassis of vehicle on which the bodies of those murdered were loaded
6. Experiments on women prisoners, Ravensbrück camp, Germany
7. Suitcase carried by Chana Fanta of Louny, Czechoslovakia. She was deported to Terezin and thence to Birkenau

4

6

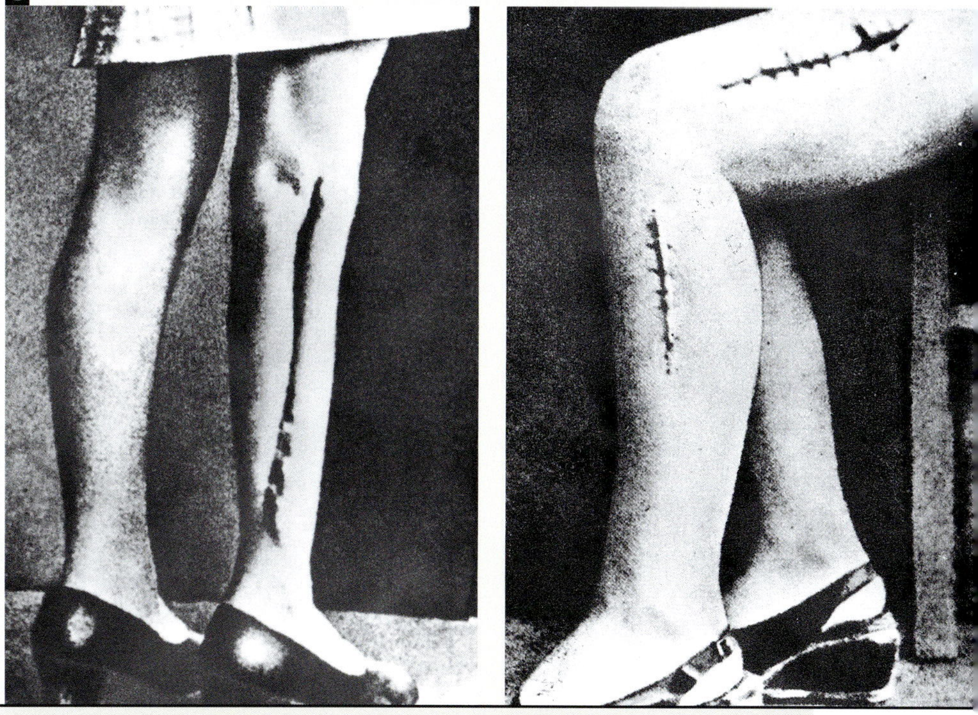

5

7

Murder and incineration of bodies in Birkenau. The photos, taken surreptitiously by a member of the Sonderkommando, were smuggled out by the camp resistance

Roza Robota

A member of the Hashomer Haza'ir youth movement, Roza Robota was deported to Auschwitz-Birkenau where she was inducted into the resistance. She undertook a hazardous mission—to obtain gunpowder from Jewish girls who worked at the Union munitions plant. Although heavily guarded, she and others managed to smuggle small quantities of explosives to members of the Sonderkommando, who placed them in hiding and eventually used them to blow up a crematorium. Roza and three of her comrades—Regina Safirsztain (Sapirstein), Ella Gartner (Gertner), and Estucia Wajcblum (Esther Weisblum)—were captured and tortured but did not betray the members of the resistance. On January 6, 1945, they were executed. Before being hanged, Roza called out, "Hazak Ve'ematz (Be strong and have courage)!"

The Sonderkommando Uprising

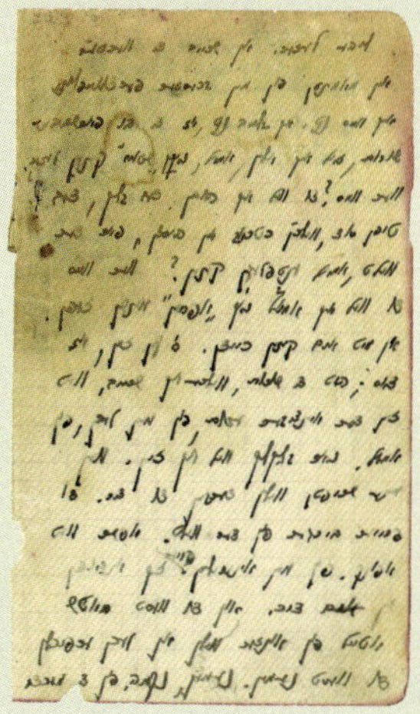

"The dark night is my friend, crying and screaming my song, the fire of victims my light, the atmosphere of death my scent. Hell is my home." Zalman Gradowski, a member of the Auschwitz Sonderkommando, wrote these words in notes that he buried near the crematoria.

The Jewish prisoners selected to work in the extermination facilities were known as the Sonderkommando (special detail). Their work included removing bodies from gas chambers and hauling them off for cremation—one of the most horrific tasks assigned to prisoners not immediately exterminated. It was this group of inmates who perpetrated the only uprising in the history of Auschwitz. Over a lengthy period of time, the rebels hoarded explosives brought to them by Jewish women prisoners working at the Union munitions plant. On October 7, 1944, the men of the Sonderkommando at Crematorium IV blew up the facility. Several cut through the barbed-wire fence and escaped but were shot as they fled. In retaliation for their act, the SS killed about 450 prisoners. None of the rebels survived but the crematorium they destroyed was abandoned.

The World's Silence

As our children wailed in the shadow of the gallows
The world's passion we did not hear
For You chose us from all nations
You loved us and held us dear.

...And as our children march to the gallows
Children Jewish, children wise,
They know their blood is not valued
They call only to mother: avert your eyes.

While the ovens were fed by day and by night,
The most Holy Father who dwells in Rome
Did not leave his palace, with crucifix high
To witness one day of pogrom.

Just to stand there, one day: "I am here, I'm with you"—
Where the child-lamb is standing, each day anew:
The anonymous Child of a Jew.

Nathan Alterman, From All Peoples, 1942

The Protest

In April 1943, British and American representatives met in Bermuda to discuss the fate of refugees in the Nazi-occupied countries. The resolutions taken were disappointing. Samuel Zygelbojm, a leader of Polish Jewry then living as a refugee in London, committed suicide in protest against the world's indifference and apathy. "May my death," he wrote, "be a cry of protest against the indifference of the world, which is watching the extermination of the Jews without lifting a finger to prevent it."

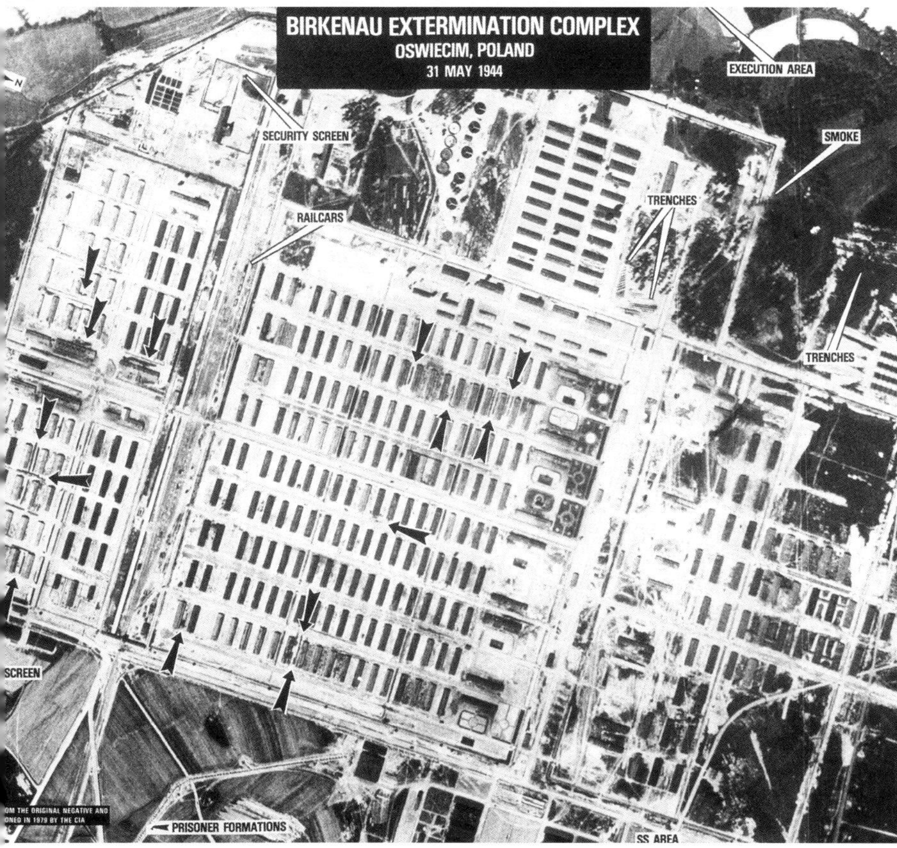

What Did the Free World Know?

In May 1942, the BBC in London broadcast information about the killing of Polish Jews. It did so again on June 26. The information that reached the Free World was accurate and readily available. The only thing needed was to identify with the victims, call for immediate assistance, and pressure the benighted regimes that had been acting with impunity. In Summer 1942 US President Roosevelt and British Prime Minister Churchill gave the Germans a public warning about the responsibility that would be laid at their feet for the murder of Jews in Europe. However, the political concept that became dominant among the politicians and generals was that winning the war came first; this would,

Aerial photos taken from American aircraft during operational sorties in the vicinity of Auschwitz by proxy, also stop the murder of European Jews.

Those who begged the Allies to bomb the extermination facilities at Auschwitz-Birkenau and the tracks leading to the camp were answered with similar rationales. The American and British rebuffed such requests by arguing that bombing the gas chambers would entail the diversion of massive resources (essential air cover for forces that were busy with crucial operations) and that an effective bombardment might have the opposite effect of that desired, i.e., Germany might treat the Jews even worse. In June 1944, American aircraft produced a set of aerial photographs over Auschwitz, in which the death facilities were clearly visible. In an air raid that actually took place on August 20, however, the bombs landed on a factory near the gas chambers, leaving the chambers intact.

The war cut off almost all relations with communities in the German- occupied territories. Jewish centers were especially affected. International Jewish organizations found it difficult to maintain any kind of contact with them, to provide them with material relief and, afterwards, to assist in rescue. Two liaison bureaus of the *Yishuv* (the Jewish community in Palestine), located in Constantinople and Geneva, maintained sporadic contact with Jewish centers in the occupied areas by means of truncated letters and veiled messages insinuated into ordinary "chatter." The resources available to them were totally inadequate for the daunting task. Furthermore, the free countries fighting Nazi Germany frowned on the establishment of any relations, private or public, with enemy countries. From their standpoint, sending money or goods to the occupied areas was indirect assistance to the enemy.

As time passed, contact between the Jews in the occupied areas and the free communities became even more tenuous. When the total extermination phase began and horrific reports about mass murder filtered to the Free World, the Jews in the free countries and in Palestine were not prepared to conduct a large-scale rescue action. Apart from a small number of parachutists from Palestine, Jews from the outside world did not enter the occupied areas and those in Europe received no guidance or efficient assistance.

The Silence of the Vatican

Reports about the murder of Jews reached the Vatican by late 1941. In March 1942, the Pope was asked to intervene in order to thwart the deportation of Slovakian Jews to Auschwitz. He took no action. The Allies, whose considerations were military and political, begged Pope Pius XII to make a statement condemning Nazi Germany's actions. The Vatican limited itself to a general, laconic statement that decried the "horrors of the war."

Bishop Eugenio Pacelli, July 20, 1933

The *Struma* Affair

The rickety ship *Struma* set sail in December 1941 from the port of Constantá, Romania, with 769 fugitive Jews aboard. Their destination was Constantinople, where they hoped to obtain entry visas for Palestine. When they docked, however, they did not receive their visas and were forced to spend ten weeks waiting aboard the ship. The British turned a deaf ear to requests to allow them to enter Palestine under the existing immigration quotas; the Turkish authorities refused to give them temporary accommodations in a camp on shore. On February 23, 1942, the ship, carrying no water, food, or fuel, was tugged into the open sea. Several hours later, it was sunk inadvertently by a torpedo from a Soviet submarine. Only one passenger survived.

Before they boarded *Struma*, Benedict and Sarah Zeitz mailed a parcel to relatives in Palestine containing belongings, photos, and a diary written by their sixteen-year-old daughter, Riva. On November 29, 1941, Riva wrote, "Is anyone listening? Some listen and are unaffected, some are unwilling or unable to listen, and some can't do a thing. All that remains is to pray...." The Zeitzes perished in the sinking of the *Struma*.

Twelve of the 19 people in the photo perished in the sinking of the *Struma*

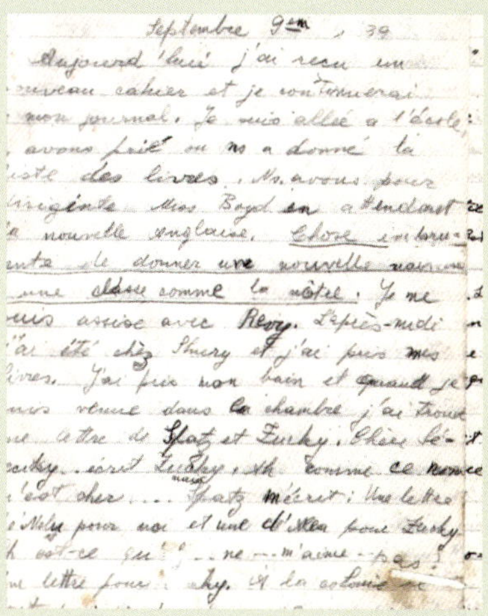

Septembre 9th, 39
Aujourd'hui j'ai reçu un
nouveau cahier et je continuerai
mon journal. Je suis allée à l'école
avons fait [illegible] a donné la
liste des livres. Nous avons pour
[illegible] Miss Boyd en attendant
la nouvelle anglaise. [illegible]
[illegible] de donner une nouvelle [illegible]
une classe comme [illegible]. Je me
suis assise avec [illegible]. L'après-midi
j'ai été chez [illegible] et j'ai pris mes
livres. J'ai pris mon bain et quand je
suis venue dans la chambre j'ai trouvé
une lettre de [illegible] et [illegible]
[illegible]
[illegible]
[illegible]
[illegible]
[illegible]

Combat and Rescue

Marko Behar (1914-1973), Partisans in winter, 1948, monotype.

Jews in Partisan and Resistance Organizations

"When we left the ghetto, suddenly there was freedom. We were young men and women, and to fight the Germans was the ideal. Yes, they were killed, they were killed, but as long as you lived, you breathed freedom."

Josef Chermetz

Despite the conditions and circumstances in which they attempted to live, Jews under Nazi occupation showed many manifestations of steadfastness, resistance and warfare. During the occupation, there were many astounding instances of mutual assistance, struggle for life, self-sacrifice, and armed self-defense. In some ghettos, an organized underground

1

2

3

was active in all areas of life. The uprising that broke out in the Warsaw ghetto was, practically speaking, the first case of armed self-defense in all of occupied Europe. Uprisings also broke out in the death camps. Most Jewish youth organizations and political parties that had existed before the war remained active during the occupation. Pioneering youth organizations continued to train teenagers, keep their allegiance, and encourage them to feel a connection with Palestine. In several locations, Zionist training farms were established in the guise of productive activity. The underground press reported developments on the fronts, called for resistance to the Nazi enemy, and urged Jews at large to maintain cohesion and public responsibility.

"When you went on an operation and thought about who you were, you were not only you, you represented your family, your friends, all of them. Whenever you fired a machine gun or a submachine gun, you shot to kill. That's how we were. It took us years to get over it."

Josef Chermetz

The population of Jewish partisans burgeoned in 1942–1943. Jews became visible participants in the French partisan struggle and resistance movements. Rescue operations for children and border-running from France and the Netherlands were organized. Jews were active in the Belgian resistance and played a considerable role in the Slovakian uprising that broke out in Summer 1944. Most Jews who fled to the mountains of Yugoslavia joined Tito's partisan army and were active in the Italian partisan movement. Tens of thousands of Jews reached the forests of Belarus and the Ukraine; they helped to establish partisan companies and fought admirably in special Jewish

1 Jews escape to the forests from ghettos in the areas of Nowogrodek and Polesie
2 Arms factory of the Bodioni brigade, Pinsk
3 Partisans in Yugoslavia: Moshe Pijada with Marshal Tito
4 Jewish partisans in Slovakia
5 Partisan unit in Italy, including Jewish members

4

5

The Minsk Ghetto and the Partisan Movement

From its establishment in August 1941, the resistance in Minsk aimed to set up a center for flight to the forests and partisan warfare. Its members, headed by the Communist leader Hirsch Smolar, first created a secret network that amassed weapons in the ghetto and established regular contact with the partisans in the forest. In the middle of 1942, as the *Aktionen* became more frequent, the escape began. Some 10,000 Jews from the Minsk ghetto, aided by the Judenrat and liaisons who had already left the ghetto and joined partisan units, reached the nearby forests. Many perished on the way but a large number of those who survived became founding members of seven partisan units that fought against the Germans.

1

2

3

4

units or in mixed battalions. In Belarus and Ukraine, family camps were established in the heart of dense forests; the fugitive noncombatant Jews who lived there were fed and protected by Jewish fighters.

"All the partisans in our brigade were Jews. Commanders were Jews; soldiers were Jews. We were in contact with Moscow and they put us under a lot of pressure to become partisans, because partisans are like soldiers in the Red Army."

Vitka Kovner

Independent partisan units were active in the Rudninki and Naliboki forests near Minsk. Many Jewish partisan commanders became renowned for their successful raids in the forests. Jews were visibly numerous in partisan units in Poland, especially in companies established or adopted by the Communist People's Guard.

"It was a glorious act, because derailing a train isn't like cutting down five telegraph poles or setting a wooden bridge on fire. A train sometimes carried hundreds of tanks, dozens of tanks.... Before the train approaches, you detonate the mine... You hear the cars... hitting each other.... You feel total satisfaction."

Baruch Shub

1 Hangings of partisans in Minsk. The Jewish partisan Maria Borisova Bruskina belonged to a resistance group that was active in Minsk. October 1941
2 **Alexander Bogen** (b. 1916), Partisan, 1944, charcoal on paper
3 Jewish partisans, Yugoslavia
4 Group of partisans, Salonika, 1943
5 Partisans in the Pinsk region
6 Jewish partisans, Vilna: Vitka Kempner, Abba Kovner, Ruz'ka Korczak

5

6

The Zorin Family Camp

Born in Minsk, Shalom Zorin escaped to the forest and joined a partisan unit commanded by his Belarusian friend, Semyon Ganzenko. Together they established a Jewish partisan unit made up of escapees from the Minsk ghetto who had fled to the forests. Apart from fighting men, Zorin allowed individuals and families to join the camp. In late 1943, their unit, which was active in the Naliboki forest, comprised some 800 Jews including 150 children. Most survived.

Were it not for several limiting factors, the Jewish partisan movement might have been even larger. However, the Jews had no weapons, and the surrounding rural population was usually hostile. In addition, the forests swarmed with bands of ruffians who attacked any Jew they encountered. Many of the non-Jewish partisan commanders refused to accept Jews, and partisan organizations affiliated to antisemitic Polish factions murdered Jewish partisans.

The Jewish Partisan
From these ghetto prison walls
Into the free forests,
Instead of chains on my hands,
I carry a new rifle.
On our rounds, this friend of mine
Hugs my neck and shoulder,
My rifle and I from this day
Will be as one, united.

The partisan Shmerke Kaczerginski

The Bielski Brothers' Family Camp

In late 1941, after the Germans had massacred the Jews of the Nowogrodek district, Tuvia, Zusia, and Asael Bielski—who had lost their parents in the slaughter—decided to establish a partisan unit in the nearby Naliboki forest in order to avenge the murders and save Jews' lives. Over time, refugee Jews from ghettos and camps, including families, gathered around them. In the summer of 1943, Tuvia Bielski's family camp had a population of about 1,200. Apart from its role in fighting the Germans, the camp became the vehicle of its inhabitants' survival. Tuvia, Zusia, and most members of the camp survived; Asael fell as a Red Army officer in combat against the Germans.

Spontaneous Resistance

On July 8, 1941, the town of Lachwa, Poland (Jewish population 2,300) was occupied, and a ghetto was established there in April 1942. The Zionist youth movements in the ghetto established an underground under the leadership of Jacob Rochczyn of the Betar youth movement. The Lachwa underground, unlike counterparts elsewhere, cooperated with the Judenrat and the Jewish Order Service (the ghetto police). On September 2,1942, the Jews discovered that pits had been excavated nearby. At dusk, the ghetto was surrounded and the inhabitants realized their deaths were imminent. At a signal from the underground, the ghetto fence was stormed and the inhabitants began to fight with axes and their bare hands. Many rushed through the gate but were gunned down by the Germans. Of the 1,000 who fled, some 600 reached the marshes; the others were led to the pits and shot.

In the Soviet territories and Yugoslavia, a large partisan movement banded together in 1942–1943. Resistance groups also formed in Eastern Poland, several parts of Slovakia, Greece, and France. In Western Europe, few Jews joined resistance groups because the groups in this area formed only after most had been sent to extermination camps.

The partisan fighter Rachel Rodnicki, Rudniki, Lithuania

The Underground in Algeria

In late 1940, after the occupation of France, an anti-Nazi underground began to form in Algeria. Most of its members were young Jews. In summer 1942, an emissary from the French resistance joined them in order to prepare for Operation Torch, the Allied invasion of northern Africa. In the main, the resistance was to paralyze communications, cut off main roads, and interfere with electricity supplies. The Allied invasion, on November 7–8, 1942, was resisted by the armed forces of Vichy France. Until then, the underground, led by Jose Aboulker, held the positions that it had seized for twenty-four hours.

American soldiers land on the coast of Algeria

Jews Rescue Jews

During the Holocaust, the universally known Biblical decree, "Love your neighbor as yourself," was manifested in its most physical sense. Although each individual was forced to conduct a daily struggle for life amidst ubiquitous violence, many Jews put this adage to the test of reality and implemented it in a manner worthy of deep respect. They risked their lives to rescue other Jews, and they epitomized the commitment implicit in the expression, "I am my brother's keeper."

Oswald Rufeisen's Rescue Enterprise

Shmuel (Oswald) Rufeisen, trapped in the town of Mir, Poland, during the

war, was named personal secretary and interpreter for the local German police. Due to his possession of a forged "Aryan" ID card and his command of languages, his commander took him into his confidence and divulged sensitive and valuable information. When he discovered the Germans' plans for the Jews of Mir, Rufeisen contacted the resistance groups and warned them about the impending *Aktionen*. The information that he obtained enabled nearly 300 Jews to flee the ghetto. Although his true identity was eventually revealed, he managed to escape.

Partisans guard an airfield in the Naliboki forest. Several were escapees from the Mir ghetto. July 1944

Zofia's Doll

In a cellar in the Warsaw ghetto, Zofia Zajczyk (Yael Rosner) played with a doll, Zusia. The doll had been made and given to her by Zofia's mother, who was busy smuggling children out of the ghetto. During one operation, Zofia's mother was injured and sent a boy to the cellar where Zofia was hiding to rescue her. The boy put Zofia into a coal sack and hoisted her on his back. Only when they were outside the ghetto did the little girl remember that she had left the doll behind in the cellar. Sobbing, she insisted on going back. "A mother doesn't leave her little girl behind," she explained. They returned to the ghetto and exited again, this time with the doll.

The "Working Group"

Gisi Fleischmann, a Zionist activist, headed the clandestine "Working Group" in Slovakia, in conjunction with Rabbi Michael Dov Weissmandel, a Haredi (ultra- Orthodox) rabbi and other public figures of various Jewish persuasions— Zionist, Orthodox, and secular. Fleischmann initiated relief and rescue operations for Jews in other countries and tried to induce the Free World to bring pressure on Germany to stop the extermination. In a letter to her daughter, she wrote, "Klal Yisrael [the Jewish people] takes precedence over all personal suffering." In the summer of 1944, when the deportations from Slovakia resumed, Gisi Fleischmann turned down an offer to save herself. In October 1944, she was sent to Auschwitz and murdered. Another leader of the group, Armin-Abba Frieder, was a rabbi in the Nove Mesto community. Using his special relations with the Slovakian Minister of Education, Frieder managed to obtain information and kept track of the fate of those deported to Poland. He survived, but his family perished.

"... I was told that a Jew from Bratislava had freed himself from a deportation transport through the intervention of Wisliceny himself, with the mediation of some Volksdeutsche, by handing over

Rescue of Children

In the summer of 1943, Myla Racine assumed command of an underground group affiliated with the Hanoar Hazioni youth movement in St. Gervais, in the Italian occupation zone. Myla helped hundreds of families that had fled to the area, helping to smuggle children to Switzerland. The last convoy she led was made up of thirty children from Nice. Stopped by a German patrol on October 21, 1943, the group was taken to a prison in Annemasse. After refusing to divulge information during torture, Myla was deported to Ravensbrück and then to Mauthausen, where she was killed in an Allied air raid. Marianne Cohen was a member of a Jewish resistance group who was caught in May 1944 while smuggling children to Switzerland. She was brutally tortured but did not give away the names of her superiors. In July 1944 Marianne was executed by the Germans. The children were saved.

To stop the deportation train

Youra Georges Livchitz

On April 19, 1943, Youra Georges Livchitz, a young Jewish doctor, and two comrades in his Belgian resistance group, Jean Franklemon and Robert Maistriau, set out for an operation of their very own: to halt a deportation train and attempt to release the Jews trapped within it. It was the twentieth transport from the Mechelen transit camp to Auschwitz-Birkenau, with 1,631 Jews aboard. Youra stopped the train and threatened the engineer with his handgun. Maistriau opened the doors of one of the cars, and seventeen Jews escaped, even as the German guards fired. It was the only attack on a deportation train during the war. In 1944, the three underground members were arrested. Jean and Robert survived the camps; Youra was tried and executed in February 1944, in Breeendonk, Belgium.

objects that were worth money, but not a great deal. I said to myself, if he takes a bribe for one individual, who says he wouldn't take a bribe for many? ..."

Rabbi Michael Dov Weissmandel

During the war, a Relief and Rescue Committee operated in Hungary. The committee, chaired by Otto Komoly, strove to forewarn Jews about the genocide being perpetrated against European Jewry and maintained connections with the Working Group in Slovakia. Rudolf (Israel) Kasztner, a member of the committee, believed that military developments in 1944 and the German occupation of Hungary would make it possible to conclude a transaction known as "goods for blood." Although his connections with high-ranking Nazis evoked disapproval, Kasztner and his associates managed to arrange the departure of a train with 1,684 Jews aboard, saving them from deportation to Auschwitz.

In France, the OSE (Oeuvre de Secours aux Enfants) had been involved in children's welfare since 1933, running ten orphanages and providing Jewish and general education. After thousands of children were swept up in arrests and deportations, the OSE began to operate surreptitiously in the detention camps to rescue children. It concealed an estimated 600 youngsters, mainly by moving them to the southern zone, where it had set up medical centers. In the summer of 1941, the OSE obtained permission to remove children aged 5–16 from the camps and house them elsewhere. The organization quickly involved itself in underground activity in the south, too, helping to smuggle the children of nonresident Jews. By establishing relations with organizations of activists such as the Garel group, it helped create another network, also Jewish, that specialized in the rescue of Jews. The Jewish scouts movement (EIF), the Zionist youth movement (MJS), and the underground "Jewish Army" (Armée Juive), which took military action, also helped further the rescue operations.

Moussa Abadi, a Jew born in Damascus who had migrated to France and operated in Nice, established a network to rescue children and hide them in

Christian institutions. His organization handled or abetted the rescue of 527 children.

1

2

1 Passengers aboard the "Kasztner train" en route to Palestine. Switzerland, 1944

2 Toy duck used by French Underground member Yehudit Geller Marcus for transferring messages

The Righteous Among the Nations

... I had to do it for myself, in order to be free....
Nancy Van Stenhoven-Spender, The Netherlands

During the Holocaust, thousands of non-Jews risked their lives to rescue Jews from the Nazis' clutches. Undeterred by German threats and their hostile surroundings, they took Jewish children into their homes, concealed and provided for entire families, established underground passage for children to neutral countries and, in particular, enabled the beleaguered Jews to believe that the qualities of humanity and altruism could overcome the indoctrination of the Fascist regimes. Many were executed for these noble deeds.

"... I thank Divine Providence for having allowed me to perform the commandment in Leviticus, 'Love your neighbor as yourself,' an incomparably important commandment of the Chosen People."
Olga St.-Blankett Baumgarten, France

Leopold Socha of Poland worked in the municipal sewage department of Lvov. After befriending Yitzhak (Jerzy) Chiger, he promised to save him from *Aktionen*. Socha kept his word, concealing 21 Jews for thirteen months in the municipal sewers. He and a friend, Stefan Wrublewski, kept the fugitives fed, and his wife, Magdalena, washed their clothes. For Passover 1944, Socha brought them a supply of potatoes and, upon liberation, invited them to a meal in his home.

Jonas and Antonina Paulavicius of Lithuania concealed a three-year-old Jewish boy in their home; their daughter, Danuta, took care of him. Jonas also sheltered the boy's parents and eight other Jews, hoping they would become a nucleus around which the community might be revitalized. In addition, two Soviet soldiers were hidden in the Paulavicius's home as well. Their neighbors reviled the family for their rescue actions, and Jonas was murdered in May 1952.

George and Magdalini Mitslioutis of the Greek island of Skopelos saved 14 members of the Leon family of Salonika by removing them to a

Jonas and Antonina Paulavicius

Dr. Adelaide Hautval

Dr. Adelaide Hautval was a French doctor who was arrested in April 1942, while attempting to cross the demarcation line between the two sectors of France without authorization. In response to her protest to the Gestapo about the treatment of the Jews, Adelaide was sent to Auschwitz-Birkenau in January 1943. There she served as a physician for women prisoners, saving many of them from selection (for murder). When she was transferred to work in the barracks where "medical" experiments were performed, she refused to take part. She was eventually transferred to Ravensbrück, which she survived. She died in 1988.

mountain hideout after the Germans established an outpost on the island.

With the assistance of the resistance, Joop and Willy Westerveel of the Netherlands managed to hide thirty-nine young Jews. When the Gestapo arrested Willy in October 1943, Joop left his job and devoted himself full-time to rescue activity. In March 1944, he was caught attempting to smuggle two young women out of the country. He was tortured in prison and executed in August 1944. Willy was liberated in Ravensbrück.

"… I know that when I stand before God on Judgment Day, I will not be asked what they asked Cain: 'Where were you when your brother's blood cried out to God?'"

Imre Bathroy, Hungary

"… My mother always taught me that God created all of us in one image…. Everyone has the right to live."

Marie Szul, Poland

"I ask you to stay with us for my sake, not yours. If you leave, I will forever be ashamed to be numbered among the human race."

Dr. Giovanni Passante, Italy

The roster of persons recognized by Yad Vashem as Righteous Among the Nations—more than 20,000 men and women—includes the names of people from many different countries. Although subjected to Nazi education and ideology, a few Germans stood up and took action, even at risk to their lives.

Oskar Schindler was a member of the Nazi party when he came to Krakow to conduct his business dealings. He acquired a factory in the Plaszow camp, employing Jewish prisoners. Seeing their terrible conditions, Schindler bribed the camp commander in August 1944 to transfer his workers to the Brünnlitz camp in the Sudetenland. Most of the people whose names appeared on "Schindler's list," survived. Schindler died in 1974, and is buried in Jerusalem.

After becoming aware of the Jews'

Raoul Wallenberg

Raoul Wallenberg, the scion of a distinguished Swedish family and a member of the Swedish diplomatic legation in Hungary, decided to mobilize his resources to rescue Jews. He issued Swedish "protective passports" to save Jews from deportation, housed many refugees in Swedish "protected houses," and, in November 1944, removed Jews from death marches to Austria. After the Red Army surrounded Budapest, he insisted on remaining in the city despite the risk. A day after liberation, Wallenberg was taken to Soviet headquarters for interrogation; he disappeared without a trace. Today it is assumed that he died in prison, but details of his fate have not been fully disclosed to this day.

suffering and the murders in Ponary, Wehrmacht Sergeant Anton Schmid decided to help Jews to the best of

his ability. Schmid arranged the release of Jews from prison, transferred food and supplies to the ghetto, and concealed Jews during *Aktionen*. Schmid was arrested by the Gestapo, convicted of treason, and executed in April 1942.

"... To help these people was the most natural thing to do... Maybe it wasn't logical but, you know, I felt a need to do it."
An inhabitant of Le Chambon-sur-Lignon, France

When the Rotenbergs, refugees from Germany living in Brussels, sought a hiding place for their four children, they contacted Father Hubert Celis of Halmaal. The clergyman responded at once, placing the two boys with his brother, Father Louis, and the two girls with his father, Joseph. Several days later the children's parents were caught and deported to their death. After two years Father Hubert was denounced and arrested. His brother sent the children to hideouts in the countryside. An older sister of the fugitives was sent to Auschwitz-

Birkenau. After the war Father Louis reunited the remaining children and arranged for their emigration to Palestine.

Rescue in Bosnia

In 1941, Mustafa and Zejneba Hardaga concealed the Kabilyo family in their home in Sarajevo. Half a year later, as the danger mounted, Mustafa removed Rivka Kabilyo and her children to Mostar, a city in the Italian occupation zone. Rivka's husband Josef found

a different hiding place, until members of the pro-Nazi Ustasi party captured him and sent him away for forced labor. In the winter of 1942, Zejneba, hearing that Josef, in shackles, was shoveling snow in the streets of Sarajevo, rushed to bring food to him and his fellow workers. Josef was captured trying to escape and sentenced to death. Before the sentence could be carried out, however, he escaped and went to the Hardagas' home, where he hid for two months, until he joined the rest of his family. Zejneba's father, Ahmad Sadeq, was arrested and executed in the Jasenovac camp. Zejneba died in Jerusalem in 1994.

Aristides De Sousa Mendes

Aristides de Sousa Mendes was the Portuguese consul general in Bordeaux during the war. When the Germans invaded and Jews attempted to obtain transit visas to Spain and Portugal, Mendes helped them, in contravention of his government's guidelines. He was expelled from his country's foreign service and deprived of all financial entitlements, which dealt a considerable blow to his economic security. Mendes died in 1954; in 1988 his name was cleared by the Portuguese government.

Rescue by Non-Jewish Individuals and Organizations

The law [under which the Jews are being arrested] is immoral. Accordingly, we must not overlook such laws and are duty-bound to resist them actively...

Father Marie-Benoit, France

Le Chambon-sur-Lignon, a small town in southern France, was the setting of an act of almost unparalleled courage during the Holocaust. Its largely Protestant population responded to the urgings of Pastor André Trocmé to aid fugitive Jews by sheltering them and smuggling them into Switzerland. Trocmé risked the lives of his family and his congregants, not to mention his own, in undertaking this mission. His cousin, Daniel Trocmé, was arrested and murdered in Buchenwald after admitting he had helped Jews. André Trocmé was imprisoned as well; he refused to stop aiding Jews, and was eventually released. Nearly 5,000 Jews found refuge in Le Chambon.

The only case in which an entire country mobilized to rescue its Jewish citizens was the rescue of 7,200 Danish Jews. After the Germans occupied Denmark

We did what we were supposed to.... It was the most natural thing to help these people.

Father Marie-Benoit, France

1

We don't know who's Jewish. We recognize only people.

Pastor André Trocmé, France

2

1 André Trocmé and his son while in hiding in the Loire region, June 13, 1944

2 Boat used by a Danish fisherman to evacuate a group of Jews from Denmark to neutral Sweden, October 1943

in April 1940, the Danish government reached an agreement with the Nazis, stipulating that the country's 8,000 Jewish citizens were not to be harmed. In August 1943, following a crisis between Germany and the Danish authorities, a state of emergency was declared, and the Reich Plenipotentiary in Denmark proposed to Berlin that the Jews be deported. The secret deportation plan was leaked to the Danes, who moved to protect and conceal their Jewish population. In October, the Danish resistance engineered the naval evacuation of the Jews to Sweden, thereby saving the community.

When the Germans took control of Italy, the fascist regime participated in the deportation of Jews for extermination and in the looting of

1

2

3

Zegota

Dr. Adolf Berman

Miriam Peleg (Maria Hochberg)

Zegota, the underground Council for Assistance to Jews, was active in Poland from December 1942 until the liberation in January 1945. With representatives of five Polish movements and two Jewish ones (the Jewish National Committee and the Bund), Zegota distributed financial aid to hundreds of individuals as well as to families of those who had perished. For the most part, however, it furnished Jews with forged papers and hiding places. It also made special efforts to rescue children by placing them in convents and with adoptive families. Some 4,000 Jews owed their survival to these actions. The secretary of Zegota was Adolf Berman.

Janina Hascheles-Altman was born in Lvov. After her father was murdered, she was confined in the ghetto with her mother. Her mother committed suicide, and Janina, now parentless, fled by choice to the Janowska labor camp. The inmates there took care of her, and the poet Michael Borwicz arranged for her escape along with other prisoners. In October 1943, she was entrusted to Miriam Peleg-Marianska, a Zegota activist, and was concealed in an orphanage under an assumed Aryan name.

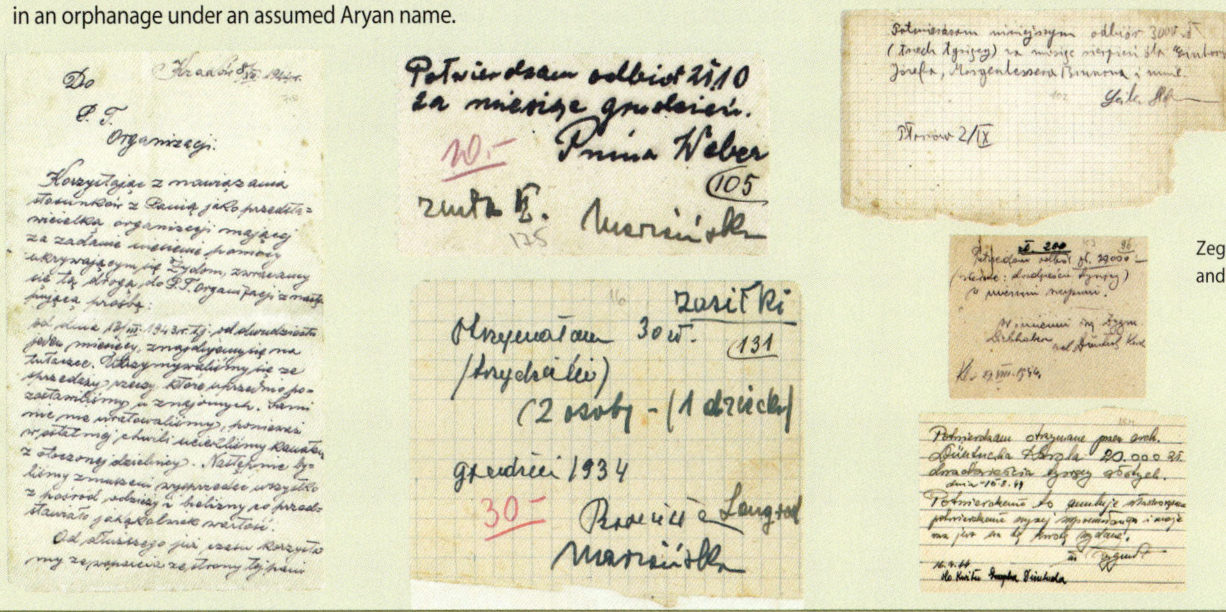

Zegota documents and letters

1 Rescue of the Jews of Denmark
2 Jewish refugees from Denmark reach the coast of Sweden
3 Anti-German demonstrations across Denmark, August 1943

Rescue of Children in Belgium

Andrée Guelen of Belgium joined the Comité de Défense des Juifs (CDJ—Committee for Jewish Defense) rescue organization after witnessing a Gestapo raid on a school to capture Jewish children. For two years she delivered youngsters to Christian families and convents, clandestinely keeping a record of their original names so they could be reunited with their families after the war. She was recognized as a Righteous Among the Nations in 1989.

their property. While Jews were being handed over, many other Italians, in particular priests and nuns, helped Jews find hiding places. Owing to this help and the possibilities of fleeing to Switzerland, along with the Allied invasion, about 80% of Italian Jewry had been saved.

Rescue in Bulgaria

In March 1941, Bulgaria allied itself with Germany and was rewarded with parts of Greek Thrace and Yugoslavian Macedonia, which both had Jewish populations. Following its patrons' lead, the Bulgarian government promulgated racial laws against its Jewish citizens. Although they were not strictly enforced, the Bulgarian authorities deported Jewish men to forced-labor camps around the country and required Jews to pin the yellow star to their garments in the middle of 1942. In early 1943, the government acceded to the Germans' demands to deport the Jews of Thrace and Macedonia to the extermination camps in Poland and prepared for the first deportation of Jews from the town of Plovdiv and Kyustendil. When the deportation plan came to light, a group of parliamentarians, church leaders (including Archbishop Stefan, a close associate of King Boris), public figures, and ordinary citizens came together to pressure the king and his government not to comply. The members of the group included Dimitur Peshev, a representative from Kyustendil and the deputy speaker of the Bulgarian parliament. On March 17, 1943, Peshev drew up a petition against the deportation and presented it to the prime minister. The pressure helped. On May 24, 1943, the plan to deport 48,000 Bulgarian Jews was revoked. The Germans did not renew their demand.

Dimitur Peshev during a visit to Kyustendil, 1942

Jews in the Allied Armies

Jewish armed resistance included service in the regular Allied armies. Approximately 550,000 Jewish soldiers fought in the United States Armed Forces during World War II. They served on all fronts, in Europe and in the Pacific. Some 28,000 were killed in combat, and more than 36,000 received citations. Many Jewish soldiers took part in liberating the camps. About 30,000 Jews served in the British army in 1939–1946, some in special units of Jews from Palestine, such as the Jewish Brigade.

Major General Morris G. Rose

Morris Rose fought in the U.S. Armed Forces during World War I. He then climbed through the ranks of command until he became an outstanding tank-units' commander. In World War II, he was chief of staff of the 1st Division in Africa and Italy, the 2nd Division in Western Europe, and the 3rd Division. Whenever he went into combat, he always led his soldiers and fought as one of them. Major General Morris Rose was killed on German soil. For his brave feats, he received many citations of excellence.

Jewish Soldiers in the Red Army

About 500,000 Jewish soldiers fought in the Red Army during World War II. Some 120,000 were killed in combat and in the line of duty; the Germans murdered another 80,000 as prisoners of war. More than 160,000, at all levels of command, earned citations, with over 150 designated "Heroes of the Soviet Union"—the highest honor a soldier in the Red Army can obtain—including Paulina Gelman, who flew hundreds of sorties as a combat pilot.

Edna Peled during her term of service with the Polish Army

The Jewish Brigade

The Jewish Brigade was a British military unit for Jewish volunteers from Palestine. Established in September 1944, through the intervention of Winston Churchill, the Brigade saw action on the Italian front and took part in the Allied offensive in Italy in April 1945, losing 57 men. At the end of the war, the Brigade was stationed in Tarvisio, near the Italian-Austrian border; some members went to the DP camps to help organize the survivors' clandestine emigration to Palestine.

Parachutists on a Rescue Mission

The British gave 110 volunteers from the *Yishuv* protracted military training for a special mission: to participate in operations of British intelligence units operating behind enemy lines in central and southern Europe. The volunteers were mainly from the German-Balkan department of the *Palmach*, *Yishuv* volunteers in the British army, and activists in pioneering youth movements. They viewed their mission as integral with another important goal: encourage Holocaust survivors to move to Palestine after the war. Thirty-eight parachutists were chosen: twelve were taken prisoner, and nine were killed in the course of their mission. Hannah Szenes, one of the parachutists who set out for Europe, had been a founding member of Kibbutz Sdot Yam. In her diary, she wrote: "... **The main thing is that I believe in Zionist fulfillment.... It will be difficult, but it's all worthwhile."**

1 

2 

1 Hannah Szenes in British army uniform with her brother Gyurry, a day before her departure on mission to Hungary, Tel Aviv, 1944

2 Parachutists from the Land of Israel.
Standing: Reuven Dafni, Tzadok Drogoyer, Abba Berdiczew.
Sitting: Sarah Braverman, Arye Fichman and Haviva Reik, Bari, Italy, 1944

The World of the Camps

Heinrich Zussmann, (1904-1986), I Remember Auschwitz Again, IV, 1960, carte grattage

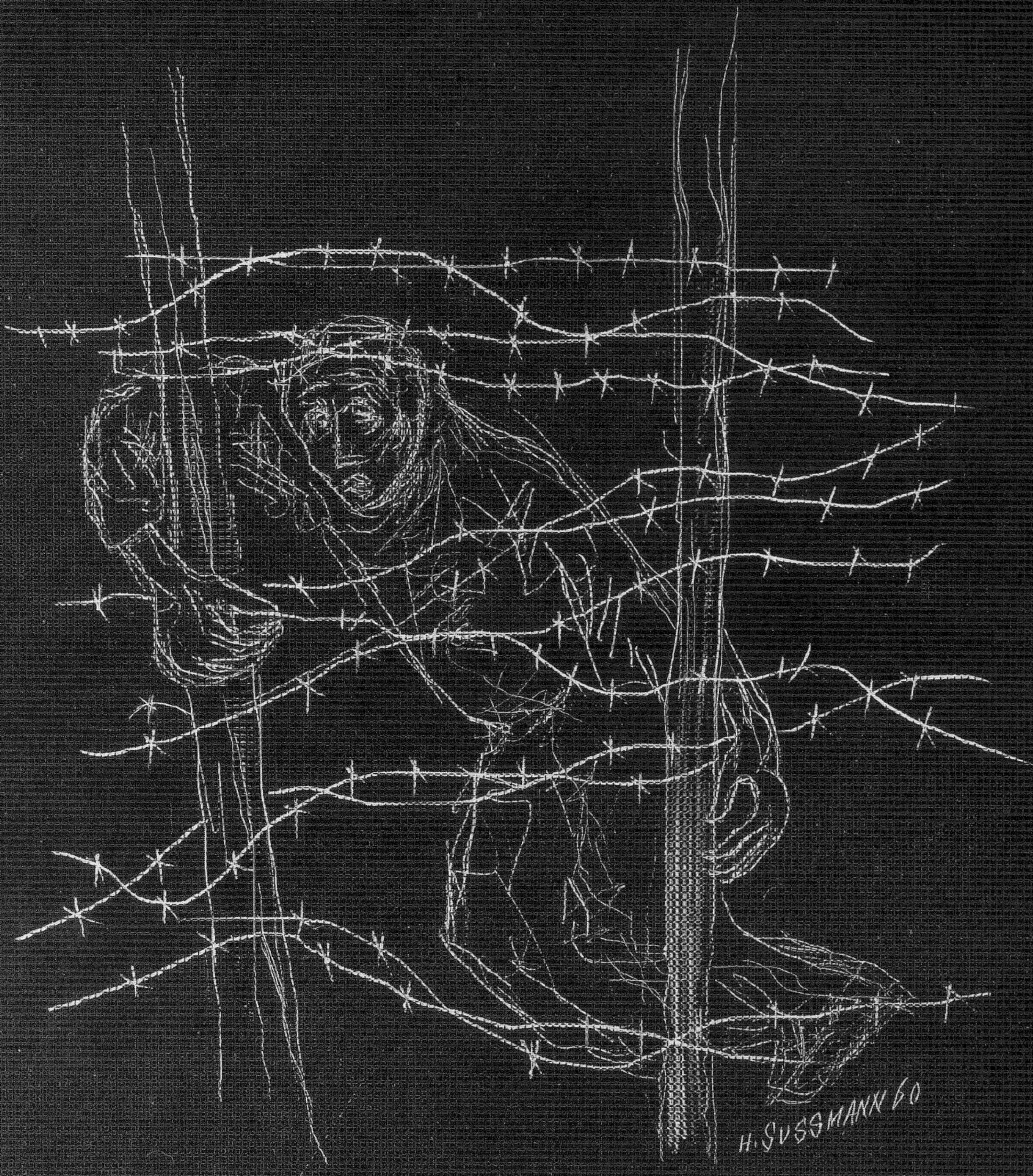
H. SUSSMANN 60

Whoever enters this place once will not remove a thing from it, not even his ashes.

Tadeusz Borowski, a Polish inmate in Auschwitz-Birkenau

1

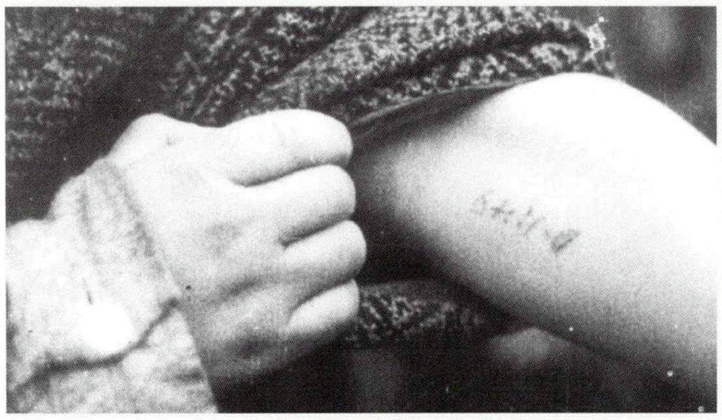

2

Despite the Germans' military reversals and the imminence of the Allied victory, the concentration and death camps continued to operate until the final downfall of the Third Reich and the end of the war. At this stage the last Jews in Europe—apart from a few

1 General view of Dachau, 1945
2 Entrance gate to the Gross-Rosen camp
3 Crematorium at the Gross-Rosen camp
4 Warning sign posted on the fence of the Majdanek concentration camp
5 Entrance to the Klooga camp. Over the gate, The inscription "An Organisation Todt Factory"
6 Flossenburg camp
7 The gate through which SS men entered the Mauthausen camp
8 Plaszow camp, Poland
9 Sign between the electrified fences that surrounded Majdanek: "Caution! Death zone"

3

ACHTUNG! UWAGA!
Lagergelände! Stehen bleiben! Fotografieren verboten! Es wird ohne Anruf scharf geschossen!
Teren obozu! Stać! Fotografowanie wzbronione! Bez
bedzie zastrzelony!

4

O. T. BETRIEBE KLOOGA
HALT!
SEIS! MUIDU LAS
СТОИ! БУДУ СТРЕ

5

6

7

8

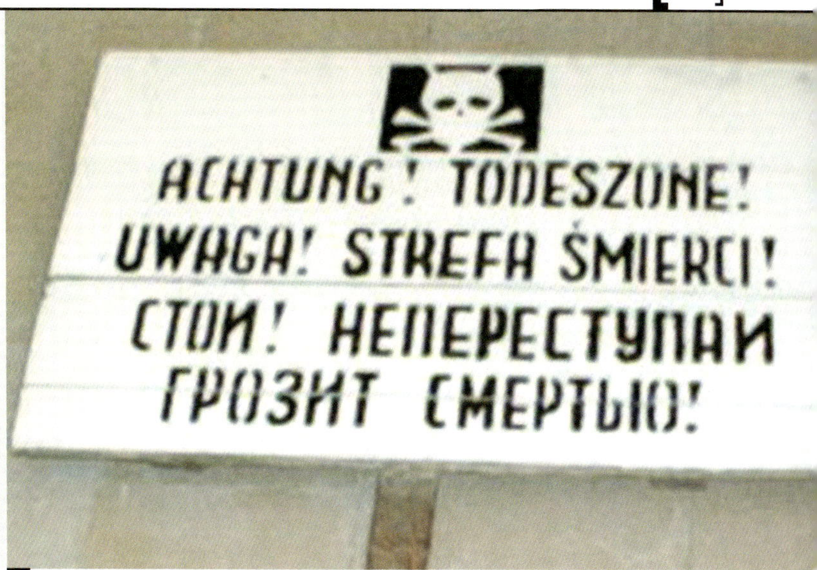
ACHTUNG! TODESZONE!
UWAGA! STREFA ŚMIERCI!
СТОИ! НЕПЕРЕСТУПАИ
ГРОЗИТ СМЕРТЬЮ!

9

who were living in hiding under "Aryan" identities, in the forests and in hideouts, or in the Soviet interior—were incarcerated in concentration and labor camps. The chimneys continued to belch smoke, and the heavy stench of cremated human bodies hovered in the air. In the extermination camps across Poland—Auschwitz-Birkenau, Majdanek, Chelmno, Belzec, Sobibor, and Treblinka—the Nazis continued to murder those who arrived and kept only small teams of prisoners alive in order to operate the facilities and collect the victims' belongings. Most Jews were murdered in two large camps, Majdanek and Auschwitz-Birkenau, which served the combined goals of concentration and extermination. Only a small percentage of those who arrived in transports were selected for dispatch to labor camps. The others—women, men, children, the elderly, and those whose strength had failed during their brief internment in the camp—were taken straight to the gas chambers.

The hierarchic structure of the concentration camps followed the model established in Dachau. The German staff was headed by the Lagerkommandant (camp commander) and a team of subordinates, comprised mostly of junior officers. One of the juniors commanded the prisoners' camp, usually after being specially trained for this duty. Male and female

1 An orchestra accompanies prisoners before they are executed. Mauthausen, Austria, July 1942
2 Prisoners' orchestra at the Janowska camp, Lvov

The Muselmann Phenomenon

"All the Muselmannner… who died in the gas chambers have the same story, or more exactly, have no story… On their entry into the camp, whether through basic infirmity, or by misfortune, or through some banal incident, they are defeated before they can adapt, they are beaten by time, they do not understand German, cannot disentangle the infernal knot of laws and prohibitions until their bodies are already in decay. And nothing can save them from selection or from death and debility."

Primo Levi

Zinovii Tolkatchev (1903–1977), Stigmatized Man, 1944, gouache, charcoal, and oil crayon on paper

guards and wardens of various kinds were subordinate to the command staff. The prisoners had a hierarchy of their own, and prisoner-supervisors were considered an elite that could wield power. The prisoners had different opinions about them: most Jewish supervisors tried to treat their brethren well; others behaved less well.

Transports and extermination continued until late 1944. Although Himmler had ordered an end to the murders in gas chambers, prisoners continued to die from exhaustion, starvation, and disease.

"They prodded us along with sticks and shouts until we came to 'barbers' who shaved us wherever we had hair. The razors had long been in use and may have shaved thousands of prisoners. The

Majdanek

Majdanek was established in late 1941, for Soviet prisoners of war and as a concentration camp for Poles. The gas chambers and crematoria were built in 1942. In the spring of that year, thousands of Jews, Slovaks, Czechs, Germans, and Poles were murdered there. The camp operated until the Soviet army liberated the Lublin area in July 1944. By then some 230,000 people had been murdered in Majdanek, including 100,000 Jews.

shaving was humiliating. After such treatment, most of the men came out lacerated and bloody.... We showered in cold water, with neither soap nor towels. We dried ourselves in the wind that blew from all directions.... After the showers, they dunked us in baths of Lysol, a disinfectant that was especially pungent. The men, cut up while being shaved, suffered from stinging when they were forced to dive into the bath."

Yehoshua Buchler

"Then for the first time we became aware that our language lacks words to express this offense, the demolition of a man.... We had reached the bottom. It is not possible to sink lower than this.... Nothing belongs to us anymore: they have taken away our clothes, our shoes, even our hair... They will even take away our name..."

Primo Levi

"We hang up our dog tags.... From this moment, we are citizens registered in the city of human suffering—Majdanek."

Tadeusz Sztabholc

"Undress! Fast! Hold only the belts and shoes.... Trembling with cold, we had arrived at true equality, the equality of the naked.... In the passageway they throw pants, a shirt, a coat, and socks at us.... Meir Katz, a huge man, received a child's trousers. A small, skinny man literally sank into his shirt. Swapping began at once."

Elie Wiesel

"There are 148 bunks on three levels... Here all the ordinary inmates live.... I do not know who my neighbor is. I am not even sure it is always the same person because I have never seen his face except for a few seconds amidst the uproar of the reveille..."

Primo Levi

1

2

3
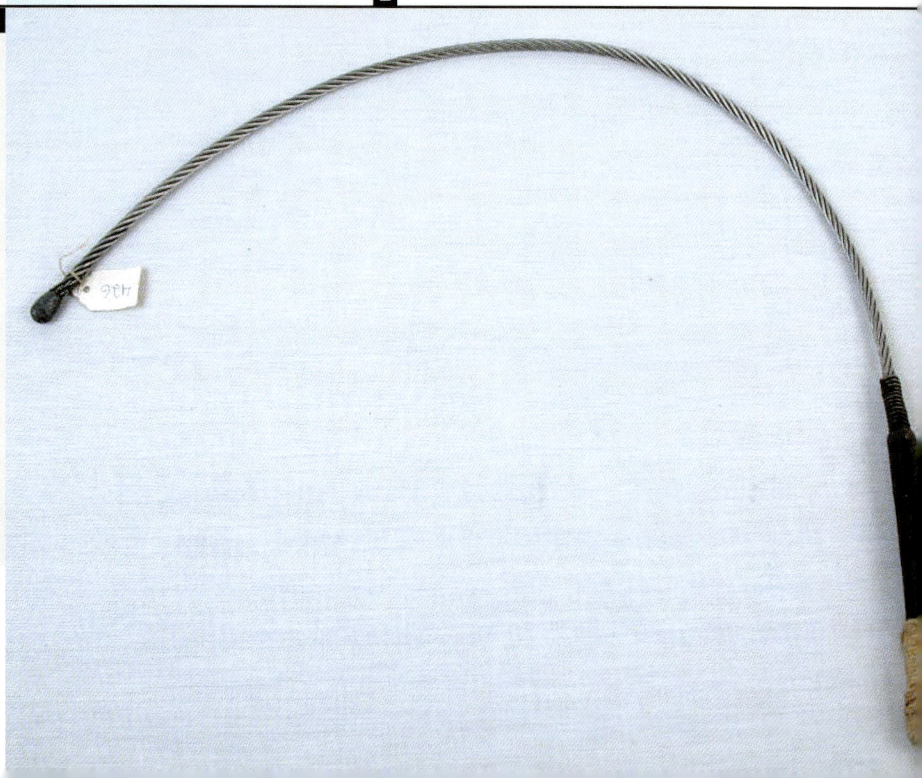

1 Prisoner's dress, Stutthof
2 Gloves made from a blanket, Bergen-Belsen
3 A lash used to flog prisoners in the camps

1

1 Lighting Hanukka candles at Westerbork
2 Mirror coated with eggshells, prepared at the Compiegne camp
3 Tefillin and pouch, taken to Auschwitz
4 Roll call before distribution of food, Flossenbürg
5 Original soup container from Gross-Rosen

"In the yard it's dark, cold. People from other barracks are running. They line up. Else lines us up, hitting people and cursing. She is helped by one SS man. Suddenly he stiffens in front of an officer who has come. He tells the officer how many and accompanies him. The officer counts us by himself."

Masha Rolnik

"They had whips. The whip was made of a metal cable with braided leather on top. The SS men and the Kapos had them, too. They used them relentlessly, at every opportunity and even without an opportunity."

Israel Gutman

"Guinea pigs, human guinea pigs, exploited by doctors for racial research! ... 'It's better this way, girls,' the veteran Greek women would tell us. 'It's better than dying.... You won't have to go out to work, you won't die!"

Giuliana Tedeschi

"'Here you have to work. Otherwise, you'll be sent to the smokestack. To the crematorium. The choice is yours.' I'll never forget the silence of the world that robbed me forever of the lust for life."

Elie Wiesel

"The confusion of languages is a fundamental component of the manner of living here: one is surrounded by a perpetual Babel, in which everyone shouts orders and threats in languages never heard before, and woe betide whoever fails to grasp the meaning."

Primo Levi

Despite their terrible conditions, cultural and religious activity continued in the

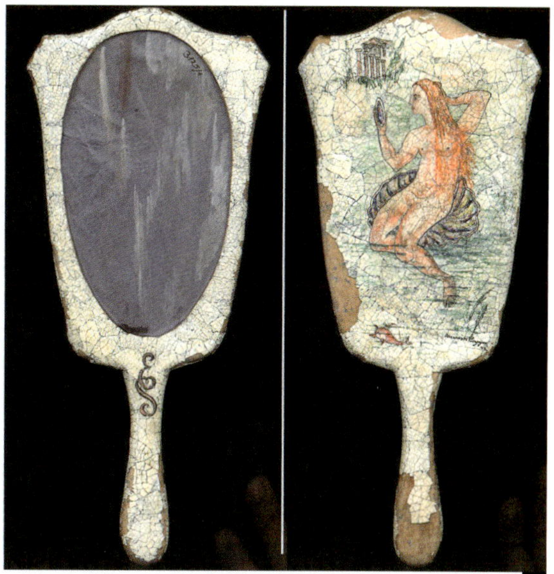

2

3

4

5

ghettos, labor camps, and even concentration camps. Literary and artistic works that survived the war reflect the Jews' lives, agonies, and efforts to maintain their human and Jewish identity. These works are direct and authentic testimonies and depict the Jewish victims' daily life during the Holocaust. Writing a diary on scraps of paper, producing drawings and illustrations of camp life, making jewelry out of copper wire, writing a Passover Haggadah, and conducting prayer services on the eve of Rosh Hashanah are all manifestations of the tremendous psychological strength maintained by these frail, starving people. Even at the end of the grueling days they had to endure, they refused to abandon their creative endeavors. Prisoners in concentration and labor camps exhibited heroism and resourcefulness in their daily lives, struggling to sustain not only the ember of physical life but also, and mainly, their humanity and basic moral values, friendship and concern for others—values that facilitated their survival.

1

2

3

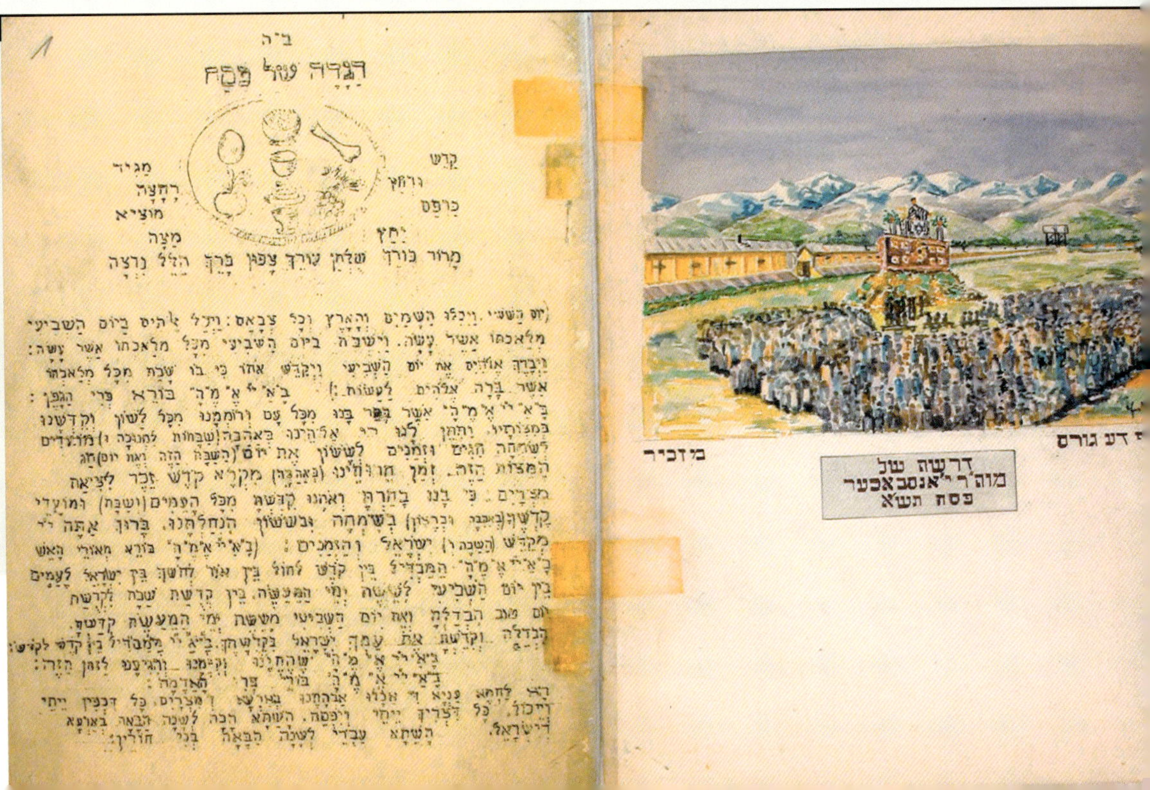

ב״ה

הגדה של פסח

קדש ורחץ כרפס יחץ מגיד רחצה מוציא מצה מרור כורך שלחן עורך צפון ברך הלל נרצה

יום הששי. ויכלו השמים והארץ וכל צבאם: ויכל אלהים ביום השביעי מלאכתו אשר עשה. וישבת ביום השביעי מכל מלאכתו אשר עשה: ויברך אלהים את יום השביעי ויקדש אתו כי בו שבת מכל מלאכתו

5

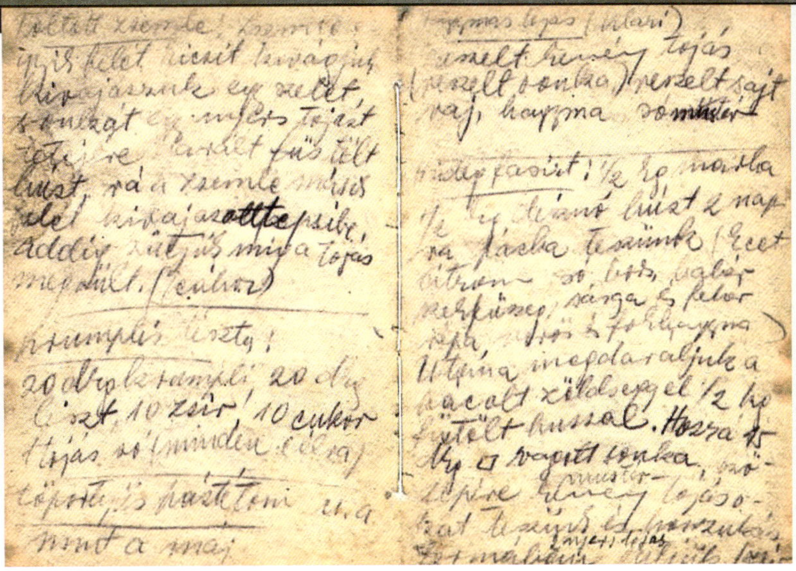

4

1. Holy Ark, carved by Leon Daniel Cohen of Altona, Hamburg. The ark was placed in the children's home in Terezin
2. Shofar made at the Skarzysko-Kamienna camp for the High Holidays, 1943
3. Passover Haggada prepared in the Gurs camp by Rabbi Leon Zuckerman, 1941
4. **Felix Nussbaum** (1904–1944), The Camp Synagogue, oil on plywood
5. Recipes written on scraps of paper in Ravensbruck by Yehudit Aufrichtig Taube

Forced-Labor Camps

"In giving us the document authorizing the appointment, Hitler pointed out that basically there could not be any such thing as a labor problem. He repeated in effect, what he had already stated on November 9, 1941: 'The area working directly for us embraces more than two hundred fifty million people. Let no one doubt that we will succeed in involving every one of these millions in the labor process.' The necessary labor force, therefore, was to come from the occupied territories. Hitler instructed Sauckel to bring the needed workers in any means whatsoever. That order marked the beginning of a fateful segment of my work."

Albert Speer

Nazi Germany exploited the labor of the occupied peoples from the onset of the occupation. More than five million people and 2.5 million prisoners of war were transported to Germany for labor. Jews were enslaved and interned in a far-reaching network of forced-labor camps across Europe, in the Reich itself, in the West and, foremost, in the East. The SS Central Office for Administration and Economy defined the new goal: labor exploitation of concentration-camp prisoners, who would be taken to hundreds of labor camps for service on behalf of the German war machine. The task of exterminating the Jewish people would be completed by means of merciless forced labor—"extermination by labor," as this "compromise" was called. Jews were made to work on farms, repair roads, clear forests and, especially, toil in industrial and armaments plants. Large concerns and private enterprises unhesitatingly exploited the labor of Jewish prisoners, who were beaten relentlessly by supervisors and were subjected to reduced and pilfered food rations by staff at all levels. Deprived of medicines and exposed to ceaseless brutality, more than half a million Jews died in the labor camps.

Miklos Bela Braun, Forced Labor, 1945, ink on paper

Wagon used at the quarries in Gross-Rosen

"From the place where we worked, we could see how this cart, heaped with corpses, made its way back and forth all day long. All the bodies were naked. Rigid limbs stuck out.... The cart didn't stop moving until evening. It was as though the corpses were being hauled from some inexhaustible warehouse. The group that performed this labor was called the "death detail." Many leaped at the opportunity [to join it] because [its members] received an additional portion of soup."

Abram Kajzer, Dornhau labor camp

"I've lost all hope, terrible hopelessness. It's mid-summer and there's not even a rumor about the end of this. Everyone looks terrible; it's been going on too long.... More work and a little less food.... The reports from home, the deportations, are very bad, but the hopelessness is even worse.... If this continues for another winter, half of us will not survive."

Fela Szeps, Grünberg labor camp

The Death Marches

As the Third Reich crumbled and the eastern front collapsed, the Germans began a comprehensive retreat to the West, towards Germany. SS Chief Himmler ordered his subordinates not to allow the Allied armies to liberate living prisoners in the concentration camps—as had happened in Majdanek, where the murders had been discovered. The evacuation of the inmates of hundreds of camps in Poland and eastern Prussia westwards, to the Reich, began in late 1944. In harsh winter weather, as artillery thundered in the distance, the prisoners were loaded aboard trains or led out on foot on murderous treks that lasted weeks, if not months. Some prisoners, those who were too weak to set out, were put to death in the camps; only a few sick prisoners were left behind. The guards who were ordered to lead the prisoners understood that these duties were an obstacle to their own escape from the Red Army; thus, they were all the more eager to kill the prisoners and get away. After the war the mass graves of thousands of murdered evacuees were found along the routes of the death marches.

The order to evacuate the prisoners

1

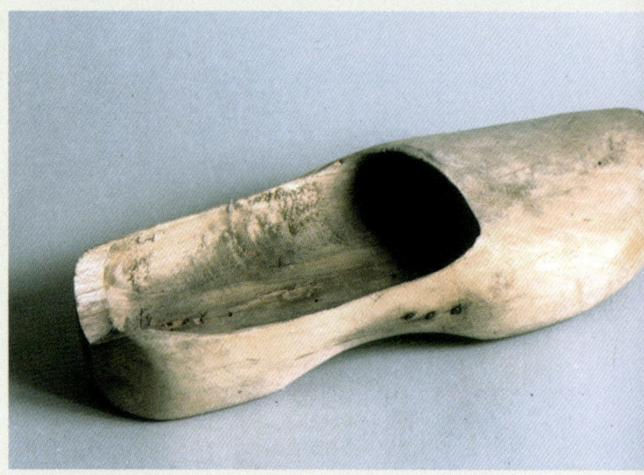

to the German interior was not issued in writing; that is, no written order has surfaced. For this reason, the local initiatives taken by guards and escorts are especially telling. Scholars suggest that the purpose of the death marches was twofold: first, they were intended as another way to continue killing Jews, to the last man and woman. And, second, until this could be accomplished, the prisoners would be concentrated temporarily in camps so as to ensure that no witnesses would be left to testify about the murders and, meanwhile, to exploit the Jewish labor force until the last possible moment. In this fashion, the mass murder of the prisoners continued until the day of surrender.

2

"I was in a terribly bad condition and the German guard stood there and watched us picking food out of the trash. [...] There was a rotten apple and we pulled it out and ate it. [...] he asked me, 'Why are you doing this?' I told him, '[...] Do me a favor. Kill me, kill me.' He said, 'I wasn't given any such order.'"

Lea

3

1 **Hellmut Bachrach-Barée** (1898–1969), Death March, Dachau to Tolz, 1945, pencil on paper
2 Death march from Dachau, April 1945
3 **Israel Alfred Glück** (b. 1921), The Death March, 1945, charcoal on paper

The Women's March from Silesia to Volary, Sudetenland

The death march of Jewish young women from Grünberg, a satellite camp of Gross Rosen, ended near the Czech town of Volary, on May 6, 1945. The women had been forced to walk some 800 kilometers in the freezing cold over a period of three months. When they were liberated a short time later, most of them required hospitalization, where many more died. After a period of convalescence, the rest returned to their countries of origin in the hope of finding family members who were still alive. Many women who returned to Poland were asked by their neighbors, "What, they didn't kill all of you?"

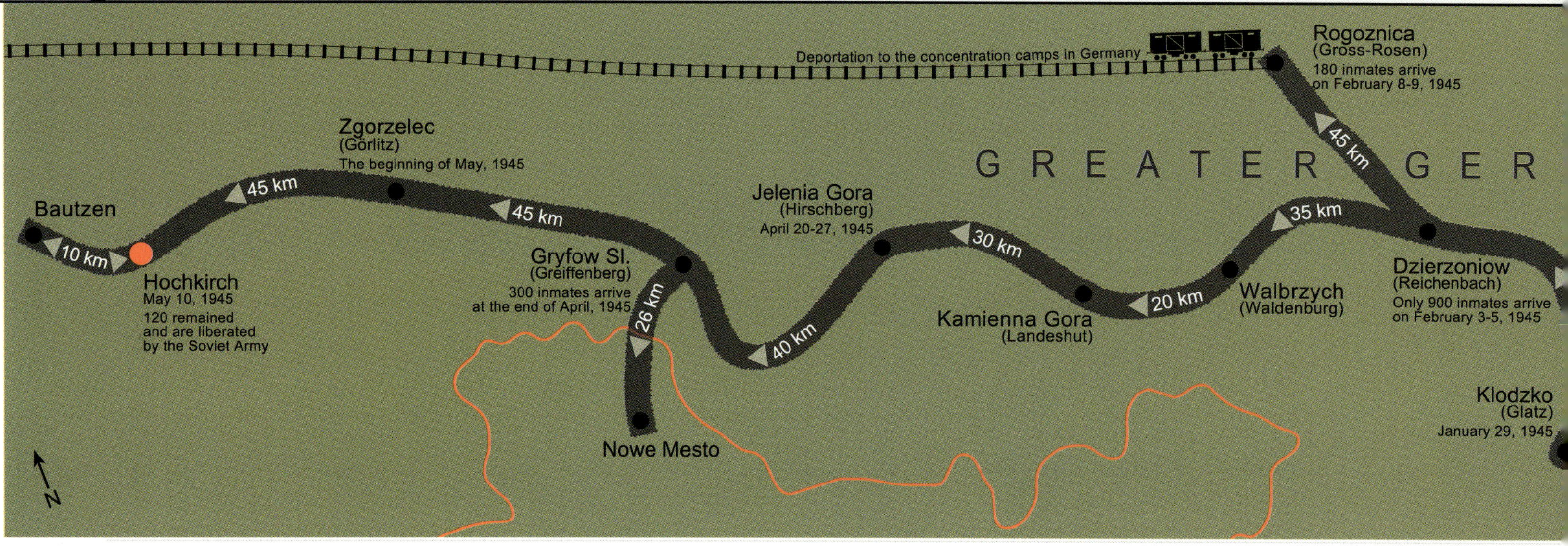

The Men's March from Auschwitz-Birkenau

On January 18, 1945, some 3,000 prisoners dressed in flimsy striped clothing were marched out of Birkenau in the heavy snow. The marchers alleviated their thirst by eating snow; they slept out in the open. After covering 59 kilometers on foot, they were placed aboard open freight cars. Many froze to death on the way. When the train stopped—possibly because the track had been damaged in a bombardment—the prisoners continued on foot. Several hundred men escaped into the forest; many were shot. During the ten days of the march, the prisoners received food only four times. After a further 368-kilometer trek, those still alive reached the Gross Rosen concentration camp. On May 9, the last day of the war, the few survivors were liberated by the Red Army. They had covered 498 kilometers in total.

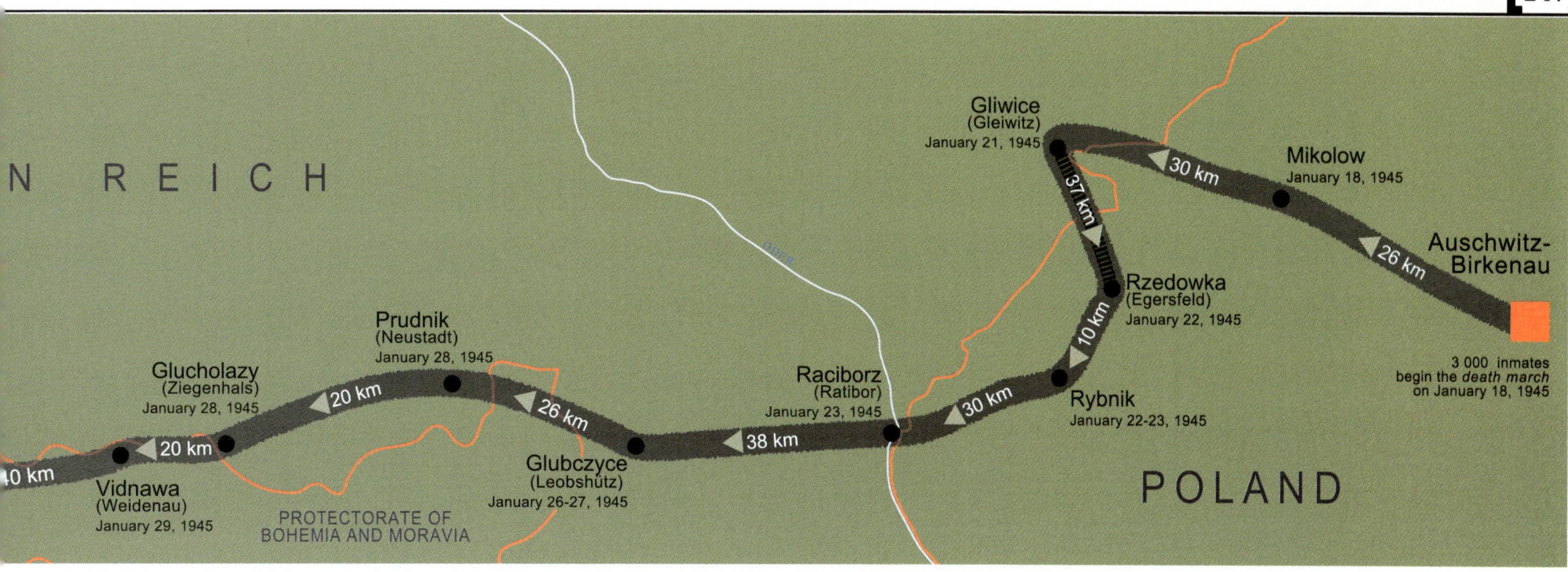

Return to Life

A soldier raises the Soviet flag over the Reichstag building, April 1945

The End of the War

1

We swore we would fight to the death and not surrender Stalingrad to the enemy.

Soviet General Vasili Chuikov

The free men of the world are marching together to Victory.

General Dwight David Eisenhower

The power of the German Reich peaked in the winter of 1942, and then began to ebb. Although the turnaround was not immediately perceptible, the Reich, which Hitler had fantasized would endure for 1,000 years, slowly but steadily disintegrated. The collapse was a gradual process, which began when the United States joined the war in 1941. It continued with the routing of the Wehrmacht at El Alamein in 1942 and in Stalingrad in the winter of 1942/3; the Allied invasion of Italy in July 1943 and with the landing in Normandy in June 1944. These campaigns reversed the course of the war. Yet even in the last phase, although Allied aircraft were bombing the gates

2

3

4

of Germany, Allied forces had landed on the coast of Normandy, and the Red Army was advancing westwards, the Germans continued to murder Jews, even attempting to thwart the rescue of those still interned in the concentration and labor camps.

"When you examine contemporary history, turn and contemplate the piles of corpses, pause for a moment, and imagine that these remnants of flesh and bones are your father, your children, your wife, someone you loved. Imagine yourself and those close to you, to whom you're devoted in your heart and soul, tossed naked onto the heap, tortured, dying, murdered."

Eugen Kogon

God bless you all. In all our long history we have never seen a greater day than this.

Winston Churchill, May 8, 1945

1 Roosevelt, Stalin, and Churchill at the Teheran Conference, November 28, 1943
2 Soviet cartoon: "Hitler's sending his soldiers to hell," 1944
3 German prisoners of war in Sicily, 1943
4 Soviet soldier raises a flag over the ruins of Stalingrad

The Allies' great offensive from the East and the West, in the first few months of 1945, ended with the occupation of Berlin, Hitler's suicide, and the defeat of the last pockets of Wehrmacht resistance. In the capitals of the occupied countries, civilians greeted the victors with cries of exultation. Jews, however, saw no reason to rejoice. The few survivors knew they had nowhere to return. The sights that terrified the liberators who entered the concentration camps, the massive pits filled with bodies, had been part of their daily lives for too long. Those sprawled corpses had been their parents, children, siblings, and acquaintances. The warehouses now pried open, were filled with the hair, clothing and belongings of those who had been murdered.

1

2

3

"As a non-Jewish German woman, I was among the first who believed that the Germans could not view the great tragedy of Hitler as a mere historical accident that could be forgotten and disavowed.... Irrespective of ideology, every German has a specific responsibility that originates in the slaughter that the Germans perpetrated against millions of human beings during the Second World War. It is not a collective guilt, passed on to the young generation, but a collective moral and historical responsibility. It was an exceptional challenge to be a German after 1945, because we were children of a humanistic Germany and also of the monstrous Germany. Each of us inherited not only our people's great achievements but also the evil that had been perpetrated."

Beate Klarsfeld, France

1 Germany on the brink of defeat, June 1944
2 The landing at Normandy, June 1944
3 American, British, French, and Soviet officers on their way to Hitler's residence. Berchtesgaden, August 1945
4 A prisoner in Bergen-Belsen after the British liberated the camp on April 15, 1945

4

To mark the complete victory over Germany today, Victory Day, Moscow, Capital of our Motherland, will salute the gallant troops of the Red Army... which have won this brilliant victory.

From Joseph Stalin's Order of the Day, May 9, 1945

The Allied armies, through sacrifice and devotion and with God's help, have wrung from Germany a final and unconditional surrender. The western world has been freed of the evil forces...

Harry Truman

The Anguish of Liberation

Liberated, but not free–that is the paradox of the Jews.

Abraham Klausner, US Army Chaplain, Dachau, June 1945

"Slowly they told me they're all gone, you've got no one left. I had survived alone. All the hope that I had a family, someone to return to, all of life, all those years, I prayed that I wouldn't remain alone in the world. That's that, the hope disappeared and then came the despair."

Herta Goldmann

"... All of a sudden Luszia came and said, 'The war's over.' I still remember the feeling. I thought, what's it for? Life isn't possible anymore, there's nothing left. Where were they before? What now?"

Miriam Akavia

1

1 Samuel Bak (b. 1933), Mother Is No More, 1946, gouache on paper

2 American forces liberate Mauthausen

2

"I'll continue to live my life that is impossible to continue.... Nothing has yet been created that is so absurd that we can't outlive it. Even now I already know that somewhere down the road, lying in wait for me like a trap that cannot be circumvented, is happiness. After all, even there, next to the smokestacks, in the intervals of time between the agonies, there was something that resembled happiness."

Imre Kertes

1

Approximately six million Jews, of all ages and from all social strata, were murdered during the Holocaust. Apart from two million Jews who remained alive in the Soviet Union, hundreds of thousands had somehow survived or had outlasted the camps. Most of them refused to return to their destroyed homes, to the soil saturated with Jewish blood and ashes, and to start life anew in exile with their sense of loss and relentless nightmares. Their first goal was to find a relative or fellow Jew who had survived the atrocities. Most failed.

2

"My eyes are riveted upon the expanse of destruction—does nothing really remain? Of all the masses, has not a person survived? Of my entire family, only I remain? How did it happen that all of them are dead and only I am alive? I, the weakest of them all?"

Dov Freiberg, a survivor of Sobibor

3

4

5

1. Prisoners on bunks in residential barracks of the "small camp," Buchenwald, after the liberation
2. Former prisoners leaving Dachau after the liberation
3. Prisoners in Auschwitz-Birkenau greet their Soviet liberators, January 1945
4. Bodies of death-march victims, Dachau, May 1945
5. Bodies of prisoners, Bergen-Belsen

Children Who Survived

At the end of the war, few Jewish children remained alive in Europe. Most were homeless orphans whose parents had entrusted them to strangers in the hope of saving their lives. They had spent years separated from their parents, living under false identities, constantly afraid of being discovered, and dependent on the good will of strangers. All this had a deep psychological impact on the children. After the war, Jewish institutions and the children's relatives made great efforts to restore them to their people and rehabilitate them. Special children's homes were established that gave them devoted care. The educators there labored to free them from their psychological distress and to rekindle their basic trust in humanity.

Reclaiming Jewish Children from Convents and Christian Homes

"They came to remove me from the convent in 1946. They told this woman, Marysa, that there's [a Jewish girl] here, and they pointed at me. At first they didn't want to answer. She's come to take some other girl whose aunt found out that she was alive, but she asked, might there be other children? They denied it. Then she told them, 'But you're doing something that shouldn't be done. You're taking children away from their religion without their parents' permission. The parents are gone; you

1

2

1 Children survivors in an OSE orphanage, Adelboden, Switzerland, after the war
2 Members of a group of approx. 160 Jewish children, concealed in Christians' homes during the war, are gathered by members of a relief unit that the *Yishuv* sent to the Jews of Greece, 1945
3 **Zinovii Tolkatchev** (1903–1977), The Savior, 1945, pencil on paper
4 Children in a Jewish orphanage in Brussels after the war
5 Friedza Rotbard

3

shouldn't do it.' She spoke to their conscience and then they pointed at me. Me? Are you kidding? I was stunned. What's this? I sobbed, I stomped my feet. Are you kidding? Is it such a big deal that I'd been a Jewish girl back then? I couldn't understand what was happening to me. When she came to remove me, kids shouted at me, 'Friedze, don't go with the Jews. They'll make matzo out of you.' The little children who were my friends all shouted, 'They'll make blood and matzo out of you.' Where did they get this from? 'Don't go.'"
Friedza Rotbard had been concealed in a convent in Turkowice.

Sela Warszawiak had been thought of as Polish, and was hidden by a Polish family. She was thrown into the street

4

5

1

2

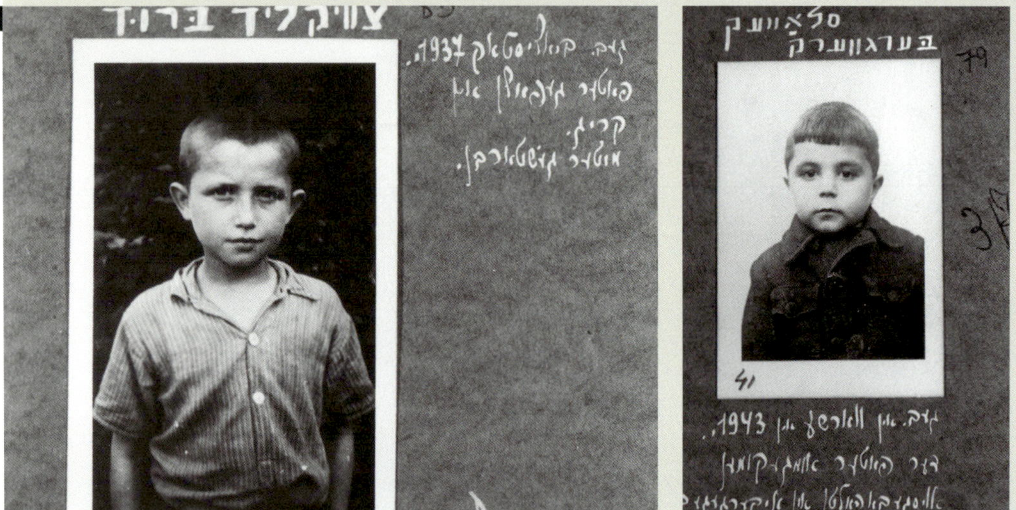

3

when her parents were deported to the camps and the money stopped coming. A Polish acquaintance of her father's spotted her and placed her in a convent with the assumed name of Irena Jablonska. Irena was moved to Krakow and adopted by a Polish couple who were devoted to her. When the war ended, relatives located her and placed her in a Jewish orphanage. However, she fled back to her adopted parents and continued to live as a Christian. Sela's grandfather pursued the matter in court and eventually took her to Israel.

"When we grouped together from the forests, the camps, and the bunkers, we felt a yearning for study.... We realized that this was the only way we could make our future lives easier.... It was abnormal to study in a mixed class because we had to master three grades of material in one year...."

Ashcze K.

1 **Zinovii Tolkatchev** (1903–1977), Dreamers and Philosophers, 1945, pencil and watercolor on paper
2 Two children who were concealed by Christians and returned to Judaism
3 Director of a Jewish orphanage in Domanovka, Transnistria, with several children, returning to Romania, 1944
4 Wall newspaper from the orphanage in Biala-Bielsko, Poland, 1947

4

Pogroms and Violence Resume

Many Jews who emerged from the camps, forests, and hideouts, or who returned from the Soviet Union under the repatriation agreement, to return to their homes received an enraged and hostile welcome. Much of the local populace was afraid that the Jews would demand restitution of the property they had stolen. In the first few months after the liberation, antisemitic gangs murdered approximately 1,000 survivors.

"... It was harder when the day of liberation came ... because then we saw moreover the destruction all around us and nonetheless that nothing had changed, the world continues to move its course.... G-d's hidden face is as it always was, we found nothing different in the world."

Rabbi Chaim Alter Ratte

The Jermis family waits for its return trip to Poland from Kazakhstan, 1946

The Pogrom in Kielce

After liberation, most Jews who had survived remained in Poland in order to psychologically and physically recover and prepare for immigration to Palestine or other destinations. Kielce, which had a Jewish population of 15,000 before the war, was home to approximately 150 Jews in June 1946. Fearing that the Jewish returnees would demand the restitution of their stolen homes and property, hate and incitement against the handful of survivors mounted among the local population. On July 1, an enflamed mob attacked Jews in their homes, murdering 42 and injuring dozens more. The local police and clergy neither stopped nor condemned the action.

Coffins of victims of the pogrom in Kielce, July 1946

As a result of their hostile reception, survivors turned to the west. Many settled provisionally near the Polish-German border and established community institutions with an eye toward continuing on to Palestine. Hospitals to treat the ill and exhausted survivors, orphanages, schools, and training farms were set up. After a period of convalescence, survivors moved on to western and southern Europe en route to the Atlantic coast. Their encounter with soldiers of the Jewish Brigade was one of their few joyous moments.

The *Bricha*

She'erit ha-Pletah (the surviving remnant), as the DPs called themselves, were unwilling to accept their fate and refused to live their lives in Europe. Exhausted from the hardships that they had endured, the lonely survivors struggled obstinately to relocate. They demanded free emigration, mainly to Palestine. The American Jewish Joint Distribution Committee (Joint) operated among the DPs, helped with food and clothing, underwrote educational endeavors, and provided money for organized emigration to Palestine, known as the *Bricha* (escape). Those who emigrated were vanguards of the Ha'apalah (clandestine immigration movement to Palestine) and played an important role in the political struggle for Jewish statehood.

Even after the war ended and the magnitude of the Holocaust was revealed, the global community continued to close its gates to Jewish migrants. Great Britain persisted in its policy of keeping Palestine off-limits, the United States allowed only relatives of American citizens into the country, and even countries that thirsted for immigrants preferred to take in only non-Jewish DPs, many of whom were Germans who had lived in Poland and Czechoslovakia; some had collaborated with the Nazis, a few had taken part in the murders. Consequently only one-third of the 300,000 Jewish DPs managed to migrate to the United States, Canada, Australia, and Latin America.

The "White Paper" policy of the British Mandate thwarted the immigration of European Jews to Palestine. However, the Jews were not deterred; even during the war, they had not desisted from trying to get there—although most failed.

Bricha activist Meyer Levin photographing the passage of survivors from Austria to Italy

DP Camps

At the war's end, the Allies placed tens of thousands of survivors in camps in Germany, Austria, and Italy. A year later, tens of thousands of additional refugees, mostly repatriates from the Soviet Union assisted by the Bricha organization, flowed to the West, hoping that, after their years of suffering, they could now live in peace and freedom. To their disappointment, they were classified as displaced persons—DPs—and placed in quarantine camps. In late 1946, there were some 250,000 DPs. Yet even in the DP camps the survivors managed to organize a vibrant Jewish life, including educational frameworks, cultural activities, religious worship, and political activism.

"… I was working in a hospital…. I see this nice guy. I hadn't yet had the feeling of 'man and woman' but that sort of thing awakened just then. That's how the romance began. Afterwards he spoke….'We'll get married.' He wants to marry me. Very well….On our wedding day, seven couples got married…."

Shoshana Roszkowski

1 A notice calling on residents of a DP camp in the American Liberated Zone to celebrate the establishment of the State of Israel
2 Mothers and children demonstrate against the British policy in Palestine, Pocking DP camp
3 Survivors in Buchenwald DP camp Welcome the Sabbath, May 18, 1945. An American military chaplain recites Kiddush
4 Protest demonstration at the Bergen-Belsen DP camp against the return of the *Exodus* refugees to Germany

1

2

3

4

The Ha'apalah Movement

After the war, hundreds of thousands of DPs fought the British White Paper policy that denied them entry to Palestine. Between 1945–1948, some 70,000 Jewish survivors made their way to Palestine, on vessels that were often unseaworthy.

"We've come from concentration camps in Europe and we refuse to exchange them for British concentration camps…. 4,000 women, children, and men are sailing under unimaginable conditions. Can you imagine the suffering of mothers who give birth on this ship? Are we criminals or murderers that you persecute us so savagely? Can you imagine a free person going to a concentration camp, albeit a British one, of his own free will?

1

2

3

We will fight for our right to live. We will fight on the beaches, we will fight in the streets, and we will fight aboard our vessel."

Cable from the Ha'apalah vessel *Knesset Yisrael*, November 1946

1 British soldiers place a clandestine immigrant aboard a deportation vessel bound for Cyprus. Haifa, October 18, 1946

2 Clandestine immigrants aboard the *United Nations* come ashore at Nahariya, January 1, 1948

3 The *Theodor Herzl* drops anchor at Haifa port, April 13, 1947

1 The *Exodus* drops anchor at Haifa port, July 18, 1947
2 Holocaust survivors from the Buchenwald camp reach Haifa port, July 15, 1945
3 Casualties from *Exodus*

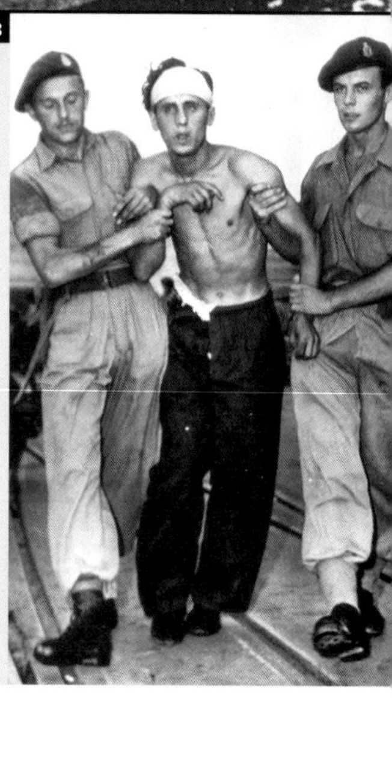

The Nuremberg Trials

Even as the war still raged, the Allies expressed their intention to bring to justice those responsible for the heinous crimes perpetrated by the Nazis and their collaborators. Once the war ended, the United States, Great Britain, the USSR and France established an international military tribunal that set, for the first time, binding legal criteria for the compulsory prosecution of perpetrators of crimes against humanity, war crimes, and crimes against peace. The wish to stress the universal dimension of the Nazis' crimes led to the inclusion of the murder of the Jews under the broad category of crimes against humanity. Between 1945-1949, a series of trials took place in the German city of Nuremberg, including a central trial against twenty-two leading German and Austrian Nazi officials. Out of hundreds of thousands Nazi war criminals, 31,651 were sentenced.

An Ending and a Beginning

Yehuda Bacon (b. 1929), To the man who restored my Belief in Humanity, 1945, Gouache, charcoal and pencil on paper

Cyprus—Detention at the Threshold to the Promised Land

After the war, as tens of thousands of survivors resisted the British White Paper policy that denied them entry to Palestine, the British responded by deporting some 52,000 clandestine immigrants to detention camps in Cyprus. This policy served another British goal: to weaken the struggle of the *Yishuv* against the Mandate. The newly deported found themselves behind barbed-wire fences in prisoner detention centers. The Joint and emissaries from the *Yishuv* mobilized to help them and maintain their link to Palestine.

1

2

3

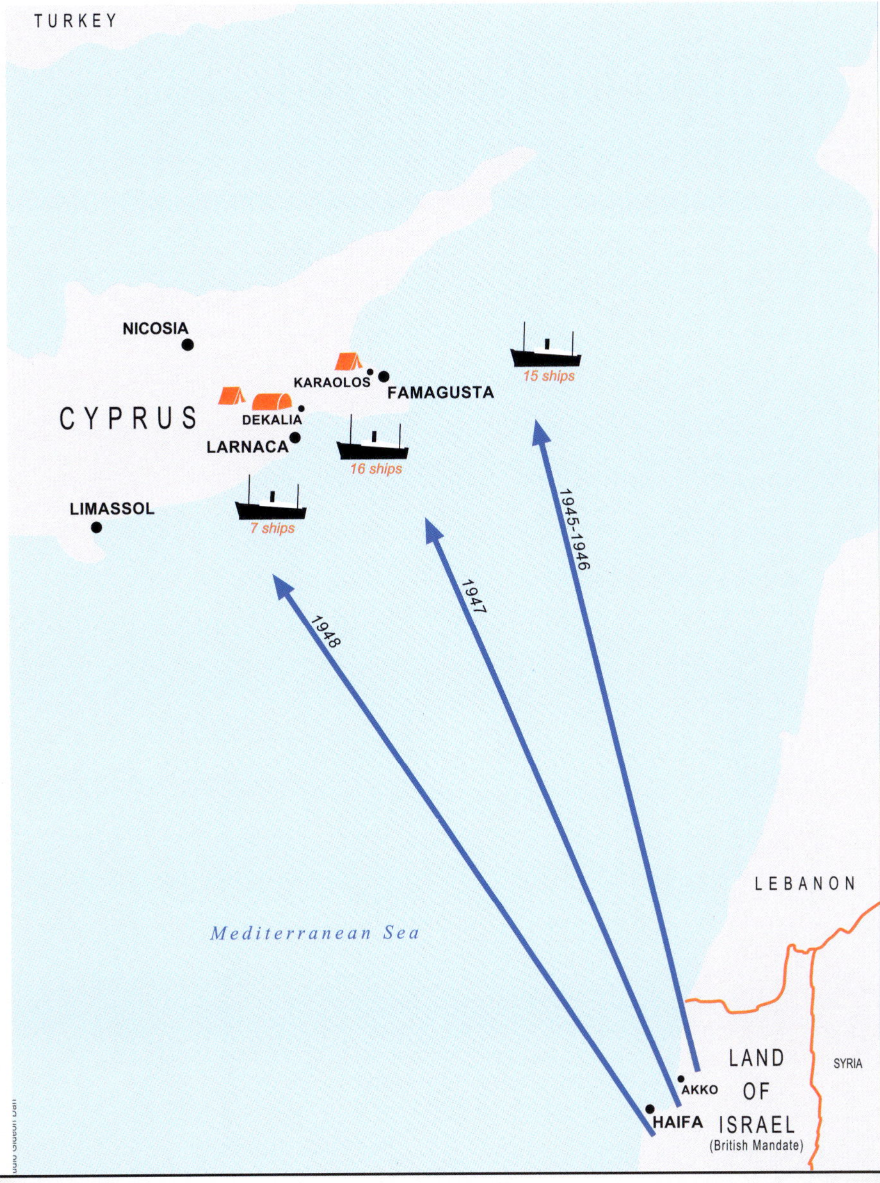

Deportations to Cyprus

4

1 Children learning Hebrew
2–4 Detension Camps in Cyprus

The Sole Survivors Fight for Israel's Independence

From the ashes of the Holocaust the nation arose, ingathered from a hundred countries, and flowed along timeless routes to the ancient homeland.

Chaim Herzog, manifesto for Israel's 40th Independence Day

On November 29, 1947, the United Nations resolved to terminate the British Mandate for Palestine and partition Eretz Israel into two states: a Jewish one and an Arab one. The following day, the Arabs declared war on the *Yishuv*, and the War of Independence broke out. Survivors played a major role in the defense of the newly declared Jewish state. These new immigrants joined units of the Haganah, Palmach, Lehi, and Etzel. Following the establishment of the Israel Defense Forces, Holocaust survivors accounted for about half of Israel's fighting force and one-fourth of combat fatalities.

Some 23,800 immigrants entered the country in 1940–1947, and a further 21,755 in 1948. In addition, some 22,100 Palestine-born Jews fought in the War of Independence. Thus, two-thirds of the fighters were recently arrived immigrants; most of them were Holocaust survivors. About 1,170 of them fell in combat.

The Silver Platter

... Then the nation, enchanted and awash in tears, asked,
And said, Who are you? And the two fall silent
And answer her: We are the silver platter
On which you were given the State of Jews

Nathan Alterman

A group of fighters in the *Yiftah* Brigade pauses before *Operation Dani* in Israel's War of Independence, Ben-Shemen forest. A number from Auschwitz appears on the arm of the soldier seated on the left. July 14, 1948.

Eretz Israel (the Land of Israel) was the birthplace of the Jewish people. Here their spiritual, religious and political identity was shaped. Here they first attained statehood, created cultural values of national and universal significance and gave to the world the eternal Book of Books.

The catastrophe which recently befell the Jewish people—the massacre of millions of Jews in Europe—was another clear demonstration of the urgency of solving the problem of its homelessness by re-establishing in Eretz Israel the Jewish State, which would open the gates of the homeland wide to every Jew and confer upon the Jewish people the status of a fully-privileged member of the community of nations...

Survivors of the Nazi Holocaust in Europe, as well as Jews from other parts of the world, continued to migrate to Eretz-Israel, undaunted by difficulties, restrictions and dangers, and never ceased to assert their right to a life of dignity, freedom and honest toil in their national homeland.

From Israel's Declaration of Independence

The Eichmann Trial

The trial of Adolf Eichmann, a principal organizer of the "Final Solution of the Jewish Question," took place in 1961–1962. Eichmann had been captured in Argentina after hiding there for years under a false identity. Many in Israel and around the world were mesmerized by the trial. For the first time since the Nuremberg trials, the Holocaust was placed under a legal spotlight. The trial also symbolized Israel's resolve to bring the war criminals to justice. On December 15, 1961, Eichmann was sentenced to death. His request for clemency was turned down, and he was hanged on June 1, 1962. His body was cremated, and his ashes were strewn over the sea beyond Israel's territorial waters. In the aftermath of the trial, there was a powerful groundswell of interest in the history of the Holocaust.

The Hall of Names

...To gather in the homeland [their] memory... and to establish a memorial and a name [Yad Vashem] to them....

From the Yad Vashem Law

"Let no person be found who knows the name of brothers and sisters, relatives, teachers and classmates, friends and acquaintances who were annihilated and who will not commit them to writing. A name is a source of strength, [as in] Yad Vashem. The strength of the nation lies in its memory, in the proficiency of its memory. This is what distinguishes man. If we wish to live, and if we wish and aspire to will life to our offspring, if we consider ourselves duty-bound to pave a way to the future, then first of all we must not forget and we must write."

Professor Benzion Dinur, *Yedi'ot Yad Vashem* [the Yad Vashem Bulletin], 1956.

In their final writings—diaries, letters and notes left behind—the victims of the Shoah pleaded for their names to be remembered. That is the motive on which the commemoration of the individual is based, expressed by the national endeavor of the Jewish people to redeem the names of all the Holocaust victims—an endeavor undertaken by Yad Vashem since its inception.

Over the years, the gathering of Shoah victims' names and their inscription on Pages of Testimony has become a focal point of Holocaust remembrance. These Pages—forms containing biographical information about the lives and deaths of Holocaust victims—were instituted in Yad Vashem's early years to redeem from oblivion the names and lives destroyed. Gathering their names brings the responsibility of preserving the memory of each victim from the family circle—which often lacked the ability to remember—to the Jewish people as a whole. Moreover, these special acid-Free Pages also serve as symbolic tombstones for the victims.

The focus on the individual takes on a special significance when compared with the unique totality of the Holocaust, as well as the Nazis' aspiration to destroy the memory of the victims—a central factor

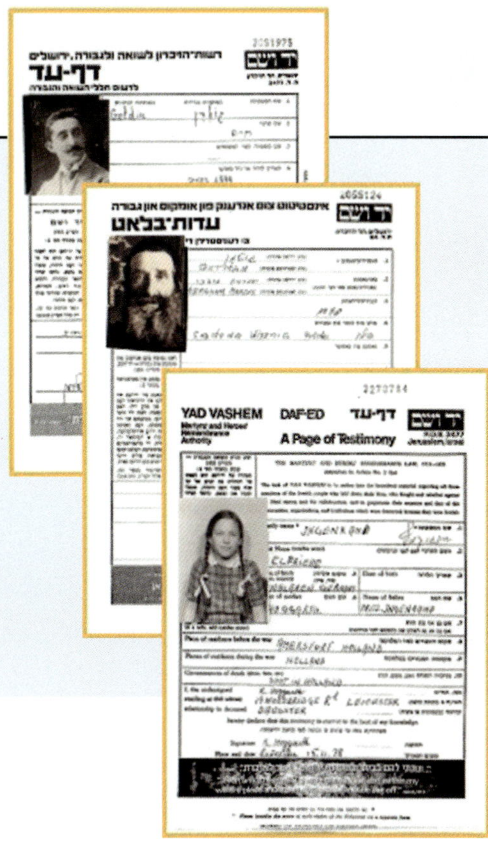

of the Shoah. Taking on the responsibility of preserving the memory of the individual obliges us to remember the victims, portray their faces and rebuild the stories of their lives and deaths. This responsibility dramatically changed the face of remembrance and instilled it with a new Jewish and public tradition.

Over the past decade, the Pages of Testimony have been scanned and digitized into the Central Database of Shoah Victims' Names (see page 290). Additional names, taken from archival lists, have been added, bringing the current total number of names in the Database to three million. In 2004, the Names Database was uploaded to the Internet (where it can be accessed via the Yad Vashem homepage: www.yadvashem.org).

New developments in technology have placed before us a renewed challenge in actualizing the vision created at Yad Vashem's inception. Enlisting technology to the service of memory adds a new active dimension to Holocaust remembrance. The mission that Yad Vashem has placed before it is to refine all existing information on every individual victim and community that was destroyed, and to bring it via a range of media outlets to every classroom, every community and every home.

In the new Holocaust History Museum, the Pages of Testimony are housed in the Hall of Names, positioned at the end of the historical narrative. Visitors enter the circular hall on a ring-shaped platform between two cones. As they stand on the platform they can see the upper cone reaching ten meters skywards, on which some 600 photographs of Holocaust victims and fragments from Pages of Testimony are displayed. These are reflected in the water in the base of the lower cone, dug deep into the bedrock. Surrounding the visitors is the circular repository, which houses the Pages of Testimony collected so far, with room for six million Pages in total.

In addition to gathering Pages of Testimony, Yad Vashem also directs the annual "To Every Person There is a Name" ceremonies, in which hundreds of thousands of victims' names are read out in many locations worldwide on Holocaust Remembrance Day.

YAD VASHEM
A Page of Testimony
Feuille de Témoignage

I happened to find a pencil and was writing on a whim, out of nostalgia, in a dream.

Primo Levi

Our twentieth century was going to improve on the others.
It will never prove it now.

Wislawa Szymborska

A man who has nothing left in this world,
still may know bliss, be it only for a brief moment,
in the contemplation of his beloved.

Victor Frankl

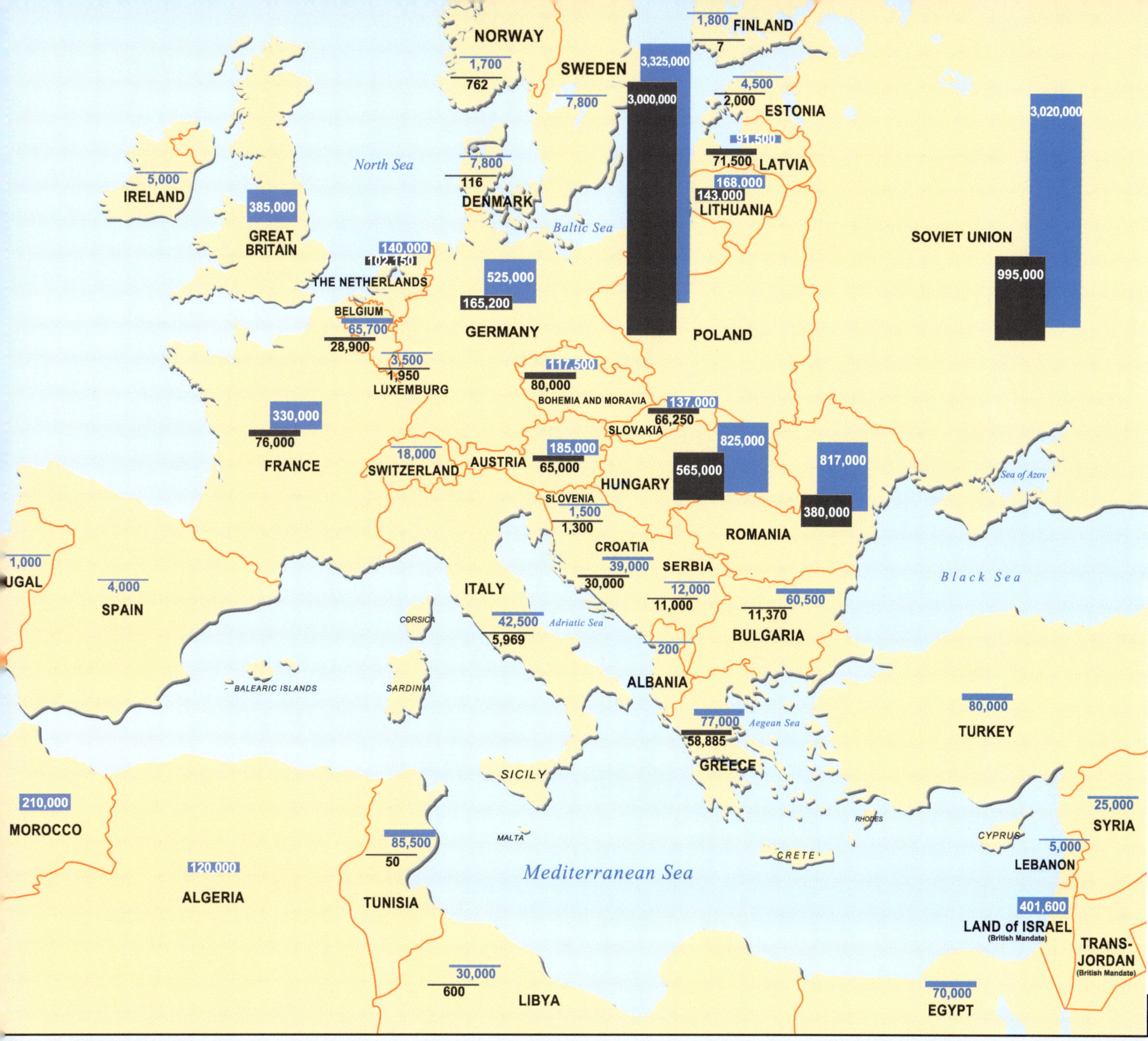

Map of Jewish communities post Holocaust

Words written by individual victims—expressions of faith, hope, yearnings and dreams—were the source of inspiration for renowned artist Uri Tzaig in designing the new Museum's epilogue. Tzaig chose to use these letters and markings, sheets and scraps of paper, as the visual platform for his video art presentation. In one corner a "virtual album" turns pages of original handwritten texts; on another wall random letters are occasionally highlighted by illuminated sentences and human images.

"I happened to find a pencil and was writing on a whim, out of nostalgia, in a dream."
Primo Levi

"Sometimes the journey takes five and three quarter hours; sometimes the same journey lasts a lifetime, until death."
Wadislaw Szlengel

"My dearest loved ones! We are all seized with an overwhelming desire to write letters before we die."
Hulda

"If all the heavens were paper and the world ink, I would be not be able to describe to you my suffering and everything that I see around me."

Haim

"The word dies wherever reality demands absolute dominion."

Jean Améry

"Perhaps it is precisely that a doomed man, in the final moment of his existence, as he glances into the abyss of annihilation with eyes stretched wide in horror, grasps the beauty of life and the power of creation."

Tusia Altman

"A man who has nothing left in this world still may know bliss, be it only for a brief moment, in the contemplation of his beloved."

Victor Frankl

"It was the battle of those who understand and love the beauty of Life and who worship their Creator, against those halfwits who destroy life and who ignore its Creator."

Jacob Barosin

"Just as no one could have imagined Auschwitz before Auschwitz, no one can now recount Auschwitz after Auschwitz."

Elie Wiesel

"Gradually, we rejoined the cycle of life, but we never recovered ourselves."

Mina

A Painting Journeys from Terezin Ghetto to Outer Space

"The cell was illuminated with a tremendous glow, and in the flame of the explosion Petr saw a spark of the great "

Petr Ginz was a boy of many talents. During his internment in Terezin he edited *Vedem* (We Are Leading), the underground newspaper put out by teenagers in the ghetto. But Petr's artistic gift was extraordinary, and his imagination ranged as far as the moon, a place many miles from Earth—and so much safer.

Petr was murdered in Auschwitz at the age of 14, cruelly denied his dream of viewing the Earth from afar. Fifty-eight years after his death, however, the first Israeli astronaut, the late Ilan Ramon, took with him into outer space a copy of Petr's "Moon Landscape," drawn during the Holocaust. Ramon's mother and grandmother survived Auschwitz, but other members of his family had been murdered. Ramon was eager to take into space an object related to the Holocaust, and he was especially moved by Petr's story.

"My voyage fulfills the dream of a boy at a distance of fifty-eight years, a dream that gives everlasting testimony to the grandness of the soul of a boy within ghetto walls that imprisoned him but could not defeat his spirit," said Ramon.

Petr Ginz (1928–1944), Moon Landscape, 1942–1944, pencil on paper

Holocaust Remembrance at Yad Vashem
Remembering the Past—Shaping the Future

The Mount of Remembrance — The Focus of Identification and Commemoration

The Hall of Remembrance

In its first decade, Yad Vashem established the Hall of Remembrance, where an eternal light burns, and ashes of victims brought from the extermination camps are buried. The Hall, designed by Architect Arie Elhanani, is situated in the center of Har Hazikaron, remains the focal point of commemoration to this day and is the site of both state and private memorial and commemorative ceremonies.

State Ceremony for Holocaust Remembrance Day

Each year Israel's national ceremony to mark Holocaust Martyrs' and Heroes' Remembrance Day takes place at Yad Vashem in the Warsaw Ghetto Square, in the presence of the president of the State of Israel, the prime minister, the speaker of the Knesset, the president of the Supreme Court, the chief rabbis, government ministers, members of the Knesset, the chief of the General Staff of the Israel Defense Forces, the inspector-general of the Israel Police, members of

the diplomatic corps, Holocaust survivors, and the general public. The assembly and the memorial ceremonies have become an expression of identification for Israelis of all walks of life.

World Documentation Center

To gather in the homeland the memory of all Jews... From the Yad Vashem Law

Jews began to document the horrors of the Holocaust even before the end of the cataclysm, and the survivors continued to do so after the war. Since its founding day, Yad Vashem has been gathering this documentation, including thousands of survivors' testimonies, diaries, letters, and documents of great historical value. Over the years the Yad Vashem Archive has become the world's largest repository of Holocaust documentation, especially in regard to the Jews' fate and Jewish sources. Yad Vashem's staff seeks out documentation in archives around the world in order to centralize all existing sources and bring them to Jerusalem for perpetual safekeeping. Today Yad Vashem's collection is composed of nearly 60,000,000 pages of documentation in forty languages, 260,000 photographs, and 40,000 testimonies in written form and on audio and video media. The Yad Vashem library, with one of the world's most comprehensive collections of publications on the Holocaust and related themes, contains 88,000 titles and a unique collection of 4,000 newspapers and journals, some of which date from the Holocaust era. A special laboratory at Yad Vashem preserves and restores archival material, lists, works of art belonging to the museum, Pages of Testimony and books.

Commemoration of the individual is expressed through the national endeavor of collecting names of Holocaust victims. In 1955, Yad Vashem began the project of collecting Pages of Testimony in Israel and around the world. Each Page is dedicated to one victim, and comprises biographical details and descriptions of the circumstances of death, expressing the effort to touch the world of each individual person. But the mission is not complete. Yad Vashem continues to collect names from every possible source in order to complete the Names Database.

International Research and Publications Center

To gather, investigate, and publish all testimony about the Holocaust...

From the Yad Vashem Law

One of the primary objectives of Yad Vashem is Holocaust research. To date, Yad Vashem has published hundreds of publications on the topic, including the *Pinkasei Hakehillot* project (winner of the 1973 Israel Prize), the *History of the Holocaust*, The *Encyclopedia of the Holocaust*, the *Encyclopedia of the Righteous Among the Nations*, studies by Israeli and foreign Holocaust researchers, documentation from the period, survivors' memoirs and memorial books. Yad Vashem's International Institute for Holocaust Research hosts international conferences, where renowned scholars from Israel and abroad discuss issues related to Holocaust history and historiography. The institute also initiates research projects, hosts scholars from all over the world, provides grants for young researchers of Holocaust-related topics, and organizes international workshops.

1

2

3

1 Prof. Israel Gutman
2 Prof. Yehuda Bauer
3 Prof. David Bankier and Prof. Dan Michman

21-24 November 2004

ALIZA BARAK-RESSLER
CRY LITTLE GIRL
A TALE OF THE SURVIVAL OF A FAMILY IN SLOVAKIA

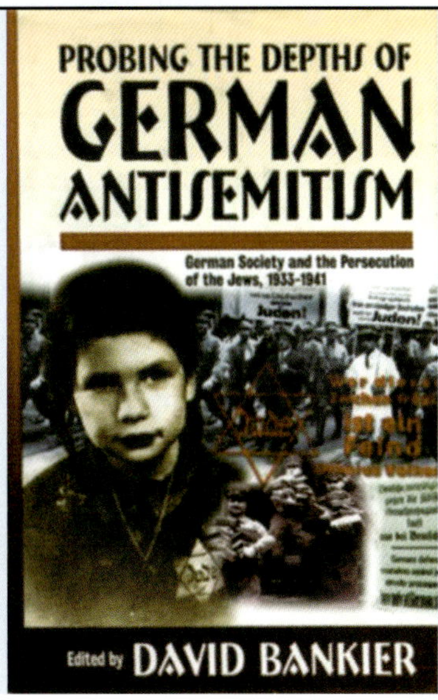
PROBING THE DEPTHS OF
GERMAN
ANTISEMITISM
German Society and the Persecution of the Jews, 1933-1941
Edited by DAVID BANKIER

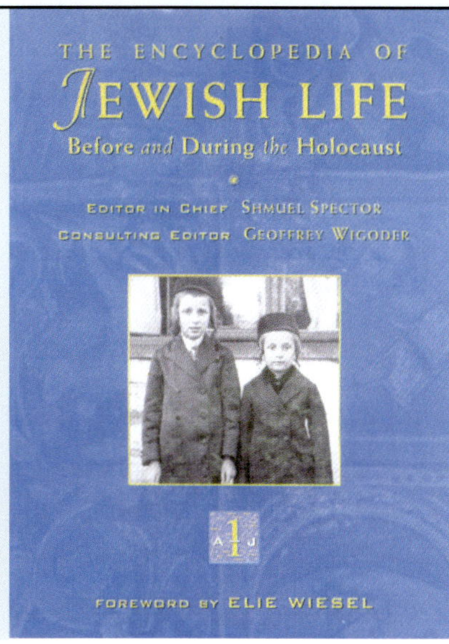
THE ENCYCLOPEDIA OF
JEWISH LIFE
Before and During the Holocaust
EDITOR IN CHIEF SHMUEL SPECTOR
CONSULTING EDITOR GEOFFREY WIGODER
1
A J
FOREWORD BY ELIE WIESEL

Educational Endeavors in Israel and Abroad—the International School for Holocaust Studies

To impart the lesson [of the Holocaust] to the nation... From the Yad Vashem Law

One of the mainstays of Yad Vashem's activities is education, spearheaded by the International School for Holocaust Studies. The school, a vibrant institution that shapes the way the subject of the Holocaust is taught in Israel, runs programs for some 800 teachers every year in many locations throughout the country. The School also offers activities for thousands of students and IDF soldiers each year, and its mobile units, which include interactive programs for students of all ages, visit schools in outlying areas in order to conduct special activity days. The Program and Curricula Development Department produces innovative learning materials in a range of languages and media.

The School also hosts seminars for overseas teachers in nine languages, tailored to the particular needs of each country, including comprehensive educational activities in the former Soviet Union. Members of staff take part in forums and conferences around the world, and graduates of the school have become leaders in Holocaust education worldwide. Once every two years, the school holds an international conference on the Holocaust and education.

The New Museum Complex

In addition to the new Holocaust History Museum, the new Museum Complex also includes the new Museum of Holocaust Art, the Exhibitions Pavilion and the Synagogue.

The New Museum of Holocaust Art

Yad Vashem's collection of Holocaust art is the largest and most wide-ranging collection in the world. It comprises some 10,000 works, most of them from the Holocaust period. In order to properly display this collection, focusing only on the works created during the Shoah, a new Holocaust Art Museum has been built. The art displayed in the new Museum allows a different view of the Holocaust—based on the experience of the individual—using a medium that appeals not just to the intellect, but also penetrates straight to the heart.

On entering the Museum, the visitor will encounter a diagonal wall displaying a range of works from different artists. The rest of the spaces are dedicated to exhibits according to subject, focusing on the human image as well as views of ghettos and camps, inside and outside. In addition, three artists have areas dedicated solely to their works: Charlotte Salomon, Bruno Schultz and Carol Deutsch. Adjacent to the exhibition hall is the world's first computerized archive and information center regarding Shoah art and artists. The center is meant for the occasional visitor who wishes to learn more about a particular artist viewed in the exhibit, as well as for researchers wishing to utilize the information for their academic work.

Creating art during the Holocaust meant risking one's life at a time when the materials needed were almost non-existent, and many of the artists were on the verge of collapse—physically and mentally—without access to even the most minimal essentials of daily life. In spite of all this, the piece was created, and sometimes managed to survive even when—as was mostly the case—the artist did not.

Most of the works were fashioned on thin scraps of paper, which demand care and periodical rotation, so as to best ensure their preservation. The Museum's display will therefore be changed every few months so that the works can "rest" in optimal dark conditions. This rotation will also allow the display of more pieces from the collection. There is no doubt that the visitor's

1

2

1 **Charlotte Salomon** (1917-1943), Port, Villefranche-sur-Mer, 1939-1941, gouache on paper

2 **Felix Nussbaum** (1904-1944), Still-life with mask, glove, and football, Brussels, c. 1940, gouache on paper

experience will be unique, both in terms of the subject matter and from an artistic viewpoint. The works displayed are not just testimonial; they express an awesome creative power. The artists who produced them knew that this was a once-in-a-lifetime chance to express all they wished to say in a few lines etched on paper.

1 **Carol Deutsch** (1894–1944), Let the Waters Bring Forth the Moving Creature and Fowl (Gen. 1:20), 1941–1942, gouache, crayon, and India ink on paper

2 **Carol Deutsch** (1894–1944), And the Tree Yielding Fruit (Gen. 1:12), 1941–1942, gouache, crayon, and India ink on paper

1

ועץ עשה פרי בר׳ א׳ יב׳

AND THE TREE YIELDING FRUIT

4e JOUR I-1-12

The Exhibitions Pavilion

The Exhibitions Pavilion will provide a showcase for interdisciplinary exhibitions focusing on historical themes that deserve broader attention than the permanent exhibits can provide. Contemporary art exhibitions on Holocaust themes will also be displayed here.

The pavilion will display a range of different materials, from large *objects d'art* to intimate artifacts. The inaugural exhibition will present a representative selection of post-Holocaust works from public collections in Israel. The works were produced by first-, second-, and third-generation survivors as well as by artists who have no personal tie to the Holocaust era. Each copes with the personal or collective memory in his/her own way and approaches the Holocaust not only as something to remember but also as a dynamic, multifaceed theme that provokes thought and debate.

1 **Roy Strassberg** (b. 1950), Black Train with Smokestacks II, 1997, clay
2 **Mark Klionski** (b. 1927), Waiting for Train, 1986, oil on canvas

2

The Learning Center

"Now it is clear that this difficult duty of preserving the memory and transmitting it to posterity cannot be accomplished by historiography alone. It requires additional tools to hoist this heavy load... Now it seems that the time has come to add to the historical questions, 'What happened?' and 'How did it happen?' a question that points in a different direction: 'What should have happened?' The Holocaust must not be left in the realm of huge numbers and generalized speech."

Aharon Appelfeld

Part of the museum complex, the Learning Center, designed by Mulli Ben-Sasson, will help visitors grapple with the educational, philosophical, and ethical questions that arise from their visit to the Holocaust History Museum and explore aspects of these issues in depth.

Otherwise known as the room where "the great questions pursuant to the Holocaust" are addressed, the Learning Center is no ordinary information center. Its design encourages visitors to embark on a personal exploratory journey. The attention of those who enter is captured by a shaft of light that projects questions into a large circle in the middle of the room. The questions, hurled onto the floor, create waves that circle the room, echoing the nature of such important questions: while one question is like a drop in the ocean, it sets many other questions in its wake. Workstations for individual or paired study are positioned around the central area, which will provide a space for group discussions. Here visitors may see and hear a range of views and opinions as presented by scholars,

philosophers, and intellectuals in various disciplines, along with Holocaust survivors.

The Visual Center

The Visual Center is a unique repository that allows visitors to view diverse materials—documentary and fictional films on Holocaust themes, as well as survivors' testimonies recorded by Yad Vashem and other bodies around the world. It includes the testimony collection of Steven Spielberg's Shoah Foundation Visual History Access Project.

The Synagogue

The new synagogue will provide visitors with an appropriate place to say Kaddish for departed loved ones, to engage in personal and shared prayer, and to hold memorial ceremonies for destroyed communities. The synagogue will display Holy Arks and artifacts from synagogues that were abandoned, damaged, or destroyed during the Holocaust.

The Avenue of the Righteous Among the Nations

To the Righteous Among the Nations, who risked their lives to save Jews.

From the Yad Vashem Law

In 1962, the Avenue of the Righteous was opened, and a year later a public commission was established so that Yad Vashem could fulfill its legal duty to award the title of "Righteous Among the Nations," in keeping with systematic criteria. The Righteous Among the Nations award is a unique honor, which recognizes and commemorates the actions of those non-Jews who risked their lives in order to rescue Jews during the Holocaust. The concept of "Righteous Among the Nations," as coined by Yad Vashem, has become a universal term, accepted the world over. In recent years, Yad Vashem has been preparing a comprehensive encyclopedia that will include all the rescue stories and summarize the Righteous project that has spanned over four decades. To date, Yad Vashem has recognized over 20,000 persons as Righteous Among the Nations.

The Garden of the Righteous Among the Nations

Commemoration

The Valley of the Communities

The Valley of the Communities highlights the names of thousands of Jewish communities destroyed by Nazi Germany and its collaborators and the few that suffered but survived in the shadow of the Holocaust. The task of architects Lippa Yahalom and Dan Tsur was to create a monument to ruin. Therefore the Valley of the Communities was excavated out of the earth, resembling a concentration of huge open graves gaping in the ground. It is as if what had been built up on the surface of the earth over the course of a millennia—a thousand years of Jewish communal life—was suddenly swallowed up. The great catastrophe that was the Shoah caused that rich world of Jewish life to suddenly disappear from sight, and sink out of existence.

The Valley itself is a labyrinth of courtyards and walls, of openings and dead ends. The names of over 5,000 communities are engraved on the 107 walls of Jerusalem stone, symbolically embedded forever in the very bedrock of Israel.

Within the site is Beit Hakehilot (the House of the Communities) an educational and research center with an audio-visual presentation and temporary exhibits on aspects of pre-war Jewish life on display.

The Warsaw Ghetto Square

This monument, designed by Natan Rappoport is identical to the sculptures at the memorial site of the Warsaw Ghetto in Poland. The first sculpture, entitled "The Warsaw Ghetto Uprising" depicts men, women and children bearing arms, and fighting courageously against the background of the burning ghetto. In the center stands the leader of the uprising, Mordechai Anielewicz, holding the flame that ignited the spirit of rebellion. To its right is the second sculpture, entitled "The Last March", which depicts the final journey of Jews to the death camps.

Memorial to the Jewish Soldiers and Partisans

Some 1.5 million Jews fought in WWII, as allied soldiers, as partisans, in the resistance movements, and in the ghettos. Hundreds of thousands fell in battle.

The monument designed by Bernie Fink, consists of six oblong granite blocks arranged in two groups and set in such a way that their inner edges form a window in the shape of the Star of David. The window, in turn, is dissected by the giant stainless steel blade of a sword. Different motifs are expressed within the monument: the six blocks stand for the six million Jews murdered by the Nazis; the Star of David represents the Jewish people; and the blade of the sword symbolizes the fighting opposition to the Nazis. Thus the monument combines the Holocaust of the Jewish people with their contribution to the establishment of the State of Israel.

The Partisans' Panorama

In the center of the Partisans' Panorama is the sculpture: "For man is like the tree of the field" – designed by the sculptor Zadok Ben-David. This silhouette of a tree towers six meters high and is alive with the figures of hundreds of men, women and children, camouflaged in its branches and disappearing amongst its foliage.

The Cattle Car – Memorial to the Deportees

This is the symbol of the partisan fighter, whose life was connected to the forest, and who found refuge among its trees. The Panorama was designed by the architect Dan Tsur.

At the center of the memorial site stands an original German cattle-car used to deport Jews to the extermination camps. Perched on the edge of a severed iron track, the cattle-car is paused on the brink of the abyss—symbolizing the journey towards annihilation and oblivion. However, facing the hills of Jerusalem the memorial also conveys the eternal hope and renewal of life after the Holocaust.

(designed by Architect Moshe Safdie)

The Pillar of Heroism

At the end of a path paved with smooth stones and bounded on both sides by six blocks of gray concrete rises the Pillar of Heroism, commemorating Jewish resistance during the Holocaust. The towering pillar is reminiscent of the chimneys of the crematoria. The inscription on the concrete blocks reads: "In memory of those who rebelled in the camps and ghettos, fought in the woods, in the underground and with the Allied forces; braved their way to Eretz Israel; and died sanctifying the name of God—now and forever."
(designed by Buki Schwartz)

Janusz Korczak Square

Located in the square is a sculpture in memory of the great Polish-Jewish educator Dr. Henrik Goldszmit (known by his pseudonym Janusz Korczak). Korczak stands in the center of a group of children and shelters them with his body and his outstretched arms. Only his face and hands are visible, uniting the group with their embrace. The children are tall and skinny, their hands long and lifeless and their heads drooping. Despite his efforts to save the children, they were sent to the Treblinka death camp in 1942.

(designed by Boris Saktsier)

The Children's Memorial

This unique memorial, hollowed out from an underground cavern, is a tribute to the 1.5 million Jewish children who perished during the Holocaust. Memorial candles, a customary Jewish tradition to remember the dead, are reflected infinitely in a dark and somber space, creating the impression of millions of stars shining in the firmament. The names of murdered children, their ages and countries of origin can be heard in the background. The Children's Memorial was designed by architect Moshe Safdie.

Dream

When I grow up and get to be twenty
I'll travel and see this world of plenty.
In a bird with an engine I will sit myself down,
Take off and fly into space, far above the ground.,
I'll fly, I'll cruise and soar up high
Above a world so lovely, into the sky....
And so, delighted by all the world's charms,
Into the heavens I will take off and not have a bother,
The cloud is my sister, the wind is my brother.

Avramek Kopelowicz,
murdered in Auschwitz at age 14

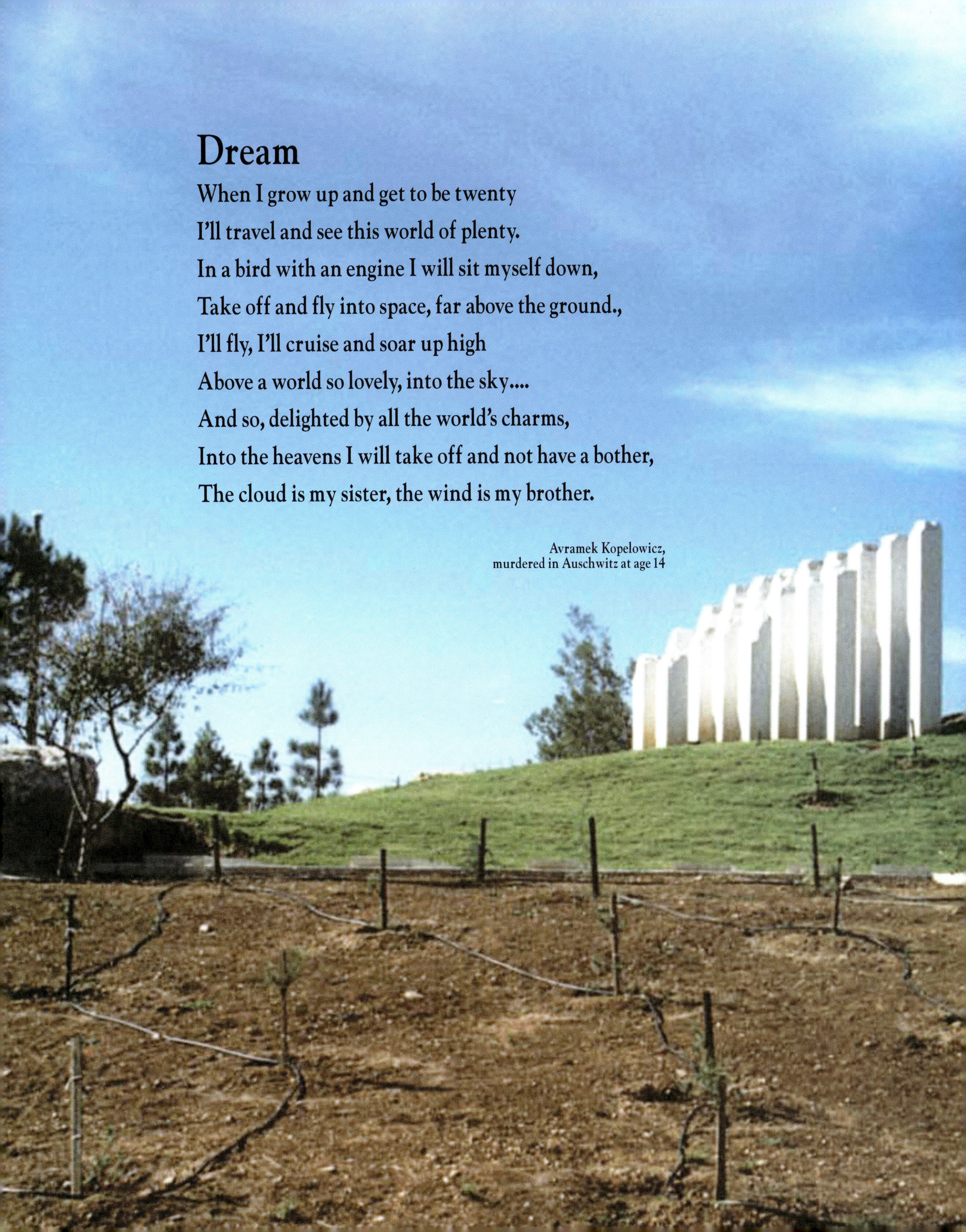

The Survivors' Manifesto

Message from the Holocaust Survivors for Posterity

For the exalted and tenacious struggle of the Jewish masses, on the brink of devastation, for their human image and their Jewish culture...

From the Yad Vashem Law

We, the generation of the Holocaust survivors, are steadily dwindling. Within a few years, no one who can give first-hand testimony—"I remember what happened in the Holocaust"—will remain on earth. Only memorial and research books, photographs, films, and survivors' testimonies will remain. At that time Holocaust remembrance will cease to be a fate that is imposed, imprinted in our flesh and souls; it will become a historic purpose that humankind and posterity must fill with content and substance.

In the spring of 1945, the sounds and horrors of World War II ceased, and we, the last vestiges of European Jewry, emerged from the death camps and the killing sites—one survivor per town and two per family, battered and embittered, orphaned, with neither communities nor homes, and without a close soul waiting for us anywhere on earth.

The war was over, but we wondered, in our perplexity and agony, whether, after the darkness of the ghettos, the death trains, and the concentration and extermination camps, we would be able to rekindle the ember of life—to love, to work, to establish families, and to mark festivals and observances.

We did not become misanthropes; we did not lust for vengeance against the innocent. This attests everlastingly to the moral values embedded in the teachings of our ancient people and to faith in the spirit of humankind and Providence. We chose life. We rehabilitated ourselves, joined the struggle for the establishment of the State of Israel, and contributed to society in Israel and the other countries to which we migrated.

Most survivors of the Holocaust chose Israel, the state of the Jewish people, as their destination. For them, this was an existential lesson of the Holocaust. Israel's foundations are bolstered not only by the memory of the six million Jews who were annihilated but also by the historical lessons that must be learned so that a Holocaust may never happen again.

Since then we have been struggling with many troubling issues that the Holocaust raises. Why and for what purpose was the horror perpetrated? Why did the Germans single out Jews as a danger to all humanity, who must be exterminated? How is it possible that amongst the German nation, a people of such apparent intellect and modern culture who produced great artists, thinkers and teachers of ethics, could arise murderers who Fashioned and operated this unprecedented killing machine?

It is true that we survivors are a pluralistic, multifaceted group with many different views. However, we share in common a deep desire to transmit to future generations the lessons of our afflicted lives before the curtain falls and the last of us leaves the world of the living. Hence it is from Jerusalem, from Yad Vashem—the Jewish people's commemorative site for the Holocaust and heroism that we speak out.

In Jewish tradition the command to remember is absolute. However, remembrance does not exist in a void; it is linked to a moral imperative. Today, as we Holocaust survivors, whose memories are burned into our flesh, pass the torch of the mission of remembrance to the next generations, we hand with it a Jewish message: that memory should lead to action and to a moral commitment; that memory should be a basis for action and a source of strength to create a better world.

"Thou shall not murder" is the supreme moral injunction with which humankind was trumpeted on Mount Sinai. By remembering the murder of six million Jews and many others by the Nazis and their accomplices, we make an unsurpassed commitment to the imperative of "Thou shall not murder." Life is a Divine creation that no human being dares to take from his fellow man, who has been created in the Divine image. Thus, as part of our Holocaust remembrance, we call for an indefatigable effort always to protect human life and to avoid bloodshed.

On our own behalf, as people whose human dignity was desecrated to dust, and on behalf of those who were doomed to ghastly humiliation before they were put to death, we urge the entire world to unite around the values of human rights and equality for all, irrespective of religion, race, nationality, social status, or sex. Tyrannical despotism, political and religious oppression, economic deprivation designed to destroy human dignity must be seen by the world community as grave sins that will not be tolerated.

There is no real alternative to the

Sculpture by Menashe Kadishman, placed in the Family Square

coexistence of people and peoples. No effort should be spared to solve problems—in the Middle East and everywhere else—by dialogue and discourse, not by bloodshed.

Antisemitism and all other forms of racism menace not only Jews but also the entire world. They carry within them propensities that may lead to genocide. At present a "new antisemitism" is directed simultaneously against Jews, Israel, and Zionism. By equating these terms the danger for Jews as a whole is exacerbated. This phenomenon is also common in propaganda emanating from the Arab world. The Holocaust showed the world the extent of the destructive power of antisemitism and racism. Holocaust denial, as well as minimization and banalization of the Holocaust, provides a means of avoiding the evident conclusions and learning lessons for the future. We, the Survivors, call upon the world to wipe out these phenomena and to combat them relentlessly.

Although the memory of the Holocaust is replete with devastation, evil, and dehumanization that threaten to inundate all human values, we, the survivors who marched through the valley of death and saw our families, communities, and people being annihilated, did not wallow in despair and did not lose faith in humankind. We wish to extract from the horror, engraved in our flesh, a positive message for our people and the world—a message of humanity, of human decency and of human dignity. The Holocaust belongs to the universal legacy of all civilized people as the benchmark of absolute evil. The lessons of the Holocaust must become a yardstick for education in human values, democracy, human rights, tolerance, and patience, and a warning against racism and totalitarian ideologies.

Thus, let the maxim voiced by Rabbi Hillel emanate from Yad Vashem to the world: "What is hateful to you, do not do to your fellow human being!"

Declaration of Remembrance
We are gathered here today, at the residence of the President of the State of Israel in Jerusalem, on the fiftieth anniversary of Yad Vashem, looking with hope to the future.
Jewish independence rose in the shadow of the destruction of European Jewry. The survivors, remnants of the inferno, burdened with grief and bereavement, became the daring immigrants to Palestine, prisoners in the camps in Cyprus, first in the ingathering of the exiles, and fighters in the War of Independence.
But a generation passed before we and the nations of the world began to internalize and to comprehend the darkness and the fall of humanity in the terrible years of the Holocaust - the development of Jew-hatred, the distorted ideas of the murderers, the apathy of the enlightened world, and the helplessness of the victims.
We now know the awesome voice that bursts forth from there, from the abyss, from the millions that were never laid to rest and from the words of the witnesses that have seared our souls. The sin and the crime give no rest and will continue to disturb humanity for all time to come.
The survivors are gradually taking their leave of us in the way of all flesh. We, the next generations, progeny of an ancient people that was forged in this land and pays a dear and ongoing price for its right to live and the hope for peace, and the people of the nations of the world, commit ourselves to remember and not to forget until the end of days. The scroll of agony to which we are heirs will accompany us, in faith in mankind created in the Divine image, and in the future.
We see education, research, and imparting the memory as essential parts of strengthening the chain linking the generations, and in firmly grounding the commitment to the existence of the Jewish people.
We commit ourselves to continuing to infuse the memory of the Holocaust with content and meaning.
We will do all within our power to extract hope from the pain, and faith from
Hope for a world that will live by the commandment "Thou shalt not kill"
Hope for a world that will fulfill the command "Thou shalt not stand by the blood of thy
Hope for a world that will inscribe on its banner a struggle against racism and antisemitism in all
Hope that the perpetual memorial flame will stand as an eternal beacon and as a warning sign -
Faith in the human spirit and in the eternal values of human civilization
Just as we endeavor to fulfill "and I will give them ... a Yad Vashem (a monument and a
we endeavor to fulfill "and I will bring peace unto the land."
17 september 2003

[318]

Yad Vashem Milestones

1953 The Knesset enacts the Yad Vashem Law

1955 The collection of names of Holocaust victims on Pages of Testimony begins

1957 The first building on Har Hazikaron is opened, housing the administration, archives, and library

1957 The first volume of *Yad Vashem Studies* is published

1961 The Hall of Remembrance is dedicated

1962 The Avenue of the Righteous Among the Nations is inaugurated

1968 The first international conference is held at Yad Vashem

1968 The Hall of Names is dedicated, housing the Pages of Testimony

1973 The Pinkasei Hakehillot project is awarded the Israel Prize

1973 The Yad Vashem Historical Museum opens

1982 The Museum of Holocaust Art is established

1985 The Memorial to the Jewish Soldiers, Partisans and Ghetto Fighters is dedicated

1987 The Children's Memorial is dedicated, commemorating the 1.5 million children who perished in the Holocaust

1992 The Valley of the Communities is dedicated, commemorating some 5,000 Jewish communities that were destroyed or damaged in the Holocaust

1993 The Yad Vashem Multiyear Development plan is launched

1994 The International Institute for Holocaust Research is established

1995 The International School for Holocaust Studies is established

1996 The Garden of the Righteous Among the Nations is dedicated, with stone slates engraved with the names of non-Jewish rescuers

1999 The International School for Holocaust Studies building is dedicated and the first international educational conference takes place

1999 Digitization of the Central Database of Shoah Victims' Names begins

2000 The new Archives and Library building, including computerized databases, is dedicated

2000 Visit of Pope John Paul II

2001 The Encyclopedia of the Jewish Communities (English) is published

2003 The first volume of Encyclopedia of the Righteous Among the Nations is published

Yad Vashem is awarded the Israeli Prize for Lifetime Achievement

2005 The new museum is dedicated on March 15

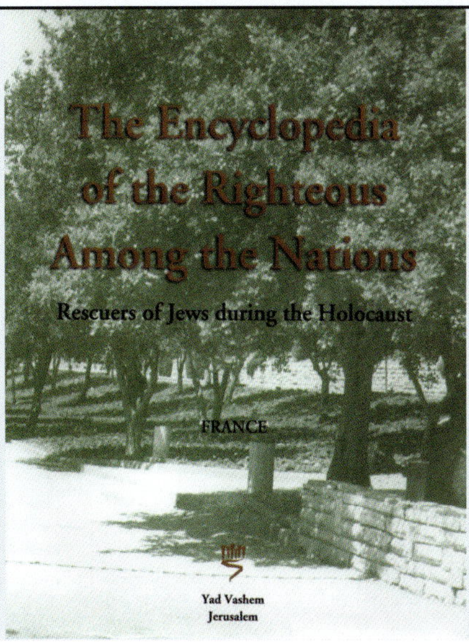

Yad Vashem was awarded the Israel Prize for Lifetime Achievement

מדינת ישראל
משרד החינוך, התרבות והספורט

על סמך המלצת ועדת השופטים מוענק

פרס ישראל

התשס"ג • 2003

על מפעל חיים -
תרומה מיוחדת לחברה ולמדינה

ל י ד ו ש ם

על מפעליו החשובים והמגוונים שהם עמודי התווך שעליהם נבנים התיעוד, המחקר, עיצוב הזיכרון וההנצחה של תקופת השואה, על תפקידו הייצוגי החשוב בהעלאת המודעות הציבורית לנושא בארץ ובעולם, על פעילותו החינוכית הענפה והייחודית ועל תרומתו החשובה לאחדות העם ולמסורת היהודית של ערבות הדדית.

לימור לבנת
שרת החינוך, התרבות והספורט

ירושלים, יום העצמאות התשס"ג

Special Thanks

The Ministry of Education, Culture and Sports

The Ministry of Tourism

The Ministry of Finance

The Conference on Jewish Material Claims Against Germany

The Jewish Agency for Israel

Friends of Yad Vashem in Israel and World-Wide

We are grateful to those donors and copyright holders—Institutions, photographers and individuals—who have given us permission to reproduce materials:

Einat Alon

Ehud Amir, Jerusalem, Israel

Denny Andrews, U.S.A

AP Photo

Apfel Gerson

Archiv der KZ-Gedenkstaette Mauthausen, Germany

Army Historical Archive in Prague

The Association of 3d Armored Division Veterans

Hellmut Bachrach-Barée

Yehuda Bacon

Samuel Bak

Jacob Barosin

Tzlila and Hadassah Bau, Ramat Gan, Israel

Jana Behar, Sofia

Tania Behar-Zacharia, Arad, Israel

Moshe Ben Dov (Weintreter), Bnei Braq, Israel

Beth Hatefutsoth Photo Archive, Tel Aviv, Israel

Bibliotheque Nationale de France, Paris

Bildarchiv Abraham Pisarek

Bildarchiv Preussischer Kulturbesitz, Berlin, Germany

Alexander Bogen

Z. Braun, Israel

Bundesarchiv, Koblenz, Germany

Charlotte Buresova

The Boris Carmi Estate, Tel Aviv, Israel

Central State Archive for Photos and Films, Kiev

The Central Zionist Archives, Jerusalem, Israel

Centrum Judaicum Archiv, Berlin, Germany

Kristine Chiger Keren, New York, U.S.A

Chronos Films, Courtesy of Von Zur Mihlen, Germany

Corbis-Bettmann

Deutsches Historisches Museum, Berlin, Germany

Dokumentationsarchiv des österreichischen Widerstandes, Vienna

Maria Eisen Leszczynska, Warsaw, Poland

Embassy of Israel, Germany

Julien Engel

Mr. Epstein, U.S.A

Estonian Central Historic Museum in Tallin, Estonia

Établissement Cinématographique et Photographique des Armées, Paris, France

Jochanan Fein, Holon, Israel

Gusti Felton, White Plains, NY, U.S.A

Neil Folberg

Anne Frank Foundation, Basel/ AFS, Amsterdam

Paul and Hilda Freund, Jerusalem

Frihedsmuseet, Copenhagen, Denmark

Henrietta Garty (Blum), Kibbutz Shluchot, Israel

Andree Geulen-Herscovici, Brussels, Belgium

Ghetto Fighters' Museum Archives

Joachim F. Giessler, Murnau Seehausen, Germany

Otto Ginz, Haifa, Israel

Dan Glass, Jerusalem, Israel

Micah Glass, Ramat Gan, Israel

Ottilie Gobel Bourne, Washington State

Zsigmond Gutman, Hungary

Hamburger Institut für Sozialforschung, Hamburg, Germany

Isaac Harari

Haus der Wannsee Konferenz, Berlin, Germany

Bequest of Ingrid Hendrickx Abrams, Chicago

William H. Hersh, Los Angeles, California

Hessisches Hauptstaatsarchiv Wiesbaden, Germany

Alex Hirt

Hungary National Museum

John Hymans, Netanya, Israel

Instytut Pamieci Narodowej

The Israel Defense Forces (IDF) and Defense Establishment Archives, Tel Aviv, Israel

Abraham Wolf Jasny Archive

Hava Jasny

Jewish Museum Brussels, Belgium

The Jewish Museum of Greece, Athens

Jewish Museum Prague

Jewish Museum, Frankfurt, Germany

The Jewish National and University Library, Jerusalem, Israel

The Jewish Record Office, London, England

Zvi Kadushin Collection, United States Holocaust Memorial Museum, Washington, D.C, U.S.A

Simcha and Shmuel Kalderon, Kfar Sirkin, Israel

Dr. Yisrael Katz, Jerusalem, Israel

Roger-David Katz and his wife Louba Moscicka, Brussels

Collection Klarsfeld–FFDJF, Paris, France

Z. Kluger Collection, Government Press Office, Jerusalem, Israel

Daisy Koeb, Rishon LeZion, Israel

Yehuda Koren

KZ Gedenkstaette Dachau, Germany

Rev. Michael Lawson, Kent, England

Library of Congress, Washington, D.C., U.S.A

Egger Lilli, New York, U.S.A

Magyar Nemzeti Muzeum Torteneti Fenykeptar

Yehudit Marcus (Geller), Petach Tikva, Israel

Menachem Maron (Marku), Raanana, Israel

Memorial Museum of Hungarian Speaking Jewry, Safed, Israel

Menkin Collection, Yad Vashem Archives

Irving Milchberg

Éva Modvál-Haimovich, Ramat Gan, Israel

Musée de l'Oeuvre Notre Dame de Strassbourg, France

Muzeum Byłego Obozu Zagłady Chełmno nad Nerem, Konin, Poland

Muzeum Gross-Rosen, Walbrzych, Poland

Muzeum Okregowe Konin, Poland

National Archives, Washington, D.C, U.S.A

Nederlands Instituut voor Oorlogsdocumentatie, Amsterdam, the Netherlands

Eilat Negev

Ruth Nussbacher (Bensinger), New York, NY, U.S.A

Richard Oestermann, Jerusalem, Israel

The Olidort family, New York

Family of William Ossipow, Geneva, Switzerland

Österreichisches Institut für Zeitgeschichte, Bildarchiv, Vienna, Austria

Leopold Page Photographic Collection

Państwowe Muzeum Auschwitz-Birkenau, Oświęcim, Poland

Państwowe Muzeum na Majdanku, Lublin, Poland

K. Passer, London

Sara Pechanac, Jerusalem, Israel

Edna Peled, Holon, Israel

Netta Porat, Kibbutz Tzora, Israel

Prague Committee for Documentation

Raccolte Storiche del Comune de Milano

Alice Randt, Grossburgwedel, Germany

Lilli Rochman-Chester, Baltimore, Maryland, U.S.A

Roger et Viollet, Paris, France

Sigmund Rolat, New York

Yael Rosner (Zofia Zajczyk), Jerusalem, Israel

Alex Rynecki, California

Nathan Samuel, Jerusalem, Israel

Prof. B. Sandler, Libourne, France

Frederike Schoenwalder, Wien, Austria

Guenter Schwarberg

Ziskin Schwarz, Ramat Gan, Israel

Daniella Sela

Pinchas Shaar

Shlomo Shafir

Ze'ev and Alisa Shek, Caeseria, Israel

Eli Shilat

Barbara and Lewis Shrensky, Washington, D.C.

Uriel and Shulamit Simon, Jerusalem, Israel

Shimon Srebrenik, Nes-Tziona, Israel

Staatsarchiv Detmold

Staatsarchiv Worms, Germany

State Archives of the Russian Federation, Moscow

Stato Maggiore Esercito Ufficio Storico

Stern Archives

David Stoliar

Roy Strassberg

David Susskind, Brussels

Tzila Szafalowa-Gorniecka, Tel Aviv, Israel

David Szenes, Haifa, Israel

Eithan Szenes, Haifa, Israel

Denise Tal

Yehudit Taube (Aufrichtig), Rechovot, Israel

Sasson Tiram

Ilya Tolkatchev, Kiev

Anel Tolkatcheva, Kiev

Jerzy Tomaszewski Collection, United States Holocaust Memorial Museum, Washington, D.C, U.S.A

Ullstein Bilderdienst, Berlin, Germany

United States Holocaust Memorial Museum, Washington, D.C, U.S.A

Raphael Uzan

Ivan Vojtech Fric Collection, Jewish Museum Prague

Bill Wales, U.S.A

Mirjam Waterman Pinkhof, Haifa, Israel

Weiner Collection, Courtesy of Tel Aviv University

West-Bohemian Museum, Pilsen

A. Wilhelm, Holon, Israel

Samuel Willenberg

Tomek Wisniewski, Bialystok, Poland

Regina Wolbrom, Florida, U.S.A

Clarette Wolczak (Vigder), Kibbutz Mishmar HaNegev, Israel

Chaim Zvi Wolnerman and Jetka Wolnerman-Ringer

Yad Vashem Archives

Yad Vashem Art Collection

Yad Vashem Artifacts Collection

Yad Vashem Library

Aaron Yermis

YIVO Institute for Jewish Research

Ettia Zait, Pardes Hanna, Israel

Mr. Zandler, U.S.A

Gerda Zondek, Jerusalem, Israel

Żydowski Instytut Historyczny Instytut Naukowo-Badawczy, Warsaw, Poland